FORT SISSETON

Harold H. Schuler

The Center for Western Studies

The Prairie Plains Series Number 5

Published by
The Center for Western Studies
Box 727, Augustana College
Sioux Falls, South Dakota 57197

The Center for Western Studies is an archives, library, museum, publishing house, and educational agency concerned principally with collecting, preserving, and interpreting prehistoric, historic, and contemporary materials that document native and immigrant cultures of the northern prairie plains. The Center promotes understanding of the region through exhibits, publications, art shows, conferences, and academic programs. It is committed, ultimately, to defining the contribution of the region to American civilization. The Prairie Plains Series is dedicated to the publication at moderate prices of essential but limited-market titles.

Library of Congress Cataloging-in-Publication Data:

Schuler, Harold H.
    Fort Sisseton / by Harold H. Schuler.
       p. cm. —(Prairie plains series : no. 5)
    Includes bibliographical references (p. 273) and index.
    Summary: Presents a complete history of the U.S. military post constructed in Dakota Territory in 1864, including its various uses since being decommissioned.
    ISBN 0-931170-62-1 (alk. paper)
    1. Fort Sisseton (S.D.)—History—Juvenile literature. [1. Fort Sisseton (S.D.)—History.] I. Title. II. Series.
F659.S679S38 1996
978.3'13—dc20   96-2048
                                          CIP
                                          AC

Photographs: Unless otherwise indicated, photographs are by the author.
Cover photograph, Commanding Officer's House, 1870.
Courtesy National Archives.

This book was made possible in part with the financial assistance of
Jack Adams, Frank Farrar, and Lee Schoenbeck.

Printed in United States of America

PINE HILL PRESS, INC.
Freeman, S. Dak. 57029

Table of Contents

PART III. LIFE AT FORT SISSETON

Acknowledgments

I would like to thank Dr. Arthur R. Huseboe and Harry Thompson, Center for Western Studies, in Sioux Falls, for their editorial assistance with this book. I would also like to thank Dr. Herbert Hoover, of the University of South Dakota, for his editorial review of Chapter 1, Minnesota Sioux War, and Dr. Tom Kilian for his review of the manuscript.

Thanks to Dr. J. R. Fishburne, former director of the South Dakota State Historical Society and the Office of History, who encouraged me to write this book.

I appreciate the help of the staff at the Military Reference Branch, National Archives, in Washington, D.C.; South Dakota Archives, Pierre; Division of Parks and Recreation, South Dakota's Department of Game, Fish and Parks, Pierre and Fort Sisseton. I would also like to thank Dave Daberkow, park manager.

My wife, Leona R. Schuler, was most helpful in proofing my manuscript.

I would also like to thank the following sponsors who helped with the publication of this book: Center for Western Studies, Sioux Falls; Jack Adams, Sisseton; Frank Farrar, Britton; and Lee Schoenbeck, Webster.

Harold H. Schuler
607 North Van Buren
Pierre, South Dakota 57501

Preface

This book reviews primarily the military era of Fort Sisseton, 1864-1889. The leasing of the fort, its restoration, and its use as a state park since military disbandment are also covered in the book.

The sources for the military part of the book are the original post records; War Department documents, made from reports provided by Fort Sisseton officers; and diaries of Fort Sisseton soldiers.

The National Archives, Washington, D.C., is the depository for the original, hand-written Fort Sisseton records. The records consisted of many letter-sized, hard-cover, rule-lined ledgers, leather-bound books, and archival boxes of correspondence. In most cases the paper was well preserved and the handwriting was very legible. I made hundreds of notations as I researched these records in the National Archives' reading room. In some cases, I obtained permission to make copies of the original documents. The National Archives' Cartographic Section, Alexandria, Virginia, provided me with additional information.

Some of the principal Fort Sisseton records in the National Archives were Letters Sent, Index of Letters Sent, Letters Received, Telegrams Sent, Index of Telegrams Sent, Telegrams Received, Post Medical History, Post Orders, Court-Martial Records, Post Fund, Quartermaster and Ordinance Records, and Post Returns. Letters and telegrams received were stored in archival boxes.

Military records in the South Dakota State Archives included a microfilm copy of Fort Sisseton's Post Returns; original War Department maps used for the restoration of Fort Sisseton; and Reports of the Secretary of War, 1862-1890. The South Dakota Adjutant General's Reports, 1887-1947, State Treasurer's Reports, 1902-1959, and other books and documents in the State Archives library provided much information about the fort since military disbandment.

What a thrill to read these original post records and walk along with the hundreds of soldiers who at one time or another called Fort Sisseton home! To share their experiences was an exciting adventure.

PART 1

HISTORICAL BACKGROUND

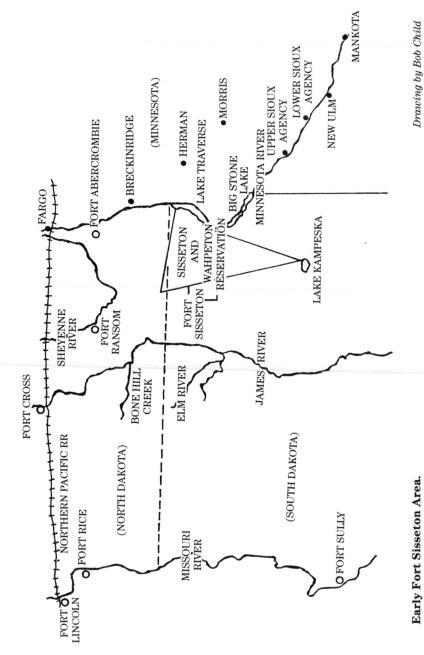

Drawing by Bob Child

Early Fort Sisseton Area.

Chapter 1

The Minnesota Sioux War

The story of Fort Sisseton, originally called Fort Wadsworth, begins with the 1862 Minnesota Sioux War, also known as the Dakota Conflict, which occurred in the Minnesota River valley. In 1851, Minnesota Sioux Sisseton and Wahpeton leaders had signed the Treaty of Traverse des Sioux wherein they agreed to sell most of their land in southern Minnesota, as well as land east of the Big Sioux River in present-day South Dakota, to the United States. These two tribes, with the Mdewakanton and Wahpekute Sioux, kept a small reservation consisting of a ten-mile-wide strip of land on each side of the Minnesota River between Lake Traverse and New Ulm. On the upper part of the reservation, federal officials built Yellow Medicine Agency for the Sisseton and Wahpeton tribes, called the "Upper Sioux." On the lower part, they built Redwood Agency for Mdewakantons and Wahpekutes, called the "Lower Sioux." Within a few years the land surrounding the reservation was filled with immigrant settlers.

The Minnesota Sioux, estimated between 4,500 and 6,200, were supposed to remain on their new reservation, peacefully changing from a hunting culture to a farming culture. It didn't work out that way. Their survival largely depended upon the government's treaty promises of providing them with annual payments for their land, annuities of food and clothing as well as farm implements. Inept policies of the United States Government helped create tension among the Sioux, culminating in August 1862, when annual land payments and foodstuffs were several months late in arriving. The relationship with nearby settlers was also strained, especially when the Sioux wandered off the reservation.

The murder of five settlers by four Sioux warriors at Acton, Minnesota, on Sunday 17 August 1862 was the spark that ignited a powderkeg of discontent on both sides. Alarmed settlers began organizing a defensive position, and the few soldiers at nearby Fort Ridgely were put on full alert. That night, the Lower Sioux, expecting reprisals for the Acton killings, met in council and decided to attack and drive the whites from their ancestral land. The next day, Chief Little Crow and his Lower Sioux warriors attacked Redwood Agency, killing many of the employees as well as looting and burning the buildings. Although many Sisseton and Wahpeton Sioux from the Upper Agency refused to join the uprising, Little Crow and his warriors attacked New Ulm on 19 August, but were repulsed. On 20 August, 400 warriors attacked Fort Ridgely, where many of the panic-stricken settlers had fled, but were repulsed. More than 800 warriors attacked the fort on 22 August, and again they were repulsed. But the warriors kept the fort under siege, while they continued to raid settlements in the area. Minnesota Governor Alexander Ramsey learned of the attack and commissioned the former governor, Henry H. Sibley, as a colonel and ordered him to organize several regiments of volunteers to quell the uprising.

On 6 September 1862, Governor Ramsey telegraphed President Lincoln with a request for military aid, reporting, "This is not our war. It is a national war. More than 500 whites have been murdered by Indians."[1] Lincoln acted the same day, creating the Military Department of the Northwest and placing Civil War Major General John Pope in charge, with headquarters in St. Paul. During September, the Sioux killed more settlers and pillaged the countryside. The conflict continued until 23 September 1862, when Sibley's force of some 1,600 men subdued and scattered Little Crow's 700 warriors at the battle of Wood Lake, which ended the uprising. On 27 September, Sibley's force rescued 269 men, women, and children at Camp Release.

Minnesota Sioux to Dakota Territory

Following the battle of Wood Lake, Little Crow, with many of his followers, Mdewakanton and Wahpekute, as well as the Sissetons and Waphetons, retreated west into Dakota Territory. About 1,200 Sioux, who had surrendered to Sibley, were taken to a fenced enclosure near Fort Snelling. Another 307 were captured, imprisoned, and tried before a military tribunal, which sentenced them to die.

Through intervention by President Lincoln, only thirty-eight were hanged, and the remainder imprisoned at Fort Davenport.

The United States Congress, by the Forfeiture Act of 1863, annulled the 1851 Treaty and reclaimed the land for the United States. That year, Congress also provided funds to transfer all of the captive Sioux in Minnesota to a reservation at Crow Creek, Dakota Territory. The forced exodus of the Minnesota Sioux was complete. Although the war with the Sioux in Minnesota was over, it was about to begin in the Dakota Territory.

Protecting the Minnesota Frontier

1863 Sully Expedition

After Wood Lake, Little Crow and his followers fled to Devils Lake in present-day North Dakota, then to Canada. Sissetons and Wahpetons, believing that the Sibley forces could not tell the difference between friendly and hostile Sioux, moved to the Coteau des Prairie, the upper James River basin, and the Missouri River drainage basin. Lakota situated along the Missouri River and Yanktonais in the upper James River area were alarmed at the turn of events for the Minnesota Sioux. Obviously, a state of war existed between Sioux people and the United States Government.

When General Pope arrived in St. Paul in October 1862, he believed there could be as many as 4,000 to 5,000 hostile Sioux warriors in the Dakota Territory and feared they might attack the Minnesota frontier. In defense of non-Indians early in 1863, Pope implemented a two-part plan. First, he would send an armed force into Dakota Territory to attack the Sioux and drive them west of the Missouri River. Second, he would order the construction of new forts west of Minnesota to keep the Sioux from returning. One of these would be Fort Wadsworth.

Pope then asked the governors of Minnesota, Iowa, Wisconsin, and Dakota Territory to expand their volunteer military forces, which would be federalized into the United States Army. His field plan called for a pincer movement against the Sioux. General Sibley would lead a force from Fort Ridgely, Minnesota, to a point on the Missouri River near Bismarck. General Alfred Sully would lead a force via Yankton and Fort Randall to the same point. Sibley led about 3,052 infantrymen, 800 cavalrymen, 148 artillerymen, Major

Joseph Brown's seventy-five Indian Scouts, and 225 six-mule-team wagons. Carrying provisions for ninety days, they left Camp Pope near Fort Ridgely on 16 June 1863.

This large force camped several times in present-day Roberts County, South Dakota, on its way to the Devils Lake area. Between Devils Lake and the Missouri River, Sibley's force fought and routed about 2,000 Sioux warriors at three battles: Big Mound, Dead Buffalo Lake, and Stony Lake. As many as 10,000 warriors and their families fled west of the Missouri River. Sibley reached the rendezvous point on 29 July. He waited three days for General Sully, each night firing signal rockets into the air without any response. Finally, Sibley returned to Minnesota, scouring the countryside for Indians along the way.

The Sully force of about 1,200 cavalrymen, 325 infantrymen, and 150 supply wagons left Yankton city on 26 June 1863 for Fort Pierre II. Because of low water on the Missouri, his supply steamboats were delayed. Sully finally left Fort Pierre II on 13 August and reached the rendezvous point near Bismarck, long after Sibley had left. Sully noted that many Sioux had already returned east of the Missouri to their old hunting grounds. He directed his force to White Stone Hill (near present-day Ellendale, North Dakota), where he fought a decisive battle with about 1,500 warriors. Sully then headed west before returning to the Fort Pierre II area on 14 September 1863. Here he ordered the construction of Fort Sully I, five miles east of present-day Pierre, South Dakota.

1864 Sully Expedition

The 1863 Sully expedition displayed the strength of the United States Army, but did little damage to the prairie tribes. Many were driven west of the river, but some tribes returned to their hunting grounds between the Missouri and the James rivers as soon as the Sully and Sibley campaigns ended. The Sully expedition forced the Sioux, including the Mdewakanton, Wahpekute, and some of the Sisseton and Wahpeton people, to unite. General Sully expected them to attack the Minnesota frontier in 1864.

During the winter of 1863-1864, General Pope moved his headquarters to Milwaukee and reorganized the Department of Northwest into three military districts: Minnesota, commanded by Brigadier General Henry H. Sibley; Iowa, (consisting of Iowa and Dakota Territory), commanded by Brigadier General Alfred Sully;

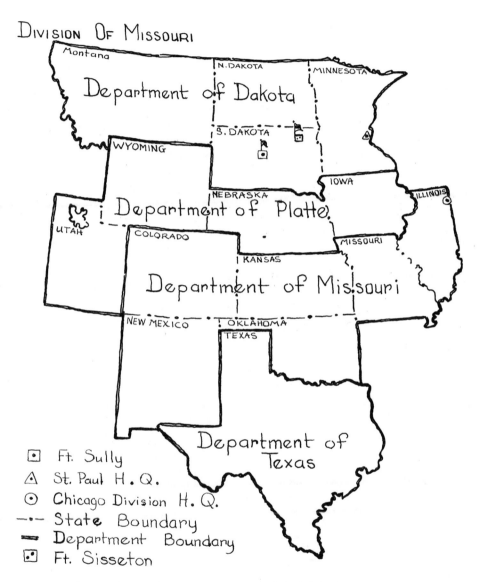

Military Division of Missouri.

Drawing by Nancyjane Marie Huehl

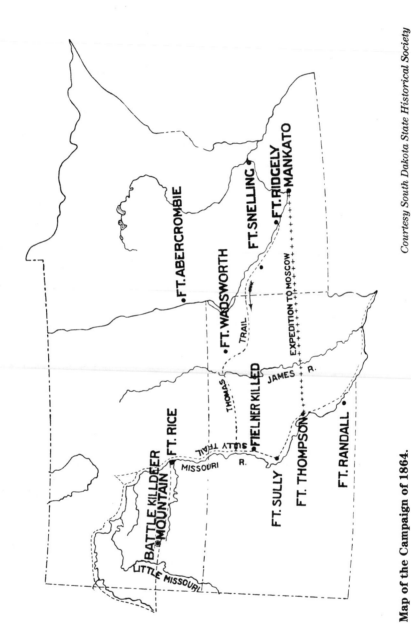

Map of the Campaign of 1864.

and Wisconsin, commanded by Brigadier General T. C. H. Smith. In February 1864, War Department officers authorized General Pope to send 2,200 soldiers into Dakota Territory to force the Sioux either to fight or sue for peace.

Pope also received orders to build more forts in Indian Country, one of them, Fort Wadsworth, close to the James River, between the head of the Couteau des Prairie and Fort Rice, on the Upper Missouri. General Sibley noted that the country between Devils Lake and Fort Wadsworth was "in the heart of the country inhabited by the powerful upper bands of (Sisseton and Wahpeton) Sioux or Dakota...within striking distance of the settlements of Minnesota."[2]

When completed, soldiers in a chain of forts—Abercrombie, Wadsworth (Sisseton), Rice, Sully I, Thompson, and Randall—would keep the Sioux far west of the borders of Minnesota, Iowa, and the southeastern counties of Dakota Territory. The Sully force would help protect immigrants traveling overland to Montana and Idaho and "sweep the whole region now occupied by the hostile Indians north of a line from Fort Sully I to Fort Abercrombie."[3]

The 1864 Sully expedition consisted of two units. The First Brigade of about 700 men included companies from the Sixth and Seventh Iowa Cavalry, the Dakota Cavalry (from Yankton and Vermillion), Brackett's Minnesota Battalion, plus a battery of four mountain howitzers, and Major Joseph Brown's seventy Indian scouts. The Second Brigade of some 1,500 men, often called the Minnesota Brigade, consisted of ten companies of the Eighth Minnesota Infantry, six companies of the Second Minnesota Cavalry, Indian scouts, and a battery of four mountain howitzers.

Under Brigade Commander Colonel Minot T. Thomas, the Minnesotans left Fort Ridgely on 6 June 1864 and marched to Swan Lake, near the Missouri River, to join with General Sully and the First Brigade. En route, Indian scouts traveled in advance as well as on the flanks of the column. Colonel Thomas took defensive measures for the brigade's nightly camps: camped on high ground; corralled the cattle, mules, and horses inside the wagons; posted artillery and guards; and dug rifle pits. The two brigades met on 30 June 1864, then marched to the confluence of the Cannonball and Missouri rivers, where they left four infantry companies to build Fort Rice.

On 28 July, they encountered a large force of Sioux at Killdeer Mountain, about ninety miles northwest of present-day Bismarck.

After a day-long battle, Sully lost five men, and the Sioux lost about 150 before they were dispersed. Colonel Thomas described the brigade's participation in the battle:

> After a few minutes the whole line advanced in the same direction, the whole brigade moving as rapidly as possible, much of the time on the run over broken ground, the firing being kept up briskly and with good effect. After advancing about two miles the enemy rapidly retreated. The Second Cavalry was mounted and pushed rapidly forward, and the Eighth Regiment closed to the right by companies and the whole line closed on the enemy's abandoned camp. The next day, Colonel Robert N. McLaren, (from Redwing, Minnesota) with four companies of the Second Cavalry...and a large portion of the First Brigade, worked with a will for six hours destroying the abandoned property of the Indians...belonging to the camp of 1,600 lodges. At dusk, two pickets, members of Company D, Second Minnesota Cavalry, were surprised and killed by a small party of Indians which is the only casualty of consequence...during the engagement.[4]

Sully continued west to the Little Missouri River, where on 8 August 1864 he again engaged and scattered the Sioux. Early in September, Private George W. Doud, of the Eighth Minnesota Infantry, described the expedition's encounter with buffalo:

> September 1—Buffalo seen in heards [sic] of thousands from 10 am to 3 pm. Just before we camped a heard ran along the lines of the 8th Minnesota. The boys let the balls fly and shot down 8 along the lines. After we camped at the lake whare [sic] was from 8 to 10 thousand buffalo in sight on the hills 1 1/2 miles off. Boys shooting all the time in every direction. Some 50 buffalo shot. September 2—Buffalo in sight in large heards of thousands all the way. Some run into the wagon train. September 6—Buffalo in sight all day in heards of thousands. Hard work to keep them out of the train. The boys shot many of the buffalo during the day.[5]

After the summer campaigns, Sully and the First Brigade headed to Fort Sully I, and Colonel Thomas and the Second Brigade turned toward Minnesota. Thomas scoured the region for Indians south of

Devils Lake, between Forts Rice and Wadsworth, both under construction. Arriving at Fort Wadsworth on 26 September 1864, Colonel Minor T. Thomas left Major Robert H. Rose (from Scott County, Minnesota) and Companies B, C, D, and H of the Second Minnesota Cavalry. Rose and his men replaced Major John Clowney and three companies of the Thirtieth Wisconsin Infantry and one company of the Second Minnesota Cavalry, who had been building Fort Wadsworth since 1 August. Major Rose and his four companies of the Second Minnesota Cavalry, consisting of seasoned Indian fighters of the 1864 expedition, continued construction of the fort and established its defensive breastworks.

1865 Sully Expedition

In 1865, General Sully led another expedition into Dakota Territory, west of the Missouri River. After receiving reports that the Sioux at Devils Lake planned to attack Forts Abercrombie and Wadsworth, while Sully was west of the Missouri, General Pope ordered Sully to Devils Lake to confront the Sioux.

Sully and about 1,000 men searched the Indian camps at Devils Lake, but found no hostile people. He then headed for Fort Rice, where on 16 July he encountered 300 lodges of Sioux, who were ready to talk peace. After a march to Fort Berthold, where he found few Indians, he returned to Fort Sully I on 13 September. He made preparations at the fort for an October peace conference with the Sioux.

A Fragile Peace

After three expeditions by Sully, both the Sioux and the United States Army soldiers were weary of fighting. Consequently, a peace conference was called for October 1865 at Fort Sully I. After long deliberations, seven Lakota tribes, as well as some Yanktonai, agreed to cease fighting, recognize the sovereignty of the United States Government, and permit the construction of roads across Dakota Territory. In turn, the Sioux would receive annuities of food and clothing in the amount of $30 a lodge for twenty years. It was a fragile peace, however, because such leaders as Red Cloud, Spotted Tail, and Sitting Bull refused to endorse the terms.

Some 200 lodges of Sisseton and Wahpeton tribes who did not participate in the 1865 peace conference were also desirous of peace. In 1867, a treaty between the two tribes and the United States was approved. Two reservations were recognized in the treaty, one at Lake Traverse and the other at Devils Lake. Members of the tribes received annuities of food, clothing, seed, and agricultural tools. The pie-shaped 918,780-acre Lake Traverse Reservation was located just east of Fort Wadsworth.

Sioux people in other parts of Dakota Territory, including some Minnesota Sioux, continued to confront United States Army soldiers. In 1866, trouble developed between United States Army forces and those of Red Cloud in the Powder River country in present-day Montana. Red Cloud, who had refused to allow federal employees to build a wagon road between Fort Laramie and Bozeman, Montana, laid siege to the area. Negotiations between Sioux tribal leaders and spokesmen for the United States resulted in the 1868 Fort Laramie Treaty. One of its provisions was the creation of the Great Sioux Reservation, which included all of the land west of the Missouri River in present-day South Dakota.

The change from a hunting and gleaning culture to a sedentary society on a reservation was difficult. Many warriors believed it beneath their dignity to farm. Consequently, many of the Sioux would not cooperate with the agency-sponsored agricultural programs. They were willing, however, to accept treaty annuities.

An uneasy peace lasted until 1874, when gold-seekers began entering the Black Hills, in violation of the 1868 treaty. United States Army troops struggled with the job of keeping thousands of prospectors out, but failed. Efforts by federal officials to obtain the Black Hills by treaty also failed. In the meantime, several thousand disgruntled Sioux warriors, tired of reservation life and the failure of the United States to enforce the 1868 treaty, left the reservations and assembled at the Big Horn River in present-day Montana.

In February 1876, Bureau of Indian Affairs leaders turned to United States Army leaders for assistance in returning Sioux people to their respective reservations. Military leaders sent three forces to Montana, culminating in the Battle of Little Big Horn on 25 June 1876. Colonel Custer and more than 200 of his men died in this battle. In the aftermath, the Sioux scattered, and many returned to the Great Sioux Reservation.

In 1877, the United States seized the Black Hills by an Act of Congress, leaving the remainder of the Great Sioux Reservation intact. (In 1980, the United States Supreme Court ruled that the 1877

Act of Congress wrongfully seized the Black Hills from the Sioux without just compensation.) Intermittent military action continued in Lakota country until the Wounded Knee tragedy of 1890.

The massacre at Wounded Knee was the last major confrontation between the United States Army troops and the Sioux. What had started in 1862 as an uprising by the Minnesota Sioux turned into a twenty-eight-year armed conflict between the Sioux in Dakota Territory and the United States Army. The military mission of Fort Sisseton during that period was significant, because it was an integral part of the United States Army's fort system.

Endnotes

1. Kenneth Carley. *The Sioux Uprising of 1862*. St. Paul:Minnesota Historical Society, 1976:59.

2. H. H. Sibley to W. S. Ketchum, July 1864. *South Dakota Historical Collections* 8:399. (Hereafter cited as *SDHC*.)

3. John Pope to Henry H. Sibley, 18 January 1864. *SDHC* 8:150.

4. Colonel Minor Thomas, Report, 1 September 1864. *SDHC* 8:379.

5. George W. Doud Diary. South Dakota Archives, Pierre, South Dakota.

Chapter 2
Military Mission of Fort Sisseton

From 1864 to 1889, Fort Wadsworth (the name was changed to Fort Sisseton in 1876) was one of several key military posts in the Dakota Territory. A military presence at the post played an important role in the non-Indian settlement of Minnesota and of North and South Dakota. Its military mission consisted of three broad charges: keeping the Sioux west of the James River to prevent raids on the settlements in Minnesota and Dakota Territory; protecting friendly Sioux and keeping the peace on the Lake Traverse Reservation; and providing military escorts.

Keeping the Sioux West of the James River

Locating Fort Wadsworth

To keep the Sioux west of the James River, General John Pope wanted to build Fort Wadsworth near the confluence of Elm Creek and the James River, which was on the main route of Sioux travel. General Henry H. Sibley, advised by his scouts, Major Joseph Brown, Pierre Bottineau, and Norman Kittson, thought there were too few trees near the proposed James River site to build a post. It would be better to build it forty miles east at the head of the Coteau des Prairie (Hills of the Prairie). Although General Pope insisted that a military post east of the James River would be out of line with Fort Abercrombie and other posts, eventually he agreed to locating it at the head of the Coteau des Prairie.

On 12 May 1864, the War Department issued General Order 197, naming the new post Fort Wadsworth in honor of General James W.

Wadsworth, who died at the Battle of the Wilderness in Virginia during the Civil War. (In 1876, to avoid confusion with Fort Wadsworth
on Staten Island, New York, the post was renamed Fort Sisseton in
honor of the nearby Sisseton tribe.) Major John Clowney, from
Mineral Point, Wisconsin, was placed in command of a detachment
of men from the Thirtieth Wisconsin Infantry. They would be
assigned the task of building the post. On 9 June, General Sibley
assured General Pope that the architect's ground plan of the post
would be given to Major Clowney to "insure the erection of suitable
buildings and defenses."[1]

Colonel Thomas and the Minnesota Brigade had left Fort
Ridgely on 6 June 1864 to join General Sully on the Missouri River.
The quartermaster at Fort Snelling then rushed to complete General
Sibley's order to equip Major Clowney's expedition. Some of the
equipage and supplies for the expedition, as well as for the construction and stocking of the new Fort Wadsworth, included building
materials, other than stone and wood available locally; horse-
powered sawmill; three cannon; tents; tools; supplies and equipment; medical supplies; a five-months' food supply to 1 November
consisting of salt pork, smoked ham and bacon, beans, potatoes,
hardtack, flour, coffee, sugar, salt; rifle and cannon ammunition;
extra clothing; and grain for Clowney's horses and the hundreds of
horses and mules that pulled George Brackett's 200 wagons. Federal
officials had hired George Brackett's transportation company to haul
supplies to the site.

Major Clowney and his wagon train left Fort Ridgely, Minnesota,
on 10 July 1864 for the head of the Coteau des Prairie, generally
referred to as "Coteau." His command of twelve officers and 311
enlisted men consisted of Companies B, E, K of the Thirtieth
Wisconsin Infantry; Company M, Second Minnesota Cavalry; Third
Section, Third Minnesota Light Battery; Surgeon Lamberton; and
Chief Scout Pierre Bottineau and twenty-five Indian scouts.
Bottineau was paid $5.50 per day for his services.

On 25 July, after marching 183 miles in fifteen days, averaging
twelve miles a day, Clowney made camp at 10:00 a.m. on Kettle
Lakes in the area of present-day Fort Sisseton. The next day Major
Clowney, following General Sibley's instructions, ordered Captain
Lewis S. Burton and 157 men to explore the James River from the
mouth of Elm River to Bone Hill River. The detachment consisted of
sixty cavalrymen, seventy-five infantrymen, Pierre Bottineau and ten

scouts, and eleven men with one mountain howitzer. Burton was to make one more determination as to whether or not there was enough timber to build a post near the James River. While Burton was absent, Clowney surveyed the Kettle Lakes area to search for an appropriate site to build the post.

On 1 August 1864, Captain Burton returned and confirmed a lack of timber along the James River, and based upon that information, Major Clowney located Fort Wadsworth that day. Clowney's site was on a knoll in the midst of rolling hills surrounded by many small lakes. There was sufficient stone and timber for buildings and fuel and clay for making bricks. The unspoiled area of oak and cotton-wood trees, grass, small lakes, and marshes was a haven for birds, wildlife, and fish. On 3 August, Major Clowney advised General Sibley in St. Paul that "the fort will front to the south, and in front has a fine slope rising from a neck between two lakes. There is a fine view in front with nothing to cover an enemy for a half a mile. There are no unfriendly Indians in the vicinity of this post; still I keep up the guards as if I expected an attack."[2]

Defense of Fort Wadsworth

Immediately after the selection of the post site, Major Clowney and his command moved to a permanent camp nearby. After the supplies were unloaded from the 200 wagons, twenty-nine men were provided as a military escort for the teamsters returning to Fort Ridgely. Major Clowney then ordered the men to erect a tent city which they would use as quarters during construction of the post. Each four-man tent, with wood-slab floors, contained a wood-burning stove. Tents were also erected for the officers and the hospital. By October, however, the officers and men and some of the supplies were quartered in temporary log huts.

Major Clowney's immediate defensive plan included stationing guards at strategic positions around the camp and the stacks of supplies. Clowney also placed the six-pound cannon and the two 12-pound mountain howitzers at three of the corners and constructed a sixteen-foot by eleven-foot log magazine, for ammunition storage. In addition, every infantryman was armed with a .58 caliber single-shot, muzzle-loading Springfield rifle. Clowney then began laying out the post according to St. Paul architect H. M. Ackeroyd's ground plan given to him by General Sibley. The first defensive measure was building the two-story block houses at the southeast and northwest corners. The following is his description of the construction of the block houses:

> Since the establishment of the post I have been making preparations for the construction of all necessary buildings by having all the men not...on guard duty, engaged in entrenching on the line as laid down on the plan, and securing and hewing the timbers for the block houses, preparing the saw mill and all the tools. Captain McKusick will have the mill in operation I think this week. Some men also engaged in burning coal and lime and some hauling rock for the foundations for block houses; two men engaged in digging a well, and all the men busily engaged.[3]

By 1 September, construction stopped on the block houses, which were then one-story high, in order to build log quarters for the men. The block houses, built with hewn oak timber seven by eight inches thick, were almost impregnable. The outside, except for the rifle niches and doors for the cannon, was covered with one-and-one-half-inch-thick oak plank. Each block house contained a twelve-pound mountain howitzer. The howitzers had been placed at two of the corners. The one-story block houses permitted a wide sweep of the terrain around the post. With the defensive positions of the post well underway, Clowney turned his attention toward defense of the area. He also executed the post's main military mission, keeping the Sioux west of the James River. Both of the missions had to be carried on during construction.

Defense of the Area

Fort Wadsworth was centered in a large area between the upper James River and the Minnesota border. General Henry H. Sibley in August 1864 reported there were many Sioux in that area: "Remnants of Mdewakanton, Wahpeton and Sisseton Sioux, who participated more or less actively in the outbreak of 1862, 450 lodges, containing 2,700; bands of Yanktonais in the region of Devil's Lake, 1,000 lodges, 6,000; Sisseton Sioux and Cut Heads who did not join in the massacres of 1862 and who are generally inclined to peace, 200 lodges, 1,200."[4] United States Army officers placed Fort Wadsworth right on the route the Minnesota Sioux traveled, to keep them from returning to Minnesota.

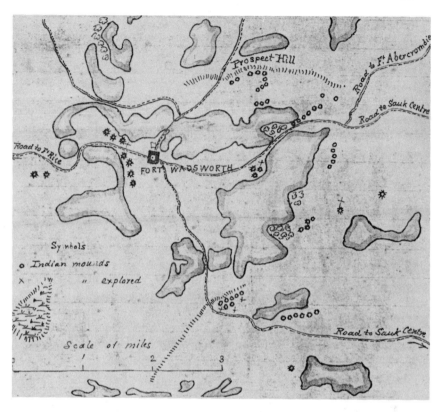

Fort Sisseton roads and Indian mounds, drawn by Post Surgeon A. I. Comfort, 1869.

Courtesy Minnesota Historical Society

Clowney used Captain John C. Hanley's Company M, Second Minnesota Cavalry, and Gabriel Renville's mounted Indian scouts to patrol the immediate area. This also provided protection for the infantrymen building the post. On 28 July 1864, Clowney's scout force was almost doubled with the arrival of Major Joseph R. Brown and twelve scouts. Brown had been Chief of Scouts with General Alfred Sully on the Northwest Indian Expedition, but was ordered to the new post to serve as Chief of Scouts under Major Clowney. On 9 August, however, Major Brown was promoted to Special Military Agent for the post and vicinity at a salary of $5.00 per day, and Gabriel Renville was named Chief of Scouts. Major Clowney was advised that the main objective of Brown's appointment was "to

have an experienced and competent person to communicate with
those Sioux Indians who are desirous of a restoration of their former
friendly relations with the government, and thus relieve you from
details...in your labors during the progress of the building. Major
Brown...will be under your general orders. Instruct Gabriel Renville,
Chief of Scouts, with those attached to him, to give all the aid they
can to Major Brown."[5]

Brown was no stranger to the area, having at one time
(1843-1846) operated trading posts in Sica Hollow, in what is now
Roberts County, and on Buffalo Lake in Marshall County. Following
the 1862 Minnesota Sioux War, he served as Chief of Scouts for
Generals Sibley and Sully in the 1863-1864 Sully expeditions. Brown
was employed by the army, and even though he did not hold a military commission, he was called "Major."

Although Clowney reported that no Indians had attacked the
post, he was very concerned about their presence nearby. His concern was evident on 10 August when he contracted Mark Donnie to
cut hay on a meadow seventeen miles west of the post for the command's 157 horses. The major provided a guard of thirty infantrymen, ten cavalrymen, four scouts, and one mountain howitzer with
six men, commanded by Captain John Klatt, for protection of
Donnie and his men.

After a survey of the area, Brown found Indians from Crow
Creek located on the Coteau, as well as Indians who had made peace
and were hunting on the Coteau. He also found hostile Indians who
had come down the James River and headed east to the Minnesota
settlements where they stole horses and interfered with the settlers.
Brown wrote to Major Clowney the following:

> Although these predatory excursions may not result in the
> loss of life and property to any great extent, they are sufficiently
> numerous and formidable to keep the [Minnesota] frontier in
> continuous ferment. Indians encamped on the Coteau, either
> above or below this post, and all that may be encamped on the
> James River flat, be immediately ordered to the west side of the
> James River and that the orders be promptly enforced. Those
> Indians being under the protection of government, should not be
> exposed to the danger of attack from the troops or scouts when
> searching for hostile Indians. A detachment of mounted scouts
> with a few troops be stationed both at the Hawks Nest on the

Special Military Agency built one mile east of Fort Sisseton by Joseph R. Brown for Frontier Indian Scout Force headquarters. When the Frontier Indian Scout Force disbanded in 1867, Brown moved the log building to Browns Valley, Minnesota. It is currently used as a museum.

Courtesy Joseph R. Brown Museum, Browns Valley, Minnesota

Coteau and Cottonwood Grove on the James River, to intercept hostile parties passing either to or from the settlements.[6]

Major Brown and his scouts began construction of what he called a "Special Military Agency" about a mile east of the post. The twenty-foot-by-fifty-foot oak log building was surrounded by a twelve-foot-high stockade with slots for musketry. The building was used for storage of scouts' guns, ammunition, and rations. It was also Brown's office and residence.

Gabriel Renville and his scouts, located at the camp at the mouth of Elm Creek on the James, continued patrolling the area searching for hostile Indians. Each of Renville's scouts was paid a daily ration of meat, flour, beans, coffee, sugar, and soap for each adult and a half ration for each child in his family. Some of the friendly Sissetons were turning themselves in at Renville's camp where they, too, received rations and protection from hostile Sioux.

Major Clowney continued construction of the post. He was also busy directing its defense and that of the area in order to keep the hostile Sioux at a distance. Each day guards were picked to serve for a twenty-four-hour period. They were stationed at various guard posts for a two-hour shift and were required to challenge anyone who approached them and ask for the countersign. He directed the Indian scout activities of Major Joseph Brown and Gabriel Renville as well as the cavalry company, all of whom conducted daily patrols of the area. On 19 August, General Sibley's adjutant wrote Clowney that the general was "pleased to learn the scouts are doing a good service. It is important the valley of the James River as well as the approaches to the Minnesota River by way of Lake Traverse be closely watched, so that the earliest information of the passage downward of war parties may be communicated through you to these headquarters. Although no hostile Indians have been discovered about Fort Wadsworth, too much care and vigilance cannot be exercised."[7]

Both Brown and Renville were concerned about the increasing number of Indians roaming the area. They believed there would be more raids by hostile Sioux, and it was imperative that defensive measures be increased to keep the Sioux from passing east to the settlements. The two scout leaders recommended to Major Clowney that more Indian scout camps be established in the region.

Change of Command

The Minnesota Brigade, commanded by Colonel Minor T. Thomas, on its return from the Sully expedition, stopped at Fort Wadsworth on 26 September 1864. Two privates with the brigade told a little about life at the post in their diaries.

Private George W. Doud described his stop as follows:

> Sunday September 25, 1864—Camp among Coteaus. Lay over all day. Co. F kills one buffalo. The scouts discover Fort Wadsworth 25 mls [sic] to the southeast. One of the scouts lost. Last night the battery throw up skyrockets to light him in. Scouts return in evening at 10. Report Fort Wadsworth 20 miles off. Skyrockets thrown up to light them in they saw them 12 mls distant.

September 26, 1864—On coteaus. Rev. [Reveille] 4 am. Mch [March] 5 am South east 18 mls camp at Kettle Lakes 2 Pm near Ft. Wadsworth. High winds and chilly, water good and wood a plenty. Co. M boys of 2 cavalry and 3 wisc boys [from Fort Wadsworth] in camp before tents were up.

Tues. September 27, 1864 at Kettle Lakes. Morn very cool. I go over to see the Ft. A very pleasant situation and Lakes on every side. There was a narrow strip of land to go in and out from the Ft. Lakes. Sandy beach. Sut [Sutler] Store at the Ft. Shoulder Straps [officers] of the drinking kind...admitted in the house. No private soldier admitted in doors. They go to a window and get down on their knees and beg for what they want.[8]

Private Lewis C. Paxon, also of the Eighth Minnesota Regiment, reports similar experiences at the post:

Sunday September 25, 1864: Hayes, Crow and myself went after plums and found only a few. Did not march today. Sent up rockets in the evening. Sermon, "Beware, lest ye fall into like temptation". I made a pair of mittens of socks, and took a general wash.

Monday, September 26, 1864: Marched 20 miles nearly south and reached Fort Wadsworth, D.T. afternoon. I bought five apple pies for $1.

Tuesday, September 27, 1864: Laid over. Went after "Return" [return from work call] to fort; paid 30 for rations; wrote to H. B. Grant. I lost and found pony. Cold and blustery.[9]

Needless to say Colonel Thomas' brigade of 1,500 men and Major Clowney's 311 men, along with hundreds of horses from both groups, created a melee of activity at the post during the three-day stop. Hundreds of tents and cooking fires dotted the landscape around the post. The post sutler, Mark Donnie, was kept busy serving the soldiers' needs. Colonel Thomas was carrying orders from General Sibley to change the command at the post. He was ordered to leave Major Robert H. Rose and Companies B, C, D, and H of the Second Minnesota Cavalry, and to replace Major Clowney and his men of the Thirtieth Wisconsin Infantry.

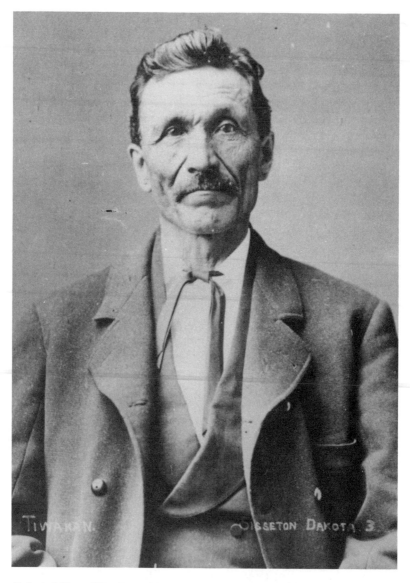

Gabriel Renville, frontier Indian scout and chief, Lake Traverse Reservation, 1884.

Courtesy South Dakota Archives

Major Rose Expands Scout Force

Rose's four battle-seasoned Second Cavalry Companies, having just experienced combat with the Sioux in the western part of Dakota Territory, turned their attention to the defense of the area and to building Fort Wadsworth. Major Rose, thirty-two years of age, was disappointed to find that little had been done in the construction of buildings. He ordered the construction of the log hospital, commissary, and magazine, and the finishing of the stockade. He also hoped to finish the men's log quarters before winter.

Major Rose soon discovered that the area was occupied with Sioux Indians, many of them hostile. He followed Major Brown's plan and moved Gabriel Renville and his twelve scouts and their families from the mouth of the Elm River, on the west side of the James River, to a new camp in the midst of a cottonwood grove on the east side and close to the James River. The James River Camp, also called Cottonwood Grove Camp, was a little south of present-day Putney, South Dakota. Not only would the new location help improve patrolling of the area, but it would serve as a better camp for surrendering Sioux.

Defense of the area between the Upper James River basin and the Minnesota border was a continuing duty for Major Rose during the fall of 1864. At the time, Major Brown, Special Military Agent, had thirty-four Indian scouts, employed by the government, at the following locations:

1. Gabriel Renville, chief of scouts, at the James River Camp, plus twelve scouts;
2. Charles Crawford, chief at the Special Military Agency east of the post, plus nineteen scouts. Samuel J. Brown, son of Major Joseph Brown, was listed as interpreter. All of the above scouts, except four men who were used to carry the mail between the post and Fort Abercrombie, were on patrol each day. Occasionally scouts were also used for courier and escort service.[10]

Many problems and incidents faced the scouts and soldiers that fall. On 15 October 1864, Brackett's train of 200 wagons with subsistence for 800 men for one year arrived at the post, requiring more men to guard the stacks of supplies.[11]

Four hostiles passed through the Coteau between the post and the hay meadow on 26 October 1864 to evade the scouts on the

James River and troops at the meadow seventeen miles west of the post. Large numbers of Indians from Fort Thompson moved east to the Coteau to hunt. Joseph R. Brown wrote to Major Rose that, "If measures are not promptly taken to send them back, the entire camp of Sioux located at Fort Thompson will be over here before the winter sets in."[12]

On 1 November 1864, Major Rose wrote to General Sibley, "I start the patrols out every morning before daylight and have them patrol around near the fort for several hours, then go back into the country and examine all places of concealment and crossings until about two hours of sun, when they return and patrol again around the fort until after dark."[13]

Later, on 3 November 1864, Rose wrote, "My scouts yesterday afternoon killed two Indians, one of Little Six's and the other of Red Leg's band. Their avowed purpose was to take the life of Gabriel Renville, chief of scouts."[14]

A few days later Major Rose also wrote to the Adjutant of the Department of Dakota:

> I have no special reason to anticipate an attack [on the post] but shall always keep a good lookout and be prepared for anything that may turn up. Saturday night a messenger was sent in from the hay field to inform me that after dark a half-blood came to the camp and told them that he had been told by two friendly Indians from up country that the Indians were getting together to attack the camp. I sent Lieutenant Hunt with twenty-five cavalrymen and one mountain howitzer to reinforce the camp. The lieutenant sent in word today. All quiet. They have a strong position and fortified. I have no fears for them.[15]

General Sibley advised General Pope on 16 November 1864, "Two hostile Indians were killed by the scouts on the James River. An attack was threatened on the party of soldiers guarding the hay at a distance from the fort. The detachment, however, had been reinforced and no danger was apprehended on their account."[16]

Among the upper bands of Sioux, there was a breach between those who wanted peace and those who wanted to fight. Those who wanted peace came into the fort for military protection. Red Feather and twelve lodges turned themselves in at Renville's camp on the James River.

In late November the second stories of the two blockhouses were completed, providing added security for the post. Because of a shortage of logs, Major Rose built a sod-revetment around the post instead of a stockade. He reported to General Sibley the following:

> I am having made in place of a stockade an embankment, to be sodded, and two 8-inch beams on top, the lower one pierced for musketry, when completed to be eight feet high, with a ditch nine feet wide in front, the entrances to have substantial gates, and the upper story of both bastions pierced for musketry, so the ditches can be swept by both artillery and musketry. When finished...we can with a small force bid defiance to all the Indians in the northwest.[17]

General Sibley on 17 November, commented on the fort's value to the region: "I am more and more satisfied that Fort Wadsworth will prove to be one of the most important military stations in the northwest. Defensive works are being constructed which will render the fort secure against attack by any force of Indians who may venture to assail it."[18]

In November 1864, both Major Brown and Gabriel Renville recommended to Major Rose that another fifty scouts be added to the thirty-four scouts then on duty. The fifty new scouts would be picked by Renville from the surrendered Sisseton and Wahpeton at his camp and placed in new scout camps in the area. Apparently, Rose was successful in convincing General Sibley of the need for additional scouts because that month Sibley advised General Pope of his policy:

> I have already employed quite a number of the friendly Sissetons for the last three months in general scouting duty and in intercepting raiding parties from the hostile camps, and they have rendered excellent service. It is my intention to increase this...force by the addition of the warriors who have already come in, and will do so during the winter, so as to have them prepared to cooperate with the troops in the spring operations against the Indians, who still maintain a defiant attitude. No pay will be allowed them, but I shall station some trusty scouts in their camp and direct that...rations shall be made to the Indians.[19]

Frontier Indian Scout Force

In January 1865, Major Brown advised Post Commander Rose that as many as 200 more lodges of Sisseton and Wahpeton who took no part in the Minnesota Sioux War were ready to turn themselves in at Renville's James River Camp. Furthermore, there were as many as 150 lodges of Yanktonai and sixty lodges of Teton at Oak Grove on the east side of the James River. There were also 300 to 500 lodges of various Missouri River bands who had settled their differences with the United States at the Fort Sully I peace conference who were hunting between the Missouri River and the Coteau.[20]

It was obvious that Major Rose's soldiers, and the two Indian scout camps, one at the James River and the other at the post, would have difficulty keeping the Sioux, not all necessarily hostile, west of the James River. In order to arrange for the surrendering Sissetons and Wahpetons, as well as increasing surveillance of other bands in the area, General Sibley, in early spring, authorized Major Rose to increase the Frontier Indian Scout Force to 100, "which will give you the means to intercept all parties of Indians bound for the settlements."[21]

Brown and Renville set up five new Indian scout camps: Hawk's Nest (Buzzard's Roost) Camp, between present-day Bristol and Andover at the foot of a butte overlooking the James River flats, led by Chief Scout Solomon Two Stars; Drifting Guts Camp, about fifteen miles southwest of the post, with Chief Scout Makacega (Jug) in charge; Lake Traverse Camp, at the south end of Lake Traverse, with Chief Scout Wasuideya; Elm River Camp, near present-day Ordway, South Dakota, with Chief Scout Joseph Roulliard; and Surrender Camp, about six miles northeast of the post near Six-mile Lake, with Chief Scout Wamdiupiduta (Red Feather).[22]

By March 1865, seventy lodges of Sisseton and Wahpeton, about ten people per lodge, had come into Surrender Camp, and by May, it reached 200 lodges, including 600 warriors. They were provided protection, rations, and seed for planting.

Most of the new Indian scouts were full-blood or mixed-blood Sisseton and Wahpeton from Renville's James River Camp. They were loyal to the government and to their superiors. They helped attract other Indians to come to the camps and surrender. There were from ten to seventeen Indian scouts and their families, who lived in tepees, at each of the camps. Each scout was paid $2.00 a day plus a daily ration of food for each adult in the family and one-half ration for each child. The chief scout was given a hand-mirror for signaling. He was instructed to build a defensive earthwork around the camp as well. The army provided muzzle-loading Smith carbines and Sharps carbines and ammunition for the scouts, but each scout was expected to provide his own horse. All the camps, some as much as a two-days' ride away, were supplied and managed from Fort Wadsworth. The Frontier Indian Scout Force helped avoid any direct attacks on the post.

The scout camps were busy in the spring and summer of 1865 patrolling their areas, as reflected in Fort Wadsworth's records: On 2 April 1865, Major Rose ordered a lieutenant and six men of Company B, with four days rations, to proceed to Hawk's Nest and assist Solomon Two Stars and his scouts to move all Fort Thompson Indians west of the James River.[23] The post scouts on 1 May 1865 killed the grandson of Inkpaduta, who was one of the principal figures in the Spirit Lake Massacre.[24]

Samuel J. Brown indicated in his diary that half-blood Jack Campbell and party passed unnoticed through the scout's line and went to Mankato, Minnesota, where they killed the "Jewett family." Campbell was caught and hanged in the courthouse square, but his party escaped and headed for Canada. The party stopped in the Coteau to relax, where they were spotted by Two Stars' scouts. Chief Two Stars, using his hand-mirror, signaled Jug at Drifting Guts to help him overtake the hostiles. Scouts from both camps on 14 May 1865 attacked and killed fifteen of the sixteen-man party, about two miles northwest of present-day Webster, South Dakota. Scout James Itewayaka was shot in the arm and was taken to the post, where Surgeon Charles J. Farley amputated it below the elbow.[25]

Solomon Two Stars related one sad story about the attack, which indicates the loyalty of the Sisseton scouts: "Our express orders were to take no prisoners, and a Sisseton always aims to obey orders. While the fight was on, one of the Santees ran up to me and begged for mercy. He was my sister's son, and I loved him but I remembered my oath and my orders, and I told one of my men to shoot him. It was the awfulest moment of my life, but I had to do it, and I would do it again if it was my orders. Two of my men were wounded but they got well. I remained in the service till the treaty was made the next year and then settled down on the reservation with my family."[26]

On 18 May 1865, three more hostile Indians were killed by scouts.[27] A party of soldiers out "gooseberrying" on 1 July 1865 was fired upon by hostile Indians. The fire was returned and one Indian was killed.[28] Captain James M. Paine and thirteen men, with ten days rations, on 18 July 1865, were sent to an encampment of Fort Thompson Indians. Paine ordered the Indians to the west side of the James River and "to never come again on this side."[29]

Post Commander Major Rose was especially annoyed with John W. Stone, Indian Agent at Fort Thompson, for authorizing Fort Thompson and Missouri River Indians to hunt east of the James River. Rose advised Stone in the strongest language that this was against army orders: "I have so notified the Indians, and also that a pass from any officer outside of this district will not be considered as an excuse; and hereafter any of the Indians from Fort Thompson or Missouri River found east of the James River will be treated as hostile, and I take no prisoners."[30]

Major Rose was pleased about the effectiveness of his Frontier Indian Scout Force but believed that it had to be enlarged to keep the Sioux west of the James River and away from the Minnesota frontier. His soldiers, of course, assisted with the patrolling and served as reinforcements at some of the camps. The use of the Indian scouts helped free many of the soldiers for the construction of the post. General Sibley also had high praise for the scout force: "The 100 men of this class now employed as scouts are more valuable for the particular service in which they are engaged than would be a regiment of cavalry."[31]

General Sibley agreed to provide funds to raise the Fort Wadsworth Frontier Indian Scout Force from 100 to 200 men. Major Rose, Major Brown, and Chief of Scouts Gabriel Renville proceeded immediately to establish another nine scout camps in the area, bringing the total to sixteen. The Frontier Indian Scout Force area covered a ninety-mile irregular square, 8,100 square miles, between the upper James River and the Minnesota border. Using present-day descriptions, the area was bounded on the south by a line running west from the Minnesota border through Watertown to Redfield, South Dakota; on the west, by the James River from Redfield north to La Moure, North Dakota; on the north, by a line from La Moure east to Lisbon, North Dakota, and east along the Sheyenne River to the Minnesota border; and on the east, by the Minnesota border.

Eight new Indian scout camps, according to Samuel J. Brown, were established during the remainder of 1865 and early 1866: Bone Hill Camp, near the James River and south of LaMoure, North

Dakota, led by Chief Scout Charles Crawford (later at Head of Coteau); Dry Wood Camp, about ten miles southerly from present-day Sisseton, South Dakota, Chief Scout Ixakiye (Red Mouth) in charge; Head of Coteau Camp, on north end of Coteau near Hillhead, South Dakota, Chief Scout Charles Crawford; Red Iron Camp, used for guarding the entrance to the post, Chief Scout Mazaxa (Red Iron-Wahpeton), later turned over to Joseph A. Renville-Akipa; Snake River Camp, near the James River opposite the mouth of Snake Creek, a few miles south of present-day Ashton, South Dakota, Chief Scout Ecanajinka (Always Standing); Sheyenne River Camp, on south side of Sheyenne River close to Dead Bolt Creek and south of present-day Lisbon, North Dakota, Chief Scout Solomon Tookansaiciye; Twin Lakes Camp, a few miles southwest of present-day Hankinson, North Dakota, Chief Scout Mazakutemani (Little Paul); Vasseur Camp, on a lake shore three-fourths mile northwest of post, Chief Scout Francois Vasseur. (Nearly all scouts at Vasseur used for mail and courier service were white men.)[32] Oak Grove Camp, northeast of present-day Mellette, South Dakota, Chief Scout Waseankas in charge, was also established.

There is conflicting information as to the number of Frontier Indian Scout Camps serving Fort Wadsworth. Samuel J. Brown, however, says there were sixteen. The sixteen scout camps were supplied from Fort Wadsworth and the Special Military Agency. Rations on hand at the Special Military Agency for Bone Hill Scout Camp in March 1866, for example, included thirteen barrels of salt pork, ten barrels of flour, 332 pounds of sugar, 121 pounds of coffee, eighty-one pounds of soap, and 3,720 pounds of oats for horses.[33]

By December of 1865, Major Rose, his men, and civilians had completed two stone barracks, a stone stable, a squared-timber hospital, and a number of other log buildings. They also performed other military duties. Rose's work of implementing the Frontier Scout Force was recognized in the 10 April 1866 *St. Paul Daily News:*

Major Rose organized and perfected a scouting system in May 1865, after which not an Indian came through the lines. These scouts have proved themselves true and trusty. Every war party on their way to the [Minnesota] settlements has been met and forced to retire, and the peace and safety of our frontier has thereby been secured. These results...characterized the administration of Major Rose as most creditable.[34]

On 13 April 1866, Samuel J. Brown, who at different times had been a scout, interpreter, inspector of scouts, and chief scout at the post, was appointed special military agent replacing his father, Joseph R. Brown. The senior Brown had been appointed a special agent of the Department of Interior to work with the Minnesota Sioux and the United States Peace Commissioners. On 19 April, Samuel J. Brown performed a spectacular effort in the line of duty as a special military agent. That afternoon he had been informed that Indians were coming down the James River planning to attack the Minnesota settlements. Brown notified his superiors at both Forts Abercrombie and Wadsworth. That night he rode to the Elm River Camp, fifty-five miles to the west, to warn the scouts of the danger. At the camp, he learned the reported raid was false, so he changed horses and rode back to the post that same night to correct his original report before alarm spread throughout the settlements. His description of his famous ride tells about the mission, countryside, landmarks, scout camps, and his intense loyalty to the scouting force.

Samuel J. Brown's Ride (Excerpts)

On the afternoon of April 19, 1866, at the military agency, near Fort Wadsworth, Dak. T., I received information that led me to believe there was imminent danger of an Indian raid. News was brought in to the effect that fresh moccasin tracks had been discovered in the vicinity of "where they cut bows," on the upper James River, a few days before, and that the tracks led in the direction of the Minnesota frontier.

I immediately reported the matter to the commanding officer at the fort and informed him that I should at once leave for the Elm River for the purpose of putting the scouts there on the qui vive. I was under most stringent orders not only from the commanding officer at Fort Abercrombie, who required me to "see that all war parties are promptly pursued and intercepted in their hostile designs against the exposed frontiers of Minnesota and Iowa," but also from the commanding general at St. Paul, who required me to "keep the scouts constantly on the qui vive." I therefore hurriedly drew on my buffalo-skin suit—jacket, leggings, and moccasins—buckled a Henry [gun] to my waist belt, hurriedly bridled and saddled my horse, which stood in the stable nearby and always kept ready for an emergency of this kind that might arise, and mounting the animal and giving it the whip, started off on a brisk gallop for the Elm River scouting station— between 55 and 60 miles away to the westward.

This scouting station was occupied by 17 lodges of scouts— regular and supernumerary—the former getting a per diem and rations and the latter rations only, and was under Joseph Rouillard, chief of scouts. The camp was located on the Elm River, west of the James, about where Ordway, Brown County, S.D., now is, and was regarded as one of the most important outposts in the service. Its location was far out in the hostile country and on the thoroughfare of travel for war parties from the northwest.

I left Fort Wadsworth, or rather the military agency half a mile east of it, at about sundown, and before I had gone far was enveloped in darkness. Indeed, when I had reached the western edge of the Coteau Hills, eight miles, utter darkness was upon me. The country from here on was a wild, level plain and almost trackless. I tried to follow an old trail which led to the Cottonwood Grove on the James [Renville's camp] and could not. But I had been over this route before and had no trouble in making my way, and, owing to the darkness, I felt safe from ambush.

The north star, which peered through the clouds at intervals, was my main reliance. It was my only guide and comforter. I galloped on at a rapid pace across the wild and trackless prairie country without any interval of rest or let up whatever, except when fording the James or pulling up the horse for a moment at a time to enable it to catch its breath, and arrived at my destination about midnight, making the distance, about 55 miles, in about five hours.

Entering the camp and going direct to the chief's lodge I dismounted and proceeded to tie the horse to a wagon near by, when Rouillard, who had been lying under it, watching my movements, rose up and called out, "Hello Sam! what's up?" I hurriedly explained matters and was quickly informed that the Indians who had been sent north a month or so before as peace messengers to the hostile Sioux had that evening passed by on their return to the Cottonwood Grove on the James, and that they had assured him peace had been made and there was no longer any danger from Indian raids.

My father [Major Joseph R. Brown] having been appointed a special agent of the Department of Interior to collect the Minnesota Sioux and assemble them at Fort Rice to meet the United States peace commissioners there, had dispatched some trusty Indian messengers to the north to endeavor to negotiate and bring them in. These were the peace messengers referred to.

I was struck dumb with surprise and mortification, for I was satisfied I had come on a wild-goose chase, and the alarm was a false one; that no war party was coming, and that the tracks or the trail of these Indian messengers had been seen and supposed to be the tracks of hostile Indians. I at once decided to return without delay. I deemed it my duty to return at once and intercept the communications which I had sent previous to my departure relative to hostile Indians, or to correct the same so as not to create unnecessary alarm at headquarters in St. Paul and throughout western Minnesota, the raid the spring before, particularly at the time of the murder of the Jewett family, near Mankato, and the capture and hanging of the half-breed Jack Campbell there having thrown the whole country into a feverish state of excitement and nervousness.

Besides, it was considered hazardous and foolhardy in the extreme to attempt to cross the prairies by day, especially when alone, owing to the danger of being ambushed and waylaid by prowling Indians. So after securing Rouillard's fresh Indian pony, which stood picketed near the lodge, and which the chief had recommended as "tough and gamy," and saddling and bridling it, and giving my own horse a parting tap with the whip, I mounted the pony and dashed away in the night, homeward bound.

There was no moon or star to be seen, and I was enveloped in utter darkness. The north star, which had peered through the clouds and had guided and comforted me on the way over, was now completely hidden behind heavy clouds, and I was left with absolutely nothing to steer by except occasional faint flashes of lightning behind me in the west; and although the dark and heavy clouds overhead, as well as in the west, indicated a storm, I was not in the least disturbed thereby, and pushed forward in the direction of the James. When I had been out an hour or so, however, and had reached the river, and had heard the noise of rushing waters before me, and the rumbling of thunder overhead and before me, accompanied by sharp flashes of lightning, and felt a few drops of rain, I became somewhat nervous.

But when I had forded the stream and had struck an old and well beaten trail and recognized the spot where I, with a few scouts and a supply train, and Lieutenant Jonathan Darrow with part of a company of soldiers, had camped a few nights before, and had found myself fairly on the James River flat, where the country before me was as level as a barn floor and free from wolf holes or gopher knolls or other impediments to fast traveling, I was not only delighted, but highly elated and very much encouraged, for I felt that I could keep ahead of any storm that might come up from the west. I whipped up the pony and dashed forward at a breakneck speed, and kept on at a very rapid pace until I had reached "the old hay meadow," a lake about halfway between the James River and the fort.

I made up my mind I would stop and crawl in among the tall weeds or rushes which skirted the lake and wait there for the rain to pass by, and pulled up. I was about to alight when the thought all of a sudden struck me that some war party passing along might already have taken refuge there. I struck the pony with my rawhide whip and went flying past the reeds and on over the prairie. I had proceeded but half a mile or so when...I was struck by one of the most terrific windstorms I ever knew. Very soon the rain came. Following the rain and close upon it came sleet, hail and snow, which in a few minutes turned into a snowstorm—a genuine Dakota blizzard.

There was nothing to be seen, nothing to be felt or heard, save wind and snow. But in spite of this I managed to keep the wind to my back and push on. Of course, no landmarks could be seen, but I knew, or thought I knew, that the range of hills known as Coteau des Prairie was before me across my way, and that I needed only to be guided by the wind to reach it. I felt that once among the hills, I could find shelter in one of the numerous wooded ravines or coulees there and be safe. Very soon my clothes began to freeze, and notwithstanding my thick clothing, which kept my skin dry, I was evidently uncomfortable.

My pony was truly "tough and gamy" as Rouillard had said. It galloped on and on in the midst of driving rain, sleet, hail, snow, and through slush and mud, and across swollen streams, and frozen and icy places. Twice I was thrown, but fortunately my hair lariat, one end of which was fastened to the bridle bit and the other tucked in under my belt, prevented the pony from getting away. At about daybreak I found myself at the foot of the Coteau Hills—the western slope—which I ascended. On reaching the top I found that the storms...seemed to have increased in fury—that is, the winds blew more furiously and the cold was more intense, but the snow was lighter and the air much clearer.

Landmarks could be seen. I discovered several familiar and noteworthy ones. Away to the northwest and about a mile distant is the ravine or coulee where Lieutenant Thomas Thompson, Second Minnesota Cavalry, with a detachment of 15 or 20 soldiers and a dozen scouts and myself, camped of a night the spring before, after wandering about on the prairie all day in search of Indians. There just to the southeast, and about five miles away, is the butte or high peak overlooking the James River flats, and called Hawks Nest or Buzzards Roost. And down there on the flats, about three miles away, is the spot where General Corse [and hunting party], the fall before, struck an immense herd of buffalo, estimated at 30,000 strong.

I found that I was about 25 miles southeast of the fort—15 miles or more off course. So fierce was the wind that I dreaded to face it. The thought that possibly hostile Indians may be lurking in one of the wooded ravines near by destroyed ideas of seeking refuge there, and whipping up the pony I dashed forward. I was now shivering with cold and had well-nigh lost all hope. Giving the pony the reins and allowing it to jog along at its own gait and picking its own way, I sat shivering and wishing I was at home.

The little pony jogged along up hill and down, across frozen creeks, lakes, marshes and swamps, until the fort, or rather the military agency, which I had left the evening before, was reached, about eight o'clock on the morning of April 20, 1866, having traveled about 150 miles during the night. I...rode up to the stockade, which was built of substantial oak posts or pickets 10 feet high, around the building, with portholes for musketry and bastions or blockhouses at the angles, for the purpose of defense in case of attack from the Indians, and dismounted, or rather rolled off the pony and fell in a heap on the ground, bereft of the use of my legs.[35]

Samuel J. Brown was able to contact the commanding officer who sent a courier to Fort Abercrombie correcting the early report of hostile Indians. As a result of this ride, Samuel J. Brown was paralyzed and disabled for the rest of his life.

Frontier Indian Scout Force Dissolved

On 7 June 1866, Major S. B. Hayman and four companies of the Tenth Infantry, after marching seventy-six miles from Fort Abercrombie, arrived at the post and replaced Major Robert E. Rose and his men. Five days later, Post Commander Hayman sent First Lieutenant John Hunter and Second Lieutenant Charles E. Jewett with forty-five men of Company C, Tenth Infantry, to the Elm River Camp. They were to assist Chief Scout Joseph Roulliard in handling a large band of Indians, who were either hunting or passing through the area. On 1 August, Hunter advised Hayman about one of the bands of Indians near the Elm River Camp:

There are now in this vicinity a large number of Indians, mostly or all from the west side of the Missouri. Their ostensible business is hunting, and some of them have papers from military commanders recommending them as friendly, none of these papers are of late date. But they do not seem to be hunting, and in fact there are no buffaloes about here and have been none since last Friday. Their principal camp is between three and four miles from here but they are constantly looking about in small parties near the Elm River Camp apparently watching our movements, and occasionally when refused admittance to the camp show considerable signs of annoyance and anger. In view of the large number (probably 400 or more) remaining in the neighborhood without any apparent object, I have thought best to defer my trip to "Two Fork" and the "Mouth of the Elm River" until their departure or until their intentions are known. If their professions of friendship are made in good faith they will probably ere long visit Fort Wadsworth to draw their rations, and if not this camp is well entrenched and supplied with plenty of ammunition, subsistence and water.[36]

Company C spent most of the summer at the camp, returning on 30 September. The remainder of 1866 was quiet around the post

because of the expectation of peace. Joseph R. Brown and Gabriel
Renville had gone to Washington to work on a peace treaty.

On 19 February 1867, the United States and the Sisseton-
Wahpeton signed a treaty. The two tribes were provided a large flat-
iron-shaped reservation of land, as well as annuities of cash and food
for fifteen years. The Frontier Scout Force and the sixteen scout
camps were dissolved. Most of the Frontier Indian Scouts moved to
the new reservation where Gabriel Renville was named chief. Joseph
R. Brown purchased the special military agency log building and
moved it to Browns Valley, Minnesota, where it is now used as a
museum. Joseph and his son Samuel became businessmen in
Browns Valley. Samuel J. Brown, who had almost given his life in
service to the Frontier Scout Force, described the scouts' work protecting Fort Wadsworth and the Minnesota frontier: "These scouts
were intensely loyal—not only to the government but also in oppos-
ing their own kin who were determined to fight the whites. They
obeyed their chief as readily as the veteran soldier obeys his superi-
or officer. Their very earnestness and steadfastness inspired such
terror among the hostile Indians that they stopped all hostile raids
thereby saving many lives."[37]

In 1867, the United States Army was authorized to have a new
Enlisted Indian Scout program whereby Indians enlisted for a tour of
duty. Although not soldiers, the Enlisted Indian Scouts received the
same pay as enlisted soldiers and were subject to the same rules.
Fort Wadsworth was assigned fifteen Enlisted Indian Scouts.

Keeping the Peace on the Lake Traverse Reservation

The 1867 Sisseton-Wahpeton Treaty and the 1868 Fort Laramie
Treaty significantly changed the military mission of Fort Wadsworth.
The Sioux, who had been roaming around Dakota Territory, frequently in confrontations with the United States Army, agreed to
give up most of their land and settle on reservations. The government would make annual payments of cash, foodstuffs, agricultural
seed, and equipment for the land acquired. In 1867 the Sisseton and
Wahpeton settled on the 918,780-acre Lake Traverse Reservation,
located east of Fort Wadsworth.

In 1868, the tribes along the Missouri River and western part of
the Dakota Territory signed the Fort Laramie Treaty and settled on

the Great Sioux Reservation—all of the land west of the Missouri River in what is now South Dakota. With four military posts, Forts Yates, Sully, Thompson, and Randall, along the east side of the Great Sioux Reservation, few Sioux were traveling east to the Fort Wadsworth area. What had been Fort Wadsworth's military mission—keeping the Sioux west of the James River—changed to keeping the peace on the Lake Traverse Reservation.

Little planting was done on the reservation the first year. The winter of 1867 and 1868 was very harsh for the 1,600 members of the Sisseton and Wahpeton tribes. To avoid starvation on the reservation, Fort Wadsworth's commanding officer was authorized to provide and deliver to the Indians 141 barrels of salt pork, 218 barrels of flour, thirty barrels of salt beef, and a large supply of hardtack.

Fort Wadsworth, like any military post located next to an Indian reservation, was charged with various military duties: keep the Sisseton and Wahpeton on the Lake Traverse Reservation; keep the settlers and other reservation Indians off the Lake Traverse Reservation; protect the Bureau of Indian Affairs' Indian agent, government employees, and property; and protect the treaty rights of the Indians. The post's commanding officer acted on reservation matters only when called upon by the Indian agent.

Following the 1867 Sisseton-Wahpeton Treaty, Fort Wadsworth was changed from a four-company infantry post of about 215 men to a two-company infantry post. The October 1869 roster listed Companies B and H, Twentieth United States Infantry, consisting of seven officers, 122 enlisted men, and fifteen Enlisted Indian Scouts. The post continued as a two-company post until its disbandment. The number of fifteen Enlisted Indian Scouts was reduced to six in 1876 and one in 1884.

Military Problems Between Reservations

Despite the fact that the Teton were supposed to stay on the Great Sioux Reservation, some wandered east to Fort Wadsworth and Lake Traverse Reservation. On 9 August 1869, a party of Teton stole six horses staked near the post. Post Commander J. C. Bates sent a mounted party of seven men and two scouts in pursuit but failed to catch them. In June 1870, Bates had a problem with a band of eighty Indians from the Missouri River who wanted rations. Government policy prohibited post commanders from issuing rations to Sioux who left their reservation, unless in extreme cases.

Therefore, Bates issued them a small supply of rations before escorting them away from the post. Bates at the time was ill equipped because of the thirty-one horses at the post only "12 are reliable for such hard duty as chasing Indians."[38]

The only raid on the post was in August 1874 when a "band of horse-stealing Hunkpapas from the Grand River Country did make a raid upon Fort Wadsworth and escaped with a few horses."[39] The incident created considerable alarm in the area. In 1875, Post Commander E. P. Pearson, still concerned about summer visits from Indians living west of the Missouri River, issued specific orders to First Lieutenant Lyster M. O'Brien in regard to protecting the livestock: "You are directed to hobble the public stock while grazing. You will also cause one of the Indian scouts to guard the herd while grazing and serve as a lookout for parties of Indians from the Missouri River. The scout will be armed and mounted near his place of lookout and...instructed in case of danger to fire his carbine repeatedly and signal the guard. Four horses should be in the stable or picketed ready to be saddled and mounted to chase after any offenders."[40]

In 1879, Fort Sisseton soldiers were sent to the James River Valley, about eighty-five miles southwest of the post, to prevent a fight between Drifting Goose's Band and white "claim jumpers." As part of a treaty, Townships 119, 120, and 121 were set aside for Drifting Goose and his band. They had built houses and were farming. In the temporary absence of Drifting Goose and his band, white settlers took control as "claim jumpers" of some of this land.

Post Returns described the use of troops in the matter:

> It has been reported to the commanding officer of this post, that white settlers had "jumped" the farms opened and cultivated in the James River Valley, D.T. by "Drifting Goose's" band of Sioux, that they occupy the houses built by the said Indians, that some of the band of Indians were trying to recover possession of their houses and farms, that both Indians and whites were trying to plant the same tracts of land and that there was danger of bloodshed. Per Special Order 63, First Lieutenant James Burns, Seventeenth Infantry, with a detachment of one sergeant, one corporal, twelve privates and one Indian scout marched from the post on the morning of 2 June for the locality of the James River. They arrived on the 4th and pitched their

camp. The peace was preserved by the presence of this detachment. On 10 June, the Indians left for Crow Creek Agency, after Lieutenant Burns held a council with them and promised their claims would be referred to the President of the United States for official action. On the 11th the detachment struck camp and marched to this post.[41]

By 1881, the counties bordering the east side of the Missouri River as well as around Fort Sisseton were filling with settlers. The Sioux made fewer forays to the Fort Sisseton area. But the post was alert for almost anything, according to Post Commander Captain C.E. Bennett: "An ounce of prevention is worth a pound of cure in the Indian business. Plenty of soldiers in the right place are sure protection against Indian outbreaks. They have a profound respect for the shooting qualities of the Springfield musket [.45 caliber breech-loading 1873 Springfield rifle]. The general disposition of the Indian tribes are believed to be friendly."[42]

Military Problems Pertaining to the Lake Traverse Reservation

The goal of the United States Government was to change the Sissetons' and Wahpetons' way of life from a hunting and gleaning culture to a farming culture. The Bureau of Indian Affairs' Indian agent at the Sisseton-Wahpeton Agency was charged with that responsibility. He also worked to improve their general welfare. The Indians were not always cooperative during this process, and at times the Indian agent had to call upon the soldiers at Fort Sisseton to assist him in keeping order and protecting government property.

Although the Sisseton and Wahpeton were not prisoners on their reservation, they could not leave it without permission. This policy was well defined by Agent Moses N. Adams in a 1872 letter to Post Commander Major J. E. Yard:

The exigencies are such as to require me to request of you that you stop all Indians belonging to this Lake Traverse Reservation and under the care of this, the Sisseton and Wahpeton United States Agency, from passing your military post without a pass westward, northward or southward, sending them back to this agency under escort. Also, that all Indians coming from any direction by way of your post to this agency,

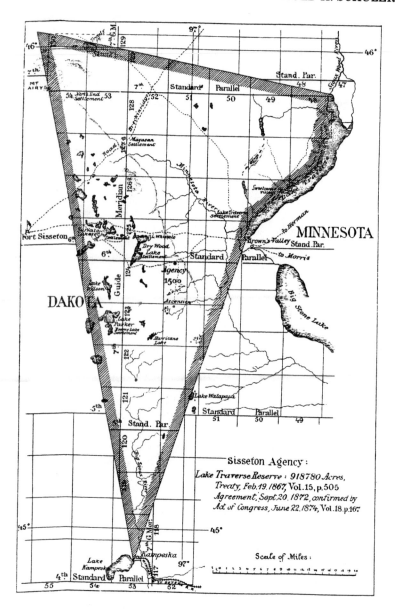

Lake Traverse Reservation.
Drawing from Report of the Secretary of War, vol. 1, 1879

Office of United States Indian Agent

FOR THE

SISSETON AND WAHPETON SIOUX,

Sisseton Agency, D. T., 28 Jany 1878

Capt Van Horn

My dear Sir

Will it be convenient
for you to detail an Officer
from your post to examine
supplies being delivered at this
agency on Friday 1st Feby /78

Very Respectfully

E. H. C. Hooper
U. S. Indian Agent

Capt Van Horn
Fort Sisseton
Dak Ter

Official letterhead of E.H.C. Hooper, Sisseton Agency, 1878.

Courtesy National Archives

Sisseton Indian women, ca. 1870. Note post hospital, built in 1868, in background.

Photo by Stanley J. Morrow. Courtesy W. H. Over State Museum

without a proper permit from their agent to do so, be detained by you there until my permission is obtained to allow them to come onto this reservation or to this agency.[43]

In 1873, Chief Gabriel Renville visited Post Commander Major Robert E. Crofton and showed him a printed copy of the 1867 treaty. Renville maintained that Article 9 was being violated "by permitting some Santee Sioux from the Missouri River to come and take claims, on his reservation and giving them cattle, wagons, and farming implements intended for his tribe. The young men want to remove the Santee by force."[44] The matter continued to ferment for three weeks before Indian Agent Moses N. Adams sent a letter to Post Commander Robert E. Crofton requesting military support. Major Crofton answered, "I regret there is a possibility of you having difficulty with your Indians. I hope it can be averted. I think that if matters can be managed without force or even the show of force, it will be much better."[45]

Major Crofton on 16 December, however, sent First Lieutenant Frank D. Garritty and thirty-two soldiers to the Sisseton-Wahpeton

Agency to protect the agent and government property from danger of attack. His instructions to Garritty were specific: "Be very cautious. Do not resort to violence of any kind unless there is no possible way of avoiding it. Do not take sides with the Indians or the agent. Preserve order and keep the peace. Make me a full report. State whether there is a necessity for troops at the agency. Don't let the men wander too far from their quarters. I believe the agent is needlessly alarmed, although the Indians are incensed at what they consider ill treatment of them. Gabriel Renville told me the Indians intended driving off the obnoxious parties."[46] Following a compromise between the parties, the agent on 20 December asked the post commander to recall the men except for a sergeant and nine privates. Not until 10 February 1874 did the Indian agent release the remaining soldiers who returned to the post.

In 1876, the post commander reported that many of the Sisseton and Wahpeton were camped near the post because provisions were scarce at the agency. "They are begging and selling berries. These Indians have no means to do much mischief, as the disappearance of large game from this vicinity has caused them, long since, to part with their rifles. The most formidable weapons they have just now are poor shot guns."[47] However, Indian scouts were posted to guard the post stables. The Indians remained at the post until new supplies arrived at the agency and the corn and potatoes were ripe.

Seventh Cavalry Assists Fort Sisseton's Seventeenth Infantry

The 1867 treaty with the Sisseton and Wahpeton required the United States to provide annual sums of cash and food for fifteen years. It was presumed that by 1882 all of the Indians would be self-supporting farmers, but that was not the case. Unfortunately, the government annuities, along with the food grown by the Indians, barely provided their food needs. Without the annual annuities of food, many of the Sisseton and Wahpeton threatened violence. In the spring of 1882, when treaty food rations ceased, 200 Sisseton and Wahpeton camped near the post and demanded food. Furthermore, a few Indians from Devils Lake and the Missouri River reservations were again moving through the settlements creating alarm. The number of settlers in the area was growing. Nearby Day County, for example, listed ninety-seven people in the 1880 census. The city of Webster, located twenty-two miles south of the post, was formed in

1881. Anticipating trouble with the Indians, Major General Alfred Terry, Commanding General of the Department of Dakota, ordered two companies of the Seventh Cavalry to Fort Sisseton to assist the two companies of the Seventeenth Infantry, if needed.

Captain Myles Maylan, commanding Troop A, and Captain Jackson, commanding Troop C, a total of six officers and 109 men, left Fort Meade, Dakota Territory, on 1 May 1882. After marching 372 miles, they arrived at Fort Sisseton on 23 May, averaging about sixteen miles a day. On a field trip, the United States Cavalry walked their horses at the same speed as the horses pulling the supply wagons. The Seventh Cavalry pitched their tents at a camp near the post. Post Commander Major C. E. Bennett had received word as early as 24 April that 115 men of the Seventh Cavalry and their horses would be temporarily stationed at the post. In preparation, Bennett ordered extra food rations, 100 pounds of No. 7 and No. 8 Globe horseshoe nails and extra .45 caliber carbine cartridges for target practice. The commander also listed the Seventh Cavalry troops on the next payroll. At the time, Fort Sisseton's roster consisted of Companies F & I, Seventeenth Infantry, six officers and ninety men.

Excitement prevailed throughout the post and cavalry camp as soldiers exchanged visits. Post Sutler John Vander Horck was kept busy selling smoking supplies, as well as Lager beer for twenty cents a quart, to the enlisted men. Officers at their bar could order whiskey by the drink or in quart bottles. One private of Troop A became intoxicated and failed to show up for water and stable call for his horse. On 1 June he was ordered to appear at a Garrison Court-Martial chaired by Captain Myles Maylan and two infantry officers. After a trial, the private was fined $2.00 and given five days of labor around the cavalry camp.[48]

At the time, over 200 Sisseton and Wahpeton were camped near the post demanding that they be provided food. Efforts to return them to the reservation had failed. To avoid an uprising in May, Captain C.E. Bennett issued ten pounds of corn to each person, along with four pounds of peas, four pounds of salt pork, and two pounds of beans to each family. Times were difficult, not only on the nearby reservation, but in other areas as well. Captain C. E. Bennett described the problems in the area:

> Owing to movement of Indians across the country through the settlers, from agencies on the Missouri River, going east to

Sisseton-Wahpeton Agency and returning west, and from Devil's Lake, Indians moving south through settlers, alarms and fears of Indian hostility were created. Troop C, 7th Cavalry, commanded by Captain Jackson, was ordered to proceed to the vicinity of Big Bend of Sheyenne River. They left the post 2 June 1882 under orders from General Terry. Troop A, 7th Cavalry was kept in reserve at Fort Sisseton. This disposition of troops at such a time was calculated to exert a powerful influence to cause Indians to preserve a peaceful attitude toward the whites. A large number of Sisseton did leave their reservation because they were in a state of starvation. The destitute Indians came to Fort Sisseton, but for judicious use of troops, a number of them might have scattered among the unarmed settlers. Troop C deployed over the country, swung around the north end of the reservation and came back to post 14 June 1882. The moving of cavalry through the country and back again did a good effect on both whites and Indians. It gave assurances to the white settlers they would be protected by the military of this section and that Indian depredations would be punished.[49]

On 20 June 1882, Captain Bennett issued ten pounds of corn, two pounds of beans, four pounds of salt pork, three pounds of peas, half pound of salt, and one pound of hard bread to each destitute Indian around the post. He placed Second Lieutenant Edward Chynowith in charge of all the Indians camped near the post. Some of the Indians wanted to work, so they were authorized to cut and haul 100 cords of wood for the post, as well as haul other freight. They were paid in small denominations of United States coins which they used to purchase food from the post sutler, or commissary.

Post Commander C. E. Bennett ordered an inspection of the post and cavalry camp for 29 June 1882. At 9:00 a.m. the infantry companies lined up on the parade ground for inspection, and at 10:30 a.m. the Seventh Cavalry, dismounted, lined up for inspection, in the cavalry camp. The next day, Post Commander Bennett received a telegram from General Terry ordering the two cavalry companies to march to Webster to board the Chicago Milwaukee and St. Paul Railway train. They were to take ten days' rations of hardtack, bacon, beans, and a half forage ration for the horses. The companies were to go west by train as far as possible and then march to Faulk County, where a massacre of whites by Indians had been reported. Captain Bennett had requested the station master to provide two train cars for troops and twelve train cars for horses, mules, wagons, and rations. Later that day, Captain Bennett received another telegram from Terry, who changed the orders, requesting Troop A of fifty men to make a forced march to Faulk County. Later, Captain Bennett received another telegram advising that the Faulk County report was false, so he sent a courier to overtake Troop A, who then returned to the post.[50]

General Terry inspected the two companies of cavalry and two companies of infantry in July. Later, he met with the representatives of the Sisseton-Wahpeton. On 3 August 1882, the Seventh Cavalry was ordered to return to Fort Meade. Preparations for their return included shodding the horses and mules, obtaining quartermaster stores for the trip, returning borrowed property to the quartermaster, and corralling a herd of beef cattle to be taken along. Captains Maylan and Jackson and the two troops of cavalry left the post for Fort Meade on 5 August.

Post Commander Bennett had high praise for the two cavalry companies: "This battalion, Troops A and C, is especially commended for an energetic, soldierly and successful performance of military duties while serving in this section of Dakota."[51] Captain Bennett later said that at the time the area was filled with unarmed settlers when General Terry ordered the two cavalry companies to Fort Sisseton, "It was a powerful influence brought to bear for the preservation of peace in this section."[52]

In time, the 200 Indians returned to the Lake Traverse Reservation and peace was restored to the area. Following 1882, there were no more incidents with the Sisseton and Wahpeton requiring Fort Sisseton soldiers to preserve order on the reservation. In 1887, Post Commander Major Frederick Mears summarized the situation on the reservation, as well as the diminishing need for Fort Sisseton: The Sisseton and Wahpeton Indians "remain peaceful and self supporting save for the very limited aid they receive from the Indian Bureau. If troops are needed it would be easier to send them from Fort Snelling by rail than the 28 mile march from here."[53]

Providing Military Escorts

One of Fort Sisseton's missions was to provide military escorts for the protection of wagon trains for government beef contractors, citizens, army quartermaster, and military units. Military escorts were also provided for inspecting generals, officers traveling between posts, and army paymasters. Fort Sisseton, a cavalry post for its first two years, provided cavalry escorts. After it became an infantry post, military escorts consisted of infantrymen on foot or mounted. A military escort always included several army supply wagons. No escort, whether infantry or cavalry, traveled faster than the horses or mules pulling the supply wagons.

Infantry officers accompanying the escort always rode horseback. Each infantry soldier was issued a knapsack, or backpack, which he strapped to his shoulders, containing an overcoat, wool blanket, rubber blanket, change of underwear, pair of socks, half of an A-shaped tent to be shared with another soldier, a few days rations, quart canteen of water, mess kit, and personal items. A soldier also carried a rifle and extra ammunition. The entire load weighed forty to fifty pounds. No infantryman, unless in a practice march or in combat, would carry such a load on his back. The knapsacks were tossed into the supply wagons and carried along with extra rations, tents, ammunition, and grain for the horses.

The first escort provided by the post was on 31 July 1864, the day before the post was located. Captain James Fisk and his wagon train of emigrants, headed for Idaho, had arrived. One newspaper report said that "during the afternoon, Captain Fisk entertained the officers of the post, while the emigrants and troopers mixed freely."[54] Major Clowney ordered Second Lieutenant Henry F. Phillips and fifty men of Company I, Second Minnesota Cavalry, to escort the wagon train to the Missouri River.

Some of the escort missions provided by the post and listed in the Post Returns included the following:

21 October 1865—Following the inspection of the post by Major General J. M. Corse, Major Rose ordered First Lieutenant Lyman B. Smith and fifteen men, fully armed, mounted, and equipped to escort the general to Fort Ridgely;

September 1867—Captain Jesse A. P. Hampson, fifty-two men of Company K, five Indian scouts, and Hospital Steward D. A. Graven, with an ambulance, left the post to escort a government beef contractor's large cattle herd to Fort Stevenson;

On 3 October, Fort Stevenson's Commanding Officer Trobriand noted in his journal: "Today the prairie around us presents the most animated sight...the line of tents belonging to the detachment which came from Fort Buford for the cattle. A little further, the mounted escort which brought it here, with its conical tents, its forges [for repair of horseshoes] and its horses out to pasture. The escort from Fort Wadsworth left this morning [5 October] to return to its post. In these trips across the plains, the detachment find an abundance of game of all kinds and for the most part live on deer and buffalo meat; but the nights are cold";[55]

July and October 1868—An officer and a company of forty men provided escorts for government beef contractors to Forts Stevenson and Totten;

22 August 1871—One captain and forty men escorted a civilian wagon train to Fort Rice. Before departure each teamster was issued a carbine and 100 rounds of ammunition;

7 June 1875—A government supply train of twenty-five wagons arrived at the post. Post Commander Edward P. Pearson deemed that it was not safe to go on to Fort Sully II without an escort of one officer, five enlisted men, and one scout. Later in June, hay and beef contractors were also escorted to Fort Sully;

1 March 1876—Captain Malcolm McArthur, First Lieutenant Frank D. Garritty, Second Lieutenant James D. Nickerson, and the forty-eight men of Company C, Seventeenth Infantry, left the post for Fort Abraham Lincoln. The mission of Company C was to protect and escort the supply train of Lieutenant Colonel George A. Custer and the Seventh Cavalry. Fort Sisseton's Company C, Seventeenth Infantry, and other infantry companies, moved out with Custer's command from Fort Lincoln on 17 May 1876. The infantry companies were left at Custer's so-called supply camp, where the Powder River meets the Yellowstone River, and did not participate in the Battle of Little Big Horn. Captain McArthur and Company C returned to Fort Sisseton on 28 December 1876.[56]

The Yellowstone Expeditions

Between 1871 and 1873, Fort Wadsworth soldiers provided military escort and assistance to surveyors and builders of the Northern Pacific Railroad Company. In 1870, the railroad had finished surveying the line from the Minnesota border to Bismarck, Dakota Territory. The following year, the railway company planned to extend the survey west to a point on the Yellowstone River near present-day Miles City, Montana. Railway officials, expecting trouble from the Indians who opposed the railroad, asked the United States Army for a military escort. The escort consisted of six companies of the Twenty-Second Infantry from several area posts and Company B, Twentieth Infantry, from Fort Wadsworth. It also included thirty Indian scouts and twenty additional soldiers manning two Gatling guns, which made a total of 450 soldiers and 150 armed railroad employees. The infantry companies assembled at Fort Rice before leaving on the expedition.

On 20 August, Second Lieutenant Edwin Turnock and nine mounted Indian scouts left Fort Wadsworth for Fort Rice to be a part of the expedition's Indian scout force. Eleven days later, Captain R. C. Bates, forty-one men of Company B, and three Indian scouts also left for Fort Rice. Enroute, Bates' detachment served as an escort for a contractor's fifty-five-wagon supply train going to Fort Rice. Captain Bates and his men later joined the Yellowstone Expedition.

The surveying expedition for the Northern Pacific left Fort Rice on 9 September 1871. Captain Javan B. Irvine, commanding two companies of the Twenty-Second Infantry from Fort Sully, listed the order of march: 1st, twelve mounted Indian scouts; 2nd, one company of infantry; 3rd, Gatling gun; 4th, three companies of infantry; 5th, engineers and supply; 6th, Gatling gun; 7th, rear guard; 8th, twelve mounted Indian scouts; 9th, two companies of infantry deployed on each side of the two lines of wagon trains. At the nightly camp, eighteen guards were on duty. The principal food on the trip was salt pork or bacon, beans, hardtack, coffee, and sugar. The menu was supplemented with buffalo killed by soldier hunting parties.

After traveling 192 miles in twenty-five days, they reached the Yellowstone River on 3 October. The expedition averaged eleven miles a day. Captain Irvine wrote, "We moved no faster than the teams walk and they being heavily loaded go at a funeral pace."[57] The expedition started its return the next day, reaching Fort Rice on 20 October. Captain Bates, Company B, and the Indian scouts returned to Fort Wadsworth on 26 October 1871. The railroad survey was completed without casualties, other than the loss of ten mules and horses. Some worn-out army wagons were also disbanded.

In 1872, the Northern Pacific Railroad construction crews had completed a line of track from Minnesota to the James River. Fort Wadsworth's commanding officer was given the responsibility of establishing a temporary military camp near the river crossing, called "Fort Cross," to protect the crews building the bridge. In May,

Captain R. C. Bates, one officer, and forty-one enlisted men of Company B, Twentieth Infantry, were sent to Fort Cross, where they remained until 1 November when the camp was disbanded.

The post also assisted in the 1873 Yellowstone resurveying expedition by protecting and escorting a herd of 600 beef cattle to Fort Rice, which would be used for food on the expedition. On 30 May, First Lieutenant William R. Maize, forty enlisted men, and two teamsters left the post and drove the herd to Fort Rice. The men returned to the post on 24 June. The post also sent Captain William Stanley and eleven enlisted men for duty at Fort Abraham Lincoln to replace other men who had gone with the 1873 expedition.

Endnotes

1. Henry H. Sibley to John Pope, 9 June 1864. *War of Rebellion Records.* Series 1, vol. 34, part 4:286. Washington: GPO.

2. John Clowney to R. C. Olin, 3 August 1864. *South Dakota Historical Collections* 8:439. (Hereafter cited as *SDHC.*)

3. John Clowney to R. C. Olin, 10 August 1864. *SDHC* 8:429.

4. Henry Sibley to John Pope, 12 August 1864. *SDHC* 8:433.

5. R. C. Olin to John Clowney, 9 August 1864. *SDHC* 8:428.

6. Joseph R. Brown to John Clowney, 23 August 1864. Sterling Papers, South Dakota Archives, Pierre, South Dakota. (Hereafter cited as Sterling Papers.)

7. R. C. Olin to John Clowney, 19 August 1864. *SDHC* 8:447.

8. George W. Doud Diary. South Dakota Archives, Pierre, South Dakota.

9. Lewis C. Paxon Diary. *North Dakota Historical Collections* II, 1908. Part 2:146.

10. J. R. Brown to Robert Rose, 9 December 1864. Sterling Papers.

11. *SDHC* 8:484,486.

12. Joseph R. Brown to Robert Rose, 26 October 1864. Sterling Papers.

13. Robert H. Rose to Henry Sibley, 1 November 1864. *SDHC* 8:502.

14. Robert H. Rose to Henry Sibley, 3 November 1864. *SDHC* 8:503, 514.

15. Robert H. Rose to R. C. Olin, 7 November, 1864, *SDHC* 8:505.

16. H. H. Sibley to John Pope, 16 November 1864. *SDHC* 8:509.

17. Robert Rose to R. C. Olin, 7 November, 1864. *SDHC* 8:506.

18. H. H. Sibley to J. F. Meline, 17 November 1864. *SDHC* 8:511.

19. H. H. Sibley to John Pope, 16 November 1864. *SDHC* 8:508.

20. Joseph R. Brown to A. S. Everest, 28 February 1865. Sterling papers.

21. R. C. Olin to Robert Rose, 19 May 1865. War Department, Department of Northwest. Letter Book, vol. 37:278.

22. Samuel J. Brown's Manuscript, Doane Robinson Papers. South Dakota Archives, Pierre, South Dakota. (Hereafter cited as Brown's Manuscript.)

23. Special Orders 1. RG 393. V. 13. National Archives, Washington, D.C.

24. Medical History. RG 94. vol. 1. National Archives, Washington, D.C. (Hereafter cited as Medical History.)

25. Brown's manuscript.

26. Doane Robinson. "Account of Solomon Two Stars." *Monthly South Dakotan.* February 1901. No. 10.

27. Medical History, RG 94. vol. 1:2.

28. Medical History, RG 94.vol. 1.

29. Special Orders. RG 393. V. 13.

30. Report of the Commissioner of Indian Affairs. 1865:221.

31. Henry Sibley to Major Charlot. 26 May 1865. *War of Rebellion Records*, Series 1, vol. XLVIII, part II:616. Washington: GPO.

32. Brown's Manuscript.

33. J. R. Brown to Samuel J. Brown, 31 March, 1866. Sterling Papers.

34. *St. Paul Daily News*, 10 April 1866.

35. Senate Document 23, 56th Congress, Second Session. 5 December 1900. Sisseton Land Claims. South Dakota Archives, Pierre, South Dakota.

36. John Hunter to S. B. Hayman, 1 August, 1866. Letters Sent. RG393. V. 7. Box 1. National Archives, Washington, D.C.

37. Brown's Manuscript.

38. J. C. Bates, 5 March 1870. Letters Sent. RG 393. V. 2. vol. 2. National Archives, Washington, D. C.

39. Doane Robinson, *History of South Dakota.* vol. 1:259.

40. E. P. Pearson to Lyster M. O'Brien, 19 May 1875. Letters Sent. RG 393. V. 2. vol. 5. National Archives, Washington, D.C.

41. Post Returns of Fort Sisseton, June 1879. National Archives, Washington, D.C. On microfilm roll 1179, South Dakota Archives, Pierre, South Dakota.

42. C. E. Bennett report. 2 September 1880. RG 393. V. 2. vol. 9. National Archives, Washington, D.C.

43. Moses N. Adams to J. E. Yard, 2 November 1872. Letters Sent. RG 393. V. E7. Box 2. National Archives, Washington, D.C.

44. Robert E. Crofton to Assistant Adjutant General, 21 November 1873. Letters Sent. RG 393. V. 2. vol. 4. National Archives, Washington, D.C.

45. Robert E. Crofton to Moses N. Adams, 13 December 1873. Letters Sent. RG 393. V. 2. vol. 4. National Archives, Washington, D.C.

46. Robert E. Crofton to Frank D. Garritty, 15 and 16 December 1873. Letters Sent. RG 393. V. 2. vol. 4. National Archives, Washington, D.C.

47. E. P. Pearson to Assistant Adjutant General, Department of Dakota, 18 July 1876. Letters Sent. RG 393. V. 2. vol. 6. National Archives, Washington, D.C.

48. General Orders, 2 June 1882. RG 393. V. 15. vol. 2. National Archives, Washington, D.C.

49. C. E. Bennett report, 11 September 1882. RG 393. V. 2. vol. 11. National Archives, Washington, D.C.

50. C. E. Bennett report, 30 June 1882. RG 393. V. 2. vol. 11. National Archives, Washington, D.C.

51. Post Order 141, 3 August 1882. RG 393. V. 15. vol. 1. National Archives, Washington, D.C.

52. C. E. Bennett to War Department, 5 October 1882. Letters Sent. RG 393. V. 2. vol. 11. National Archives, Washington, D.C.

53. Frederick Mears to Assistant Adjutant General, Department of Dakota, 1 September 1887. Letters Sent. RG 393. V. 2. vol. 15. National Archives, Washington, D.C.

54. *St. Paul Press*, 9 August 1864.

55. DeTrobriand, Philippe. *Army Life in Dakota.* ed. Milo Milton Quaife. Chicago:The Lakeside Press, 1941:120.

56. General Hoyt Sanford Vandenberg Jr. United States Air Force (Ret.), Tucson, Arizona. Letter to author, 1994.

57. Captain Javan B. Irvine, Letters to his wife, 10 September 1871. South Dakota Archives, Pierre, South Dakota.

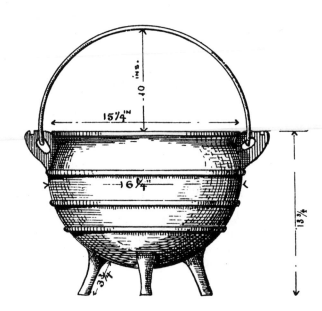

Chapter 3

The Army Chain of Command, 1864-1889

Following the Civil War, the United States Army divided the country into four military divisions: Atlantic, South, Pacific, and Missouri. The Military Division of Missouri, with headquarters in Chicago, consisted of fifteen states in the Midwest. It was further divided into four departments: Texas, Missouri, Platte, and Dakota. The Department of Dakota, with headquarters in St. Paul, included Minnesota, Montana, and North and South Dakota.

One of the twenty military posts within the Department of Dakota was Fort Sisseton. Originally, Fort Sisseton was under the command of the Department of Northwest, commanded by Major General John Pope. In 1866, the Department of Dakota replaced the Department of Northwest.

At the bottom of the chain of command ladder was the military post, commanded by a captain, major, or colonel. A post usually consisted of four companies, 200 men, and ten or twelve officers. Post Returns show that, at first, Fort Sisseton was manned by four companies of cavalry, but in 1866 four companies of infantry replaced the cavalry. In 1867, the post's strength was reduced to three infantry companies. It was further reduced to two infantry companies in 1869. Fort Sisseton continued as a two-company infantry post with an average strength of six officers and 100 men until it closed in 1889. The number of Enlisted Indian Scouts on duty after 1869 varied from fifteen in 1872, six in 1876, to one in 1884.

Post Administration

One military post operated the same as any other, because officers were required to follow "The Book" of army regulations, which rigidly controlled all aspects of military life. For example, in 1881 there were 2,793 regulations. After an 1889 recodification there were still 1,861 regulations. Regulations pertained to conduct, procedures, training, supplies, ceremony, and administration, to name a few. Fort Sisseton officers carefully followed these army regulations.[1]

Regulations, for example, prescribed procedures and forms for ordering, storing, and inventorying food, supplies, and equipment. Some of the Fort Sisseton monthly reporting forms sent to the Department of Dakota included the following: medical and hospital property, camp and garrison equipage, animals and forage, subsistence stores, and ordnance.

Other monthly reports that Fort Sisseton's adjutant filed with the Department of Dakota were inspection, pay roll, sanitation, school, and post returns. The monthly post return was a detailed report compiled by the post adjutant from the daily morning report. The return listed the number of officers and enlisted men present and absent. It also showed the number of weapons, horses, and wagons on hand. One part of the return listed the events of the month plus the number of official letters received.[2]

An 1872 post inventory listed thirty-six blank copies of post returns on hand in the adjutant's office. The adjutant general in Washington frequently asked Fort Sisseton's adjutant for more detailed information on the post return. One Washington request regarding the December 1875 post return wanted an explanation of why Lieutenant Lyster M. O'Brien reported himself on leave since 14 December whereas the post return showed him on leave since 15 December.

Post Adjutant

The post's commanding officer and adjutant officed in a twenty-foot by thirty-foot cut field-stone building on the south side of the parade ground. It was built in 1867 and consisted of three rooms and a north side porch.

The control center for the post was the adjutant's office. Under the supervision of the commanding officer, the adjutant, usually a first lieutenant, was in charge of all official correspondence, records, and post orders. Some of the reference books and pamphlets on hand in the adjutant's office at the post were Army Regulations, Artillery Tactics, Outpost Duty, Lieber's Target Practice, General Orders, Bayonet Exercises, McClellan's Rifle Tactics, Instructions to Mustering Officers, and Recruiting Guidelines.[3]

Uniform-sized leather-bound record books were provided to the post by the War Department. Fort Sisseton records in the National Archives show that the principal record book at the post was Post Letters Sent. It measured 12 inches wide, 16 3/4 inches long, and 1 1/4 inches thick. A copy of an original letter was written into this rule-lined book, before the letter was mailed, by the adjutant or his assistant. A Post Index of Letters Sent was also kept. There was also a record and index for post telegrams sent. Letters and telegrams received were kept on file in the office.

A separate Post Order Book was kept for circulars and special and general orders of the post commander. There were three classes of orders: special orders pertained to duty assignments, post care, and garrison court-martials; general orders consisted of transfer of officers and enlisted men, escort duty, and special duty; circulars resembled special orders and were used infrequently at the post. The commanding officer signed the original order as well as the one copied into the Post Order Book.

Post commander's orders were posted on the bulletin board or read at troop formations. One of Captain William Van Horn's orders, dated 4 February 1878, was posted to the bulletin board. It reminded all officers and enlisted men that any papers or passes requiring his signature must be left with the post adjutant before 9:00 a.m. Any arriving after that time would be signed the following day.[4]

The commanding officer compiled an annual report for the Department of Dakota, a copy of which was filed in the adjutant's office. Fort Sisseton officers, despite the fact they were all within walking distance of each other, often wrote official letters to one another. For example, a company commander would write to the quartermaster officer requesting supplies for escort duty. This kind of letter was, obviously, sent and kept as proof of request or delivery.

Endnotes

1. *Regulations of the United States Army*, 1863, 1881, 1889.

2. Post Returns of Fort Sisseton. National Archives, Washington, D.C. On microfilm roll 1179, South Dakota Archives, Pierre, South Dakota

3. RG 393. V. 7. Box 1, National Archives, Washington, D.C.

4. Circular 3. 4 February 1878. RG 393. V. 16. vol. 1:16. National Archives, Washington, D.C.

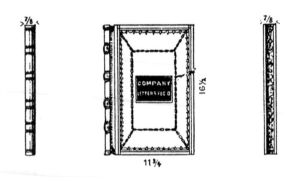

PART II

BUILDING THE FORT

(CIRCULAR LETTER.)

Headquarters Department of Dakota,

St. Paul, Minn., November 12th, 1877.

Commanding Officer,

Fork Sisseton,

Sir:

The Commanding General directs that you report to these Headquarters, at as early a date as practicable, the character and dimensions of the storage-room set apart at your post for the use of the Subsistence Department; the material of which the store-houses have been constructed; the amount of cellar, root-house room, and sale-room; whether or not the cellar is impervious to frost; the number of storage-rooms under separate roofs; the distance of the store-house or store-houses from other buildings and from each other; the means in use to afford protection from fire; and the portion of the storage which has been constructed since January 11th, 1876.

I am, Sir,

very respectfully,

your obedient servant,

Assistant Adjutant General.

Official letterhead, Department of Dakota, 1877.

Courtesy National Archives

Chapter 4
Building the Fort

Supervised by Major John Clowney

The site for Fort Sisseton (originally called Fort Wadsworth) was selected on 1 August 1864. Major John Clowney, eleven officers, and 311 men of the Thirtieth Wisconsin Infantry, Second Minnesota Cavalry, and a Section of the Third Minnesota Battery began construction of the post immediately.[1] Major Clowney staked out the location of the buildings according to the ground plan drawn by St. Paul architect H. M. Ackeryod. General Sibley had approved Ackeryod's architectural fee of $150.00 on 29 June 1864.[2] The plan, after some changes, located the officers' quarters and physician's house on the west side of a block-square parade ground. Directly across the square on the east side would be the enlisted men's barracks. On the north side would be the hospital, laundresses' quarters, mule barn, and other service buildings. Located on the south side would be the adjutant's office, guard house, more laundresses' quarters, magazine, and commissary. The layout of the buildings on the four sides of a parade ground was typical of military posts.

Major Clowney had to arrange for the defense of the area because it was occupied with Indians, many of whom were hostile. In constructing the post, he ordered his men to build two blockhouses, one in the northwest corner and one in the southeast corner. The plan also called for the construction of a log stockade surrounding the post buildings.

Clowney then ordered construction of the men's barracks, which he hoped would be finished before the onset of the cold winter, four months away. At first, the men lived in cotton-duck army tents but moved into temporary log huts before winter.[3] Each log hut held five men and was equipped with a wood-burning stove. The men slept on straw- or hay-filled bed sacks on wooden floors. Principal rations that winter included salt pork, smoked ham, flour, beans, hardtack, salt, coffee, and sugar. At first, potatoes, dried apples, and vegetables were scarce, resulting in a few cases of scurvy. Private Peter Gulbranson, Company B, Second Minnesota Cavalry, died of scurvy on 3 December 1864.[4] Post Surgeon First Lieutenant Charles J. Farley appealed to the Department of Dakota for potatoes, onions, and pickles to help contain an outbreak. The food items were provided before the disease got out of hand. Water was carried from nearby Kettle Lake and stored in barrels.

On 17 August 1864, the mule-powered saw mill began operating. Oak timber was cut for the blockhouses, magazine, blacksmith shop, and headquarters building. Other soldiers began hauling rocks for the foundations. By 1 September, two blockhouses were one-story high, built with hewn-oak timber seven-by-eight inches thick.

Supervised by Major Robert Rose

On 28 September 1864, Major Robert Rose and the Second Minnesota Cavalry replaced Major Clowney and his men. The four companies of the Second Minnesota Cavalry consisted of ten officers and 200 men. Rose was disappointed to find that only the foundation of the log warehouse and part of the squared-timber hospital had been completed, although considerable timber had been cut ready for use. Captain Arthur H. Mills used the soldiers and some hired civilians to do the work.[5]

Each day Major Rose issued a special order that was posted on the bulletin board. The orders listed the soldiers who were assigned to work on construction in one of the several job categories: carpenters, brick kiln operators, stone haulers, stone cutters, stone masons, bricklayers, and sawyers. An examination of 1864 and 1865 Post Returns show that an average of ten civilian craftsmen were employed at $70 a month to assist the soldiers with the work. However, during the busy month of November 1864, twenty-eight craftsmen were listed on the payroll.[6] The building materials, such as limestone for mortar, clay for bricks, wood, and stone, were obtained and manufactured locally. Construction material hauled from Fort Ridgely to the site by Brackett's wagon train included window frames and glass, nails, hinges, finishing lumber, and tools.

Fort Sisseton, looking east, ca. 1870. Note bastion, left center.
Photo by Stanley J. Morrow. Courtesy W. H. Over State Museum

On 5 October 1864, Major Rose reported that

The work on the buildings is progressing as rapidly as circumstances will permit. Next week the quartermaster, commissary and hospital will be completed and occupied. The quarters of the men we will complete at the earliest day possible. The boys are taking hold with a will. For the present the men are comfortably quartered in temporary [log] buildings. The [log] building for the officers' quarters will answer hereafter for laundresses etc. My greatest apprehension now is that the mill will break down. The cogs in one of the most important wheels have commenced breaking.[7]

After finishing the second stories of the two blockhouses, Major Rose found there was also a shortage of logs to build the post stockade. Instead of a log stockade, he ordered the construction of a six-foot-high earth embankment with a six-foot-deep ditch in front. Two eight-inch wood beams, the lower pierced for rifles, were placed on top of the sodded embankment.

On 23 November 1864, Company F, First Regiment, United States Volunteers Infantry, made up of three officers and eighty-one enlisted men, arrived at the post. The company consisted of Confederate prisoners who did not want to continue fighting in the Civil War.[8] Major Rose and his 210 men of the Second Minnesota Cavalry, along with the eighty-four men of Company F, continued construction of the post. Work was suspended for the winter after completing the stone foundations for the men's barracks.

Work began in earnest the following spring of 1865 and continued throughout the year. Rose, aware of a shortage of timber, had obtained approval to use cut field-stone and brick for some of the buildings. The area near the fort contained an abundance of native stone as well as materials for making bricks. Major Rose reported extensive building during 1865. With the aid of a steam-powered sawmill and shingling machine, the soldiers prepared and used 221,000 feet of lumber and 214,000 feet of shingles. The men with teams hauled 2,507 perch of native stone. Stonecutters cut and faced the stone before it was laid in place by the stonemasons. The men in the brickyard manufactured 215,000 bricks. Nine hundred barrels of lime were manufactured and used.[9] The eighty-four men of Company F, First Regiment, United States Volunteers, left the post on 28 September 1865.[10]

By 9 December 1865, the men had finished sixteen buildings: two cut field-stone barracks, one cut field-stone stable, brick guard house, squared timber hospital, two board stables, two log bastions, board enclosure for the steam sawmill, log warehouse, log magazine, separate log shops for carpenters and wheelwrights, and two shops for the blacksmiths. Major Rose and the men of the Second Minnesota Cavalry continued construction on the post until 7 June 1866. At that time, Major S. B. Hayman and four companies of the Tenth United States Infantry, five officers, and 224 enlisted men, replaced Major Rose and his men.[11] Major Hayman continued the construction program.

General Sherman Orders Permanent
Fort Wadsworth

General William Tecumseh Sherman, commanding officer of the Military Division of Missouri, was at Fort Snelling on 27 May 1866 inspecting the status of some military forts in the region. After reviewing Major Robert Rose's 9 December 1865 history and report on Fort Wadsworth, Sherman wrote the following endorsement on the back of Rose's history and report: "Post [Fort Wadsworth] seems of great importance. Should be made permanent; a thorough examination should be made, plans and estimates prepared and submitted for 4 Co's of Inf. and 2 of Cav."[12]

Following Sherman's endorsement, Colonel David I. Scott on 23 June 1866 sent the following letter to Wadsworth's Post Commander S. B. Hayman: "The Brigadier General commanding directs me to enclose a copy of the endorsement, that Major General Sherman made on the history of Fort Wadsworth, and to say that you will take the necessary steps to carry out his views, and report to these headquarters."[13] With Sherman's endorsement, Major Hayman doubled his efforts to finish the construction of the post.

By November 1866, the S. P. Folsom and H. Von Minden Fort Sisseton plat showed that another thirteen log buildings had been constructed: commanding officer's house, three houses for officers, surgeon's house, three houses for laundresses, ice house, bakery, and three buildings for the post sutler.[14] Some of the log buildings were replaced with stone and brick structures during the next two years.

F. Sturnegk's 1871 Fort Sisseton plat showed that thirty-eight buildings were completed at the post: five cut field-stone, four brick, and twenty-nine log or wood structures. Cut field-stone buildings included two barracks (1865), one stable (1865), one magazine (1867), and one adjutant's office (1867). The commanding officer's house (1867), officers' quarters (1867), hospital (1868), and guard house(1865) were made of brick.[15]

Additions and Repairs

There were thirty-nine buildings in place in 1883, one more than in 1871. However, there had been many changes through the years. Wood or stone buildings had replaced worn-out log buildings. Other

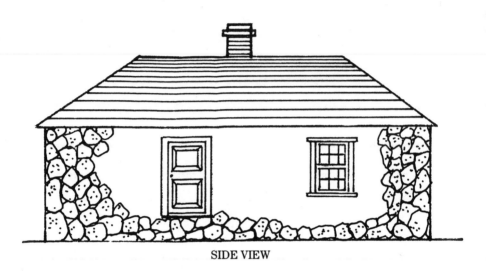

SIDE VIEW

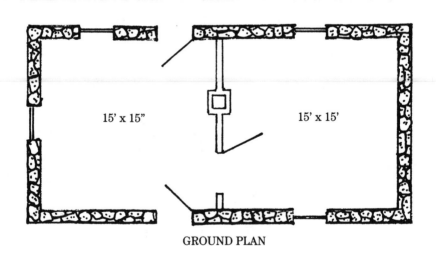

15' x 15"   15' x 15'

GROUND PLAN

**Original Plan. Commissary
Sergeant's Quarters, 1882.**

Drawing by Bob Child

buildings were repaired or extensively remodeled. A July 1873 wind-storm blew off, either partially or wholly, the roofs of the command-ing officer's house, men's barracks, guardhouse, mule barn, and adjutant's office. The hospital had 118 window panes broken. The storm damage was repaired before winter.

In 1875 the fortification embankment and ditch around the post were leveled. Department of Dakota gave approval to dismantle the northwest blockhouse in 1878. The wood was used for fence posts behind the officers' quarters.[16] The men planted 250 trees. In 1880, two new brick buildings were completed: blacksmith and carpenter shop; and school, library, and court-martial structure. A brick physi-cian's house was built in 1881. A cut field-stone commissary sergeant's quarters, a coal shed, and a root cellar were built in 1882.

Captain C. E. Bennett noted that the men used hammer and sledge as well as chisels and tools for cutting and dressing the boul-ders. He said,

> The hauling of stone for the foundation for the coal store-house, commissary sergeant's building and root cellar required an immense amount of hard work. The stone near the post had been picked over and the best building stone hauled when the post was built. To get a stone with anything like a "face" on it, the teams had to haul two or three miles. The masons preferred a large stone with at least something like one face, a stone that took four men to load. All the teams kept hauling stone, sand, water and wood. The stone...on the outside of the building pre-sents a very fine appearance and the work of laying was well done. The masonry work was done by Private August Rosenbush and three others.[17]

When August Rosenbush's enlistment at Fort Sisseton expired, he settled in Webster and continued building brick and stone build-ings.

In 1883, a wagon shed, bath house, and a 200-barrel cistern were built. The hospital, officers' quarters, barracks, and stable were also repaired. Captain David Shooley, however, advised the Department of Dakota in 1884 that "many of the buildings are badly out of shape from the effects of frost, their foundations not put down deep enough. The effects of this action has been remedied by trusses of iron rods and stone buttresses."[18]

Aerial view of Fort Sisseton, 1969.

Courtesy South Dakota Archives

The interior of the commanding officer's brick house was redecorated with new wall paper and painted woodwork in 1885 at a cost of $45.00. In that same year, an 854-foot boardwalk replaced the gravel walkways that surrounded the four sections of the parade ground that had a flag staff and sun dial in the center. The brick hospital was remodeled in 1886.

Fort Sisseton's Commanding Officer, Major Frederick Mears, recommended to the Department of Dakota in 1886 that all of the buildings, except four, were in need of repair. For that reason, he recommended the post be closed.[19] A new cut field-stone oil house was built in 1888, the last building constructed on the post.

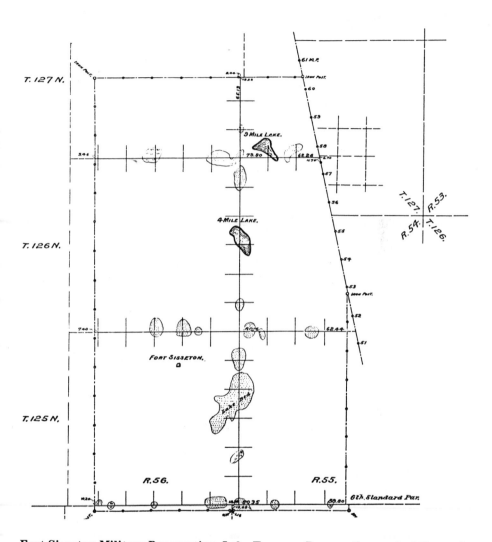

Fort Sisseton Military Reservation. Lake Traverse Reservation east of diagonal line.

Courtesy South Dakota Archives

Military Reservation

On 1 October 1867, the Department of Dakota designated the military reservation surrounding the fort. General Order No. 41 decreed it would consist of a tract of land nine miles wide by fifteen miles long, or 86,400 acres. Shortly after, a sliver of land along the northeast side of the military reservation was transferred to the Lake Traverse Indian Reservation. President Grant then approved the modified military reservation of 82,112 acres on 7 February 1871.[20]

In 1883, First Lieutenant H. S. Faber, United States Engineers, resurveyed the military reservation. He, with an eight-man crew, using two four-mule wagon teams, put in iron corner posts. They also replaced the old wooden mile-posts along the boundary and painted the tops of the new posts black. After the survey was completed, the men placed mounds of earth around the new wood mile-posts to protect them from prairie fires. The six-inch-square iron corner posts were bluish gray, and on one side contained the raised letters "Fort Sisseton Military Reservation, D.T."[21] Herman Chilson of Webster, South Dakota, in 1964 found the four iron corner posts intact in their original locations.[22]

At first, the unspoiled reservation consisted of rolling hills, lakes, grass, and trees. In time the landscape changed, especially after the large trees were used for construction of the fort. Lieutenant J. M. Burns described a different landscape in 1879:

> The surrounding country consists of high rolling prairie, interspersed with many lakes, whose margins are sparsely timbered with scrub oak, water elm and cottonwood. The soil is a rich black mold, slightly sandy and is well adapted to cereals and vegetables. Grass abundant and suitable for hay. The water in the lakes is fast drying up and is almost totally unfit for drinking and cooking, on account of its alkaline qualities. Stock thrives on it. The command is supplied with water from cisterns and by cutting and melting ice. The nearest available timber for fuel is at Wah-Bay [sic], 22 miles southeast of the post, except a very small amount which borders the lakes and which is of inferior quality.[23]

Fort Sisseton soldiers used the military reservation for training marches. They also used it for hunting, fishing, and picnicking. The post sutler used the grassland for grazing and cutting hay for his herd of cattle. Some of the hay and farm ground were leased to nearby settlers after 1882.

Water Supply

Fort Sisseton, although located within an area of many lakes, depended upon rain water for drinking and cooking. Lake water was not fit for drinking or cooking. Spring and fall prairie fires left the soil covered with ashes from plants. Following rain, the ash-covered soil drained into the lakes, making them alkaline. Army Surgeon B. Knickerbocker described the contamination of the lake water:

> The waters of the lakes are rendered alkaline from surface-drainage of an ash-covered soil; in the larger lakes not so much to be unpalatable, but in the smaller lakes it becomes offensive, and in the warm months putrefaction is rapidly set up in alkaline waters. There is an abundant supply of water, brought daily in a wagon from the neighboring lake, but of poor quality. The water of melted ice is used almost exclusively in summer by a great number of the command in consequence of the unpalatableness of the warm lake water. The hospital is well supplied with soft water from a galvanized sheet-iron cistern of about 100 barrel capacity.[24]

In 1871, there were eleven cisterns used to store rain water. Each cistern, lined with galvanized sheet-iron, was located next to a building and had a capacity of 200 barrels. Later, some cisterns were lined with zinc-covered sheets. Thirteen new cisterns with gutter spouts were built in 1879. Seven were fourteen feet deep by fifteen feet in diameter and held 200 barrels of water each. Six other cisterns held 100 barrels of water each and were nine feet deep by twelve feet in diameter.[25] A Rumsey force-pump was placed in each cistern to pump the water.

Cistern water had a degree of contamination also, according to Captain David Schooley's 1884 report to the Department of Dakota:

> Rain water, especially during the summer season, is used for all purposes, drinking, cooking and washing. To say nothing of the filth from birds, worms and all sorts of insects washed from the roofs of buildings into the cisterns. This form of supplying

water is both troublesome and expensive. Constant care and attending are required to keep the trough, pipes and cisterns in order. I know of no good reason why water cannot be had by boring or sinking a well.[26]

A sixty-foot well had been dug in 1875 but no water was found. A seventy-foot well was dug in 1887 but the water was unfit.[27]

A large water wagon was used daily to haul lake water for laundry, bathing, scrubbing, livestock, and fire protection. The water was stored in barrels throughout the post. An 1886 report indicated that the mule-pulled large water wagon made one round-trip a day to provide water for the post. The 131 inhabitants each used two gallons of water per day.[28]

In winter the men cut blocks of ice in the nearby lakes. The first log icehouse was completed in 1865 and had room for 700 tons. A new icehouse was built in 1878. In 1883, 257 loads of ice were hauled and stored in three icehouses. The ice was covered with hay and sawdust. Melted ice water was used instead of lake water for drinking and cooking.[29]

In 1886, there were twenty-seven metal-lined cisterns on the post. With 3,300 barrels of water stored in the twenty-seven cisterns, as well as 257 loads of ice on hand, there was an ample water supply to withstand any kind of Indian attack.[30]

Sinks

The army referred to outhouses as "latrines" or "sinks." A sink, covered by a wood frame shelter, was located sixty feet east of the men's barracks. A brick sink, twelve feet by six feet, was attached to the rear of the officers' quarters. A similarly sized brick sink was built behind the commanding officer's house.

The post medical officer made weekly inspections of sinks. There was also an occasional inspection by the medical officer of the Department of Dakota.

Post Medical Officer C. E. Munn noted in one of his weekly inspections in August 1870 that the sinks in the rear of the officers' quarters and the commanding officer's house needed three inches of dirt put over them.[31] New sinks were built for the laundresses in 1874.[32] In December 1874, the medical officer of the Department of

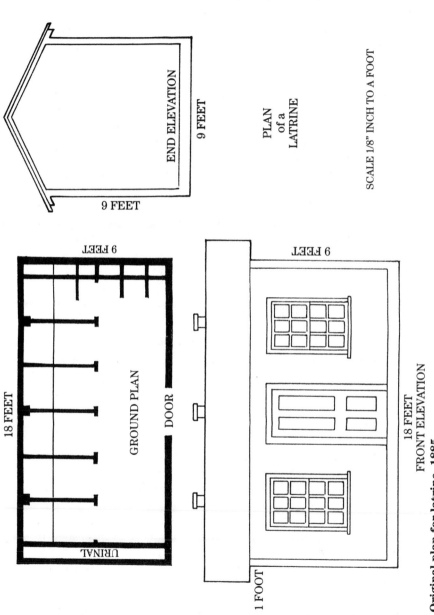

END ELEVATION

9 FEET

9 FEET

PLAN
of a
LATRINE

SCALE 1/8" INCH TO A FOOT

Drawing by Bob Child

9 FEET

9 FEET

18 FEET

GROUND PLAN

DOOR

URINAL

1 FOOT

18 FEET
FRONT ELEVATION

Original plan for latrine, 1885.

Dakota recommended that the sinks east of the men's barracks, used since 1869, be filled in and new ones built.[33]

Post Medical Officer Surgeon Charles E. McChesny in March 1876 advised the commanding officer that "a new sink should be erected for the scouts' use and the present one filled in and the wood work burned."[34] Commanding Officer Charles Bennett was so concerned about the conditions of the post sinks that on 24 July 1879 he issued Special Order 13: "The officer of the day will each day inspect the [sinks] used by the enlisted men and will see that they are kept in a proper state of cleanliness and are properly disinfected."[35]

In 1883, five new sinks were built for the enlisted men; however, the unsanitary condition of sinks was a continuous problem. Post Surgeon First Lieutenant C. Macauley alluded to the problem in a 26 April 1885 report: "The company latrines are unfit for use. As soon as new ones can be built, the old houses over the sinks should be burned where they stand, the ruins covered with a solution of sulphate of iron and then covered with earth."[36] A sink built in 1885 was eighteen feet long by nine feet wide and cost $358.

Fire Protection

Fire protection consisted of placing barrels of water, buckets, and ladders near the hospital, officers' and enlisted men's quarters, commissary, and other buildings. Buckets and barrels of water were also placed near cooking and heating stoves. In winter, the barrels of water were placed inside to keep them from freezing. Fighting a fire at the post followed army procedures:

> Following the cry of "fire," the guardhouse drummer sounded the "long roll." Company drummers then took up the signal. The sergeant of the guard and half the guards, with one ladder, one fire hook and a supply of buckets, immediately raced to the fire. The other guards remained at the guardhouse. At the same time, all the men of the companies, without arms, marched to the parade ground and awaited further orders. If more help was needed, the men from the companies grabbed the remaining fire-fighting equipment and helped fight the fire.[37]

Fort Sisseton obtained a portable Babcock chemical extinguisher in 1873 for the commissary, but Major Robert E. Crofton believed it was useless. In 1874, portable Johnson hand-force water pumps were added to the fire-fighting equipment. They were placed near barrels of water in the post adjutant's office, quartermaster's office, commissary, and stable.[38]

The effectiveness of the Johnson pumps was demonstrated in an October 1880 prairie fire: "It was a terrible sight to witness; the wind was from the south, sweeping north and brought the fire directly toward the post. The command successfully met and fought the terrible line of devouring, sweeping, roaring flame. It was a heroic struggle. The Johnson hand-force pumps were used with great effect."[39]

Other fire-prevention methods included mowing and plowing strips around the post, placing ashes into barrels and cooling them before dumping, and burning a fire break around the post. The fire break method almost turned into a disaster in October 1888, when it burned out of control and worked its way into the post grounds before it was extinguished. It didn't cause any damage except to scare the people living at the post.[40] Similar fire-prevention and fire-fighting procedures continued until the post closed in 1889.

Post Cemetery

The 100-foot square cemetery was located about a quarter-mile west of the post and was enclosed by a picket fence. It was later increased in size to 150 square feet. Private H. S. Benedict, Company C, Second Minnesota Cavalry, was the first man buried in the cemetery. He was buried 24 September 1864.

Army regulations defined procedures for funerals of soldiers. The commanding officer appointed an armed escort consisting of a corporal and eight privates. The order of march for the funeral was first, the band followed by the escort in reverse arms; and second, the horse-drawn ambulance containing the coffin, followed by other soldiers and officers. An officer read the service at the grave, after which the escort fired three volleys.[41]

There were forty-four funerals conducted at Fort Sisseton. Post records noted some of the funeral procedures:

20-21 February 1866—"Cold today. We dug a grave for Corporal. L. G. Harkness (froze to death on march.) We dug four feet and did not get through the frost. Next day warm and thawing. Buried L. G. Harkness" [Co. A, Second Minnesota Cavalry];[42]

12 January 1869—"Funeral of Private William Condon, Co. C tomorrow in school room at 10:00 a.m. All officers and men invited to attend. Escort furnished by Company C, 10th";[43]

30 December 1869—"The funeral of Private Philip McCarty, late of Company H, 20th Infantry, will take place at 2:00 p.m. 2 January 1870. All enlisted men will attend with overcoats and side arms. Company H will furnish the escort";[44]

13 July 1872—"Indian Scout Wanatakanakan, alias Friday, 22 years old, died in the post hospital of heart disease. He will be buried in the post cemetery with military honors";[45]

21 October 1885—"The funeral of Private George Gaylord, Company G, 25th Infantry, will be held at 1:00 p.m. tomorrow. The escort will consist of one corporal and eight privates from Company H. All work at the post will be suspended during the funeral."[46]

After the post surgeon certified the death of a soldier or civilian, the body was prepared for burial. Post records before 1882 do not indicate who prepared the body for burial. One of the enlisted men that year was listed as a part-time embalmer. At one time, coffins were made at the post, but by 1885 they were requisitioned from the Quartermaster Depot, Jeffersonville, Indiana. The plain coffins were delivered in pieces and assembled at the post.[47]

Post interment records reviewed four of the deaths in 1886 and 1887. At the time, two companies of seventy-four Black soldiers of the Twenty-fifth Infantry were stationed at the post. The interment record listed the nationality of each of the deceased:

1. Ten day old baby James E. Williams, sixth child of Sergeant John Williams, {Black}, and his wife {White}, died on 26 August 1886 from an infantile convulsion. John Williams was with the Twenty-fifth Infantry;

2. Corporal Richard Pratt, {American}, died of pneumonia on 16 May 1887 at 40 years of age. Pratt was from Maryland and with the Twenty-fifth Infantry;

3. Private Marshall Phillips, {Black}, died from exposure in a blizzard 14 March 1887. Phillips, from Virginia, was a member of the Twenty-fifth Infantry;

4. Michael Duggan, {Irishman}, Company F, Seventeenth Infantry, said to be married to an Indian woman on the reservation, died from congestion of the lungs 7 May 1886.[48]

Forty-four people—one officer, one surgeon, thirty-four soldiers, one Indian scout, three infants, four women, two of whom were laundresses—were buried at the post cemetery during its existence. The remains of Lieutenant Robert Wood, Post Surgeon Lewis Taylor, and Indian Scout Wanatakanakan were removed and reburied elsewhere before the post closed.[49] After the post closed, the remains of the forty-one others were reburied at Custer Battlefield National Cemetery in Montana.[50]

Small, wooden headboards marked most of the graves. A few were marked with marble headstones. A soldier's headboard contained his name, rank, unit, and age.

Endnotes

1. Post Returns, August 1864. National Archives, Washington, D.C. On microfilm roll 1179, South Dakota Archives, Pierre, South Dakota. (Hereafter cited as Post Returns.)

2. H. H. Sibley Papers. Roll 12, Minnesota Historical Society, St. Paul, Minnesota.

3. Andrew Fisk Diary. Roll 81, Minnesota Historical Society, St. Paul, Minnesota. (Hereafter cited as Fisk Diary.)

4. Cemetery Record. *Fort Sisseton.* Schumucker, Paul, Nohr & Associates, Mitchell, South Dakota. 1974:43. (Hereafter cited as Cemetery Record.)

5. Robert H. Rose to R. C. Olin, 28 September 1864. *South Dakota Historical Collections* 8:477. (Hereafter cited as *SDHC*.)

6. Post Returns, November 1864.

7. Robert H. Rose to Captain Olin, 5 October 1864. Department of Northwest, Book 66:27. National Archives, Washington, D.C.

8. Post Returns, November 1864.

9. Robert H. Rose to Captain Olin, 15 December 1865. Department of Northwest. Book 66:154. National Archives, Washington, D.C.

10. Post Returns, September 1865.

11. Post Returns, June 1866.

12. General Sherman 27 May 1866 endorsement on back of History of Fort Wadsworth 29 December 1865 letter by Robert H. Rose. Letters and Telegrams Received. RG 393. V. Vol. 7. Box 1. National Archives, Washington, D.C.

13. David I. Scott to S.B. Hayman, 23 June 1866. Letters and Telegrams Received. RG 393. V. vol.7. Box 1. National Archives, Washington, D.C.

14. S. P. Folsom and H. Von Minden Fort Sisseton Plat, November 1866. South Dakota Archives, Pierre, South Dakota.

15. F. Sturnegk Fort Sisseton Plat, October 1871. South Dakota Archives, Pierre, South Dakota..

16. Department of Dakota to William Van Horne, 29 May 1878. RG 393. V. 7. Box 4. National Archives, Washington, D. C.

17. C. E. Bennett to Department of Dakota, 10 January 1883. Letters Sent. RG 393. 2. vol. 12: 1-11, 131-141. National Archives, Washington, D.C.

18. David Schooley to Assistant Adjutant General, Department of Dakota, 5 September 1884. Letters Sent. National Archives, Washington, D.C.

19. Frederick Mears to Adjutant General, Department of Dakota. 1 September 1886. *SDHC* 31:147.

20. P. H. Sheridan. *Army Posts in the Military Division of Missouri.* Chicago:Military Division of Missouri,1876.

21. C. E. Bennett to Department of Dakota, 15 September 1883. Letters Sent. RG 393. V. 2. vol. 12:131-141. National Archives, Washington, D.C.

22. *Watertown Public Opinion,* 17 October 1964.

23. J. M. Burns Report, 29 September 1879. National Archives Cartographic Division, Washington, D.C.

24. B. Knickerbocker. "A Report on the Hygiene of the United States Army." Circular No. 8, 1 May 1875. Surgeon General's Office, Washington: GPO.

25. RG 393. 23. Box 9. 17 April 1879. National Archives, Washington, D.C.

26. David A. Schooley to Adjutant General, Department of Dakota, 5 September 1884. Letters Sent. National Archives, Washington, D.C.

27. Frederick Mears to Department of Dakota, 1 September 1887. Letters Sent. RG 393. V. 2. vol. 15. National Archives, Washington, D.C.

28. John McMartin to Post Quartermaster, 13 October 1886, Letters Sent. RG 393. V. 2. vol. 14. National Archives, Washington, D.C.

29. C. E. Bennett report, 17 December 1883. RG 393. V. 2. vol. 12. National Archives, Washington, D.C.

30. Post Medical History, June 1886. RG 94. V. 1. vol. 3. National Archives, Washington, D.C. (Hereafter cited as Medical History.)

31. Medical History, August 1879. RG 94.V. 2. vol. 1.

32. Medical History, 1874. RG 94. V. 2. vol. 1:195.

33. Medical History, 1874. RG 94. V. 1. vol. 1:198.

34. Medical History, 1876. RG 94. V. 2. vol. 2:258.

35. Special Orders. RG 393. V. 13. 24 July 1879. National Archives, Washington, D.C.

36. Medical History, 26 April 1885. RG 94. V.2. vol. 3:265.

37. Harold H. Schuler. *Fort Sully, Guns at Sunset.* Vermillion, South Dakota:University of South Dakota Press, 1992:66.

38. Medical History, August 1874. RG 94. V. 2. vol. 2:182.

39. Clarence E. Bennett Report, 24 September 1881. RG 393. V. 2. vol. 9. National Archives, Washington, D.C.

40. *The Britton Sentinel,* 12 October 1888.

41. *Regulations of the United States Army,* 1881.

42. Fisk Diary, 20-21 February 1866.

43. General Orders. RG 393. V. 11. vol. 1. National Archives, Washington, D.C.

44. Special Order 2, 30 December 1869. RG 393. V. 13. National Archives, Washington, D.C.

45. Medical History, 13 July 1872. RG 94. V. 2. vol. 1:254.

46. RG 393. V. 15. vol. 4. 21 October 1885. National Archives, Washington, D.C.

47. RG 393. 23. Box 9. Depot Quartermaster, Jeffersonville, Indiana, 10 October, 1885. National Archives, Washington, D. C.

48. Post Interments. RG 393. V. 19. Box 8. National Archives, Washington, D.C.

49. Cemetery Record: 43.

50. Fred Trende. Fort Sisseton Reburials at Custer Battlefield National Cemetery, Fort Sisseton Visitors' Center. Fort Sisseton, South Dakota.

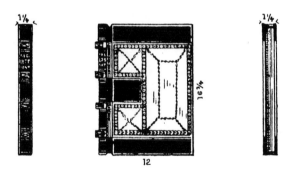

PART III

LIFE AT
FORT SISSETON

Captain Clarence E. Bennett, Seventeenth United States Infantry, Commanding Officer at Fort Sisseton, 1878-1884.

Courtesy James I. Muir, Jr., and family

Chapter 5

People at the Post

Officers

A United States Army officer received a second lieutenant's commission either as a graduate of the West Point Military Academy or by field appointment. Fort Sisseton officers were typical of army officers at frontier military posts. Like officers at Fort Sully II, they "wore distinctive uniforms, lived in separate quarters, rarely socialized with the enlisted men, liked pomp and ceremony, were trained to lead, and lived by the army's axiom that all inferiors must strictly obey the lawful orders of superiors. They were guided by tradition and believed firmly in duty and service to their country."[1]

Post Returns between 1864 and 1889 show that 138 officers served at Fort Sisseton. Fifty-two officers were volunteers with Wisconsin and Minnesota units, and three officers were from the First Regiment United States Volunteers, all of whom served at the post between 1864 and 1866. Eighty-three other officers were members of the Regular Army of the United States and served at the post between 1866 and 1889. (See Appendix A for a list of all of the officers who served at Fort Sisseton.)

Volunteer Officers

Post Returns between 1864 and 1866 show that volunteer officers served in the following units at the post: Thirtieth Wisconsin Infantry, Second Minnesota Cavalry, Third Minnesota Battery, and First Regiment, United States Volunteers Infantry. The average age of the officers of the Second Minnesota Cavalry was twenty-seven.

Wisconsin and Minnesota officers received their commissions from the governors of their states. It is not known how the three officers of Company F, First Regiment United States Volunteers Infantry, received their commissions. Company F consisted of three officers and eighty-one enlisted men. It was made up of Confederate deserters and prisoners who did not want to continue fighting in the Civil War. Company F was stationed at the post between 23 November 1864 and 28 September 1865.

Many of the volunteer officers from Wisconsin and Minnesota served with distinction in the Minnesota Sioux War. They also served with distinction with General Alfred Sully in his three expeditions into Dakota Territory. One of those officers was former Sergeant John Jones, who was stationed at Fort Ridgely at the outset of the 1862 Minnesota Sioux War. A Minnesota newspaper praised Jones' skill as an artillerist at Fort Ridgely:

> He was in command there in 1862, at a time when the fort was manned only by a mere handful of new and undisciplined troops. It was a very critical time, but the brave Serg. Jones did not flinch. He at once put the fort in as good a state of defense as it was possible. Barricades were hastily thrown up and every man about the post put under arms. The next day small parties of Indians were observed gathering near the fort...but were driven off by shells thrown by the cannon of the fort, manned by Serg. Jones. But the danger was not over. The Indians gathered all the reinforcements which they could, and a couple of days later again attacked the fort. The howling Indians surrounded the post, commenced a furious assault that would have certainly carried it, but for Serg. Jones' coolness. He loaded and fired his guns so rapidly, and with such fatal effects to the redskins that they were appalled, and after a couple of hours of vain attempts to storm or stampede the little garrison, they gave up the attempt and withdrew. Thus it was only through the coolness and skill of Serg. Jones, as an artillerist, that the fort with its garrison and 200 or 300 fugitives [settlers] were saved. Serg. Jones was soon after commissioned by Gov. Ramsey as captain of the Third Minnesota Battery.[2]

Captain John Jones was sent to Fort Sisseton on 3 November 1865 and commanded the Third Minnesota Battery. Jones was placed in charge of Fort Sisseton's four twelve-pound mountain howitzers and one six-pound brass field gun.

Regular Army Officers

Eighty-three Fort Sisseton officers were members of the Regular Army of the United States and served at the post between 1866 and 1889. They received their commissions as follows: fifteen from the United States Military Academy, West Point, and sixty by field appointment. There is no information on the other eight. Twenty-one of the officers who had received their commissions by appointment had worked their way through the ranks as non-commissioned offi-

Uniform of Captain David Schooley, served at Fort Sisseton, 1884-1888.

Courtesy Edward J. Jarot

Captain David Schooley served at Fort Sisseton, 1884-1888.

Courtesy Edward J. Jarot

cers. Companies from the Tenth, Twentieth, Seventeenth, Twenty-fifth, and Third United States Infantry Regiments served at the post.[3]

Thirty-one of the eighty-three regular army officers at the post had battlefield experience in the Civil War. These battles included Gettysburg, New Market, Fall of Richmond, Wilderness, Bull Run, Shiloh, Petersburg, and Atlanta. Two officers with Civil War experience received the Congressional Medal of Honor for valor in battle. Captain John H. Patterson received his medal at the Battle of Wilderness and First Lieutenant J. M. Burns at the Battle of New Market. Burns' act of bravery is cited: "While a sergeant under a heavy fire of musketry from the enemy he voluntarily assisted a wounded comrade from the field of battle, thereby saving him from capture by the enemy."[4]

**First Lieutenant John S. Allanson served at Fort
Sisseton, 1869-1870.**
Courtesy Joseph R. Brown Museum, Browns Valley, Minnesota

Seventy-nine of Fort Sisseton's regular army officers were from
twenty-six states east of the Missouri River. There were fourteen
officers from Pennsylvania, eleven from New York, five from Illinois,
three from Iowa, three from Virginia, three from Wisconsin, four
from Massachusetts, four from Ohio, and thirty-two from eighteen
other states. One regular army officer was from Kansas, two from
Ireland, and one from Canada. Eight of the post officers served as
either a brigadier or a major general during their army careers.[5]

In 1881, the monthly pay for regular army officers at Fort
Sisseton was $116 for a second lieutenant, $125 for a first lieutenant,

$150 for a captain, $208 for a major, and $291 for a colonel. Free living quarters were provided for each officer. They were eligible to buy food and clothing items at reduced prices at the post commissary. One commanding officer, Major Robert E. A. Crofton, owned two horses that were fed and quartered in the stone stable. Free forage was provided for two horses.

Each regular army officer at the post was required to pay for his uniform, sword, and scabbard. The required dress uniform consisted of light blue trousers, with an inch-and-a-half stripe along the sides and a dark blue double-breasted coat with two rows of buttons in front. The officer's rank determined the number of buttons on the coat. For example, a lieutenant and captain wore two rows of seven buttons, and a general wore two rows of twelve buttons. An officer was required to wear his dress uniform at guard mount, inspections, parades, and retreat. Post Commander Robert E. A. Crofton admonished his officers on 12 April 1877 that "hereafter all officers and men will wear their proper uniforms in and about the garrison."[6]

Officers' Duties

The post commander at Fort Sisseton, usually a major or a captain, was in charge of all post operations. He had complete authority over the officers and men and enforced army regulations. Whenever the commanding officer was sick or on detached service, the next ranking officer became the commanding officer. In early 1871, for example, Commanding Officer Captain J. C. Bates was ordered to serve on a general court-martial at Fort Snelling. In his absence, Captain J. S. McNaught served as commanding officer. (See Appendix B for a list of Fort Sisseton commanding officers.)

A captain or first lieutenant led each company of men and was responsible for their discipline, training, and care of equipment. Either a first or second lieutenant was assigned the job of post adjutant. He was in charge of the headquarters' office including all of the records.

Other part-time jobs assigned to officers by the commanding officer were the following: ordnance officer, quartermaster officer, officer of the day, a member of the post council of administration, a member of the board of survey, rifle range officer, commissary store officer, treasurer, and a member of a court-martial board. A chaplin and post surgeon completed the officer corps of the post.

Officers' Housing

Commanding Officer's House

The first four commanding officers, between 1864 and 1867, lived in a log house. Major S. B. Hayman, Tenth United States Infantry, was the first commanding officer to live in the new two-and-one-half story brick commanding officer's house. It was completed in 1867. The first and second floors, connected by a stairway, each contained four painted rooms with wood trim. Each room had a fireplace and several windows. There were also four small attic rooms under a gable roof. On the east side of the house there was a large covered porch facing the parade ground. After it was built, each commanding officer and his family lived in this house.

Commanding Officer C. E. Bennett had a bed-bug problem in his house in 1879. He blamed it on swallow's nests on the side of his house and ordered Lieutenant Edgar Howe to get rid of the swallows as soon as practicable.

> One side of my house is covered with bed bugs. The swallow's nests are covered with bed bugs, tear down the swallow's nests. In my house I have tried scalding water, fumes of sulphur, salt, quail oil, white washing and lime paste. The family is employed nightly burning them from the walls with flames of lighted candles. We have killed over a 1,000 a night in the last three nights. I have been informed there are powders that kill, if there is such a destroying agent, some should be furnished here.[7]

A week later, Captain Bennett gave permission to the officer of the day to pitch a tent next to the guard house, because the guardhouse was full of bed-bugs.

In 1880 the house provided ample room for Commanding Officer Cyrus S. Roberts, his wife Mary, two sons, and one servant. Several times when extra officers were at the post, the house was shared with another officer.[8]

Each commanding officer furnished the house at his own expense. Post Commander Major Frederick Mears, Twenty-fifth United States Infantry, had his furnishings hauled to the house in 1885. When he was transferred to a new army post in 1887, he elected not to ship his belongings but to sell them instead. The following

Restored Fort Sisseton commanding officer's house.

**Stairway in restored
commanding officer's
house, Fort Sisseton.**

advertisement, which ran twice in Britton's *Dakota Daylight*, shows the type of furnishings in the commanding officer's house: "Major Frederick Mears, Fort Sisseton, on account of departure for the east offers for sale all of his household effects; consisting of elegant parlor, dining, bed room and kitchen furniture. An upright piano, carpets, bedding, portieres [curtains], bronze and brass figures and ornaments, Japanese and Chinese curio's [*sic*], tableware and kitchen utensils, all can be seen on the premises."[9] The commanding officer's house was large enough to entertain the post's officers and families. The commanding officer and spouse often had parties for visiting officers, dignitaries, and generals.

Officers' Quarters

During post construction, the officers lived in three log houses completed in late 1864. These uncomfortable temporary quarters were used until 1867 when a new brick building with a mansard roof was completed. The new story-and-a-half building contained four adjoining sets of quarters. It was 100 feet long and thirty-seven feet wide. A covered wood porch was built along the east side facing the parade ground.

In the first floor of each of the quarters, there were two large rooms connected by folding doors. Each room had a fireplace and several windows. Each set of quarters had a small entry hall with a stairway to a large upstairs room. On the west side of each set of quarters was a wood frame twelve-foot by twenty-four-foot kitchen and store room with the servant's quarters above. At the rear of the store room was a covered brick sink shared with the adjoining set of quarters. There was a small cellar under each set of quarters. Officers were required to furnish their own quarters. Each paid for wood used for cooking and heating. After 1882, officers paid for the coal used in their new Garland coal stoves.

There were only six to seven officers at the post at the same time after 1869. The four sets of quarters, the commanding officer's house as well as the physician's house, usually provided adequate space. One officer was quite critical of the officers' quarters: "Four sets of officers' quarters are similarly constructed; all being under the same roof with the lower floors on a level with the ground. It is really difficult to conceive of a worse arrangement considering the great advantages of air and light which are everywhere so plentiful, cost nothing and should be enjoyed to the fullest extent."[10]

Restored Fort Sisseton officers' quarters.

Children playing in front of Fort Sisseton officers' quarters, 1870. Note twelve-pound mountain howitzer, carriage, and limber on each side of picture.

Courtesy National Archives

Commanding officer's house, Fort Sisseton, 1870.

Courtesy National Archives

Restored adjutant's office, Fort Sisseton.

Officers' quarters before restoration, Fort Sisseton, 1930.
Courtesy South Dakota Archives

Restored officers' quarters, Fort Sisseton.

Post Surgeon's House

Twenty-six post surgeons, either army officers or civilians, served at the Fort Sisseton hospital. The surgeons had the same privileges as the post officers and lived in the officers' quarters. In 1879 and 1880, Dr. James B. Ferguson, his wife, son, and one servant lived in one of the officers' quarters.

A new one-story brick surgeon's house was built near the hospital in 1881. The house contained four large rooms with a kitchen and servants' quarters in the rear. A fireplace heated each room. Dr. Ferguson and his family were the first to live in the new house. On 15 June 1883, Post Surgeon Victor Biart, his wife, their two children, and two servants moved into the surgeon's house. The post surgeons continued using this house until the post closed.

Restored surgeon's residence, Fort Sisseton.

Officers' Families

Military duty was a hardship for the families of married officers. Some of the hardships were poor transportation, inadequate quarters, and loneliness. Spouses and children of army officers, however, followed along and coped with these challenges. When officers changed posts, they usually sent their families and furnishings ahead. The officers, however, had to travel with their men. Sometimes an officer's spouse and family arrived at a new post long before the officer.

It is doubtful if any officer brought his family to Fort Sisseton before completion of the new brick quarters in 1867. The new quarters were designed to accommodate families. Officers' families began arriving in 1868. An 1870 photo shows five children playing in the front yard of the officers' quarters. First Lieutenant William Hawley and his wife used their quarters and post facilities to host a number of guests for their daughter's wedding, on 20 April 1870.

Rent-free quarters were provided for the officers, but they supplied their own household furnishings. In October 1878, Lieutenant Daniel Brush arrived for duty with the Seventeenth United States Infantry. He had left his baggage and personal belongings at the Breckinridge railroad depot. The post adjutant advised the shipping officer to "ship such baggage as Lieutenant Brush may have except his piano, which will be brought up by government teams, after the vegetables for the post have been delivered."[11]

In 1880, the Seventeenth Infantry officers filled the officers' housing. Captain Cyrus S. Roberts, wife Mary, two sons, and one servant occupied the commanding officer's house. One of the four apartments of officers' quarters was occupied by First Lieutenant George H. Roach, wife Flora, two sons, and one servant. First Lieutenant George Ruhlen, wife Ella, one son, one niece, and one servant lived in another apartment. An apartment was shared by Second Lieutenants Edward Chynowith and Robert W. Dowdy, both single. Post Surgeon Dr. James B. Ferguson, wife, one son, and one servant occupied the fourth apartment. The post surgeon's house was not completed until 1881.[12]

Each of the officers' quarters had separate rooms for a servant, often called a maid or housekeeper. Prior to 1870, officers had used enlisted men as servants, but the practice was discontinued by the United States Army. After that, post officers hired servants and paid them from $17 to $25 a month plus free room and board. Prior to the arrival of settlers in the area in 1882, servants were hard to find. Sometimes, wives of enlisted men worked as servants for officers. Some officers' hired a family member for this purpose or brought a servant with them. Hiring a servant away from another officer in 1881 so aroused the ire of Commanding Officer Clarence E. Bennett that he issued a special order forbidding the employment of officers' servants without the officers' permission.[13]

After 1881, more settlers arrived in the area, and some of these men and women found jobs at the post. Mrs. John P. Opitz, of Eden, South Dakota worked for an officer and his family from about 1885 to 1887. Her husband worked for the post sutler during this same period. Christena Schiedt worked for a major and his family before marrying James H. Tobin, of Langford.

In 1872, the nearest telegraph and railroad station was in Morris, Minnesota, eighty miles east, or Lake Kampeska, sixty-five miles to the southeast. However, much of the freight was shipped to Breckinridge, Minnesota, about sixty-five miles northeast. The freight was then hauled to the post with team and wagon. It was necessary for officers and their families to travel by train to visit distant relatives. It was a rough and dusty three-or-four-day wagon ride to the train station at Breckinridge or Morris, Minnesota. The Chicago, St. Paul and Minnesota Railway gave free passes to families of officers and half fare to officers who were changing stations. This practice ended on 1 January 1879 when the railroad began charging full fare.

In the spring of 1881, the Chicago, Milwaukee and St. Paul Railway began serving Webster, Dakota Territory. Now the twenty-two mile wagon ride to the Webster train station took less than a day. With easy access to transportation, officers and their families were eager to take leave and travel east. In 1884, passenger trains left Webster at 9:27 a.m. and 4:40 p.m. daily, except Sunday.

Post records and the *Webster Reporter and Farmer* indicated considerable traveling by Fort Sisseton officers and their families:

September 1883— First Lieutenant George Ruhlen and family left the Webster station for Columbus, Ohio, where he would serve temporarily as a military professor at a local university;

18 April 1884—Captain Clarence E. Bennett sent his family and furnishings ahead when he and two companies of the Seventeenth Infantry were transferred from Fort Sisseton to Fort Totten;

Fort Sisseton officers and families in front of the officers' quarters. ca. 1870. *Courtesy North Dakota Historical Society*

28 August 1884—Second Lieutenant H. D. Reed, of Fort Sisseton, returned from a visit east;

16 April 1885—First Lieutenant John McMartin left Webster enroute to his home in New York for a four-month leave of absence;

13 August 1885—Second Lieutenant James O. Green and his family left on the train to visit his parents in Wisconsin;

28 October 1886—Second Lieutenant James O. Green left on a month's vacation for Wisconsin to hunt deer. A number of Webster hunters planned to join him later.

A daily stage ran between Britton and Webster via Fort Sisseton, in 1885. The Webster and Britton Stage Line charged $2.00 a person from Webster to Fort Sisseton and $1.75 per person from Fort Sisseton to Britton. The Chicago, Milwaukee and St. Paul Railway began serving Britton in 1886. Using the new stage, officers and their families began exchanging social visits with people in the two cities. Both cities competed for the business of the people living at the post. In 1888, Britton claimed that they were the "headquarters for the Fort Sisseton people. Most of the families now at the fort get their supplies from our city."[14]

Enlisted Men

After May 1869, there was a daily average of 100 enlisted men and six officers stationed at Fort Sisseton. The enlisted men, listed as "EM" on the official records, came from all walks of life: farmers, laborers, clerks, the unemployed, and adventurers. The following requirements had to be met to enlist in the United States Infantry: five-feet-four-inches and up in height, between 120 and 180 pounds, able to see a three-foot diameter black center on a white background from 600 yards, and between seventeen and thirty-five years of age. An enlistment was for a five-year term.

Enlisted men were administered an Oath of Enlistment and Allegiance at the induction center. The 1876 enlistment affirmation before a United States Army officer was as follows:

> I do hereby acknowledge to have enlisted as a soldier in the Army of the United States of America for a period of five years, unless sooner discharged by proper authority, and do also agree to accept from the United States such bounty, pay, rations and clothing as are or may be established by law, and I do solemnly swear, that I am (age) and know of no impediment to my serving honestly and faithfully as a soldier for five years under this enlistment contract with the United States. I do also solemnly swear that I will bear true faith and allegiance to the United States of America, and that I will serve them honestly and faithfully against all their enemies or opposers whomsoever, and that I will observe and obey the orders of the President of the United States and the orders of the officers appointed over me, according to the Rules and Articles of War.[15]

In 1870, there were seventy Fort Sisseton soldiers counted in the Dakota Territory Census. Their average age was twenty-six; eight could not read or write. Twenty-nine were from fifteen eastern states: one each from Connecticut, Tennessee, Michigan, Illinois, Rhode Island, Massachusetts, South Carolina, and Iowa; two each from Maryland, Louisiana, and Wisconsin; three from Ohio; five from Pennsylvania; and seven from New York. Forty-one were foreign born: one each from Denmark, Scotland, Switzerland, and France; two from Canada; three from Germany; four from Russia; eleven from England; and seventeen from Ireland.[16]

The United States Army during the Fort Sisseton era maintained a troop strength of 26,000 men and 1,500 officers. Each year, between 1880 and 1888, the army lost a third of its soldiers from desertions, discharge, death, or retirement. To replace the loss, the army each year accepted 6,700 enlisted men: 6,200 were white and 500 black; 4,200 were native born and 2,500 foreign born.[17]

Post Records show that forty-one recruits arrived in Fort Sisseton during August 1870. The recruits had originated at David's Island, New York, one of three Army recruiting depots. Five men had deserted en route between Fort Snelling and the post, two of whom were caught later. The post medical doctor said that the forty-one men were "fair looking men": seven German, ten Irish, seventeen American, four English, one French, and two Canadian.[18] It was not unusual for recruits to enlist at the post. In 1882, a man enlisted and was assigned to one of the companies of the Seventeenth United States Infantry stationed at the post. In 1886, four men enlisted at the post before recruiting officer First Lieutenant Henry P. Ritzius. These men were assigned to other posts.

Enlisted Men's Pay

A private was paid $13 per month, a corporal $15, a sergeant $17, and a first sergeant $22; all received free room and board and a clothing allowance. They earned an extra $1 a month for the third, fourth, and fifth year of the enlistment. It was not a large salary but more than many could earn in civilian life. The soldiers at Fort Sisseton were paid in cash every two months by an army paymaster from Fort Snelling. A detachment of soldiers from a nearby post escorted the paymaster on his spring wagon to the post. An 1880 Post Circular directed that the men be paid at the quartermaster office in the following order: Company F, Company A, Medical Department, and Indian Scouts beginning at 1:00 p.m. Because of the cold the men were required to wear overcoats, fur caps, and gloves.[19] The army paymaster Major William Smith was "a most agreeable, cultured and companionable gentleman,"[20] according to a local newspaper. After the paymaster paid the men, it was the duty of Fort

Sisseton's commanding officer to provide a mounted armed guard to escort him to the next post.

Enlisted Men's Quarters

The men lived in army tents when they first arrived at the post in the summer of 1864. They constructed five-man log huts and moved into them before the first winter. Sergeant Andrew F. Fisk, who arrived at the post on 13 November 1865, noted in his diary, "Company D left for Fort Snelling to be mustered out. Our men moved into their log huts until the new quarters are completed. Five of us in one hut."[21] The men finished the cut field-stone barracks and moved into them on 9 December 1865. Sergeant Fisk described some events during December and January in the new barracks: "Men had a big time in the new quarters. Corporal French started a writing school. Inspection in quarters. Thank the Lord we have got good warm quarters."[22]

Each barracks, 183 feet long by forty-five feet wide, held two companies of about eighty men. A barracks contained a dormitory, wash room, kitchen, mess room, and an orderly room for each company of men. Barracks furniture was limited to wooden bunks, benches, and tables all built by the men. Heat was provided by iron-box wood stoves, which were replaced by coal stoves in 1882. Ten spittoons were conveniently placed in each of the company quarters. Lamps and lanterns were used for lighting. When the post in 1869 was changed to a two-company post of about 100 men, the south barracks was used for a commissary.

The men slept on bed sacks filled with hay or straw. Each man was allocated sixteen pounds of hay or straw per month for bedding. Post Physician Charles E. McChesny, in 1873, required the men to wash their bed sacks and replace the straw or hay each month. Blankets had to be shaken and aired from time to time. Every morning the bed sack was neatly rolled and placed at the head of the bunk. The blankets were folded into five or six uniform folds and placed near the bedsack.[23] New iron bedsteads were received in 1873, but it was not until 1884 that cotton linter replaced hay and straw for bedding. In 1885, new beds with bed springs replaced the iron bedsteads.

Drinking water was obtained from nearby cisterns. Lake water for bathing and washing clothes was stored in barrels. The men

Courtesy Larry F. Ness

Enlisted men's barracks, Fort Sisseton, ca. 1930.

Fort Sisseton soldiers in front of north barracks, 1870.
Courtesy National Archives

Restored Fort Sisseton north barracks.
Courtesy South Dakota Archives

bathed in nearby lakes in the summer. In winter they heated water in the kitchen and bathed in tubs in the wash room. Post Surgeon Charles E. McChesny, in 1875, recommended "a room should be set aside as a bath room for the men. At the present time no facilities are afforded the men. The bath room should be supplied with tubs, barrels and buckets. A small log building near the hospital could be used for that purpose."[24]

Not until 1883, however, was a coal-heated bath house built in the rear of the stone barracks. Post Surgeon Victor Biart logged in his journal on 31 December 1883, "the new bath house for the use of the men is a great acquisition to them, and it is much used, the great draw back is the question of water supply."[25]

Captain David Schooley complained in 1884 that the barracks did not have enough light: "The barracks are so constructed that the kitchens and dining rooms of the two sets of company quarters, all under the same roof, constitute one side of the building, and the two First Sergeants' rooms at ends of the other half leaving the men's quarters in the middle with only one side for doors and windows."[26]

Fort Sisseton married men's quarters, 1870.
Courtesy National Archives

Enlisted Men's Families

In 1870, there were nine one-story log houses with gable roofs used by laundresses and married soldiers. Each log house contained from one to four rooms with low ceilings. Only a few married enlisted men, usually non-commissioned officers, lived at the post. Sometimes the wife of a married soldier worked as a maid for an officer or as a laundress for the enlisted men. Married soldiers were provided rent-free quarters. Their families also received free medical care at the hospital. Soldiers' children attended the post school. Between 1870 and 1872, five boys and one girl were born at the post.

The 1880 Federal Census lists two married soldiers living in log houses at the post. One soldier had a wife and a sister who worked as a servant. The other soldier had a wife and one daughter. Eighty-one of the enlisted men were single and lived in the stone barracks.[27]

Enlisted Indian Scouts, United States Army

The United States Congress, in 1866, authorized Indians to enlist as Enlisted Indian Scouts in the United States Army for a tour of duty. The scouts were paid $13 a month, the same as an army private. Each scout was given a small clothing allowance. At first, scouts preferred to wear their own clothes rather than the army uniform. Enlisted Indian Scouts and their families lived in separate quarters at Fort Sisseton.

There was also a Frontier Indian Scout Force employed by the Army to help defend Fort Wadsworth (Fort Sisseton) and area between 1864 and 1867. Enlisted Indian Scouts were members of the United States Army; members of the Frontier Indian Scout Force were not. The services of the Frontier Indian Scout Force are described in Chapter 2.

Nine Enlisted Indian Scouts, United States Army, arrived at Fort Sisseton in April 1867. Wacehin (Soft Feather) enlisted as a scout at the post in May 1872. That same year scout Wanatakanakan died in the post hospital. He was buried in the post cemetery with military honors. In February 1873, Akaukinajin and Tacuhupawakav also enlisted as scouts. An analysis of the records of twenty-two Enlisted Indian Scouts who served at the post indicated their average age was twenty-three when they enlisted. Thirteen of the scouts were from Dakota Territory and nine from Minnesota.[28] The number of Enlisted

Indian Scouts on duty at the post varied from year to year: thirteen in 1868; fifteen in 1872; six in 1875; and two in 1880.

The scouts served the post in such ways as accompanying patrols and escorts, carrying mail, or guarding livestock. In June 1872, Fort Sisseton troops were ordered to protect the workers during construction of a Northern Pacific Railroad bridge crossing the James River in present-day North Dakota. Company F, three officers, fifty-four enlisted men and fifteen scouts made up the detachment for "Fort Cross" at the James River crossing. When Fort Sisseton's post office temporarily closed in 1873, two scouts carried the mail between the post and the Sisseton Agency, twenty-eight miles away.

Scouts Sdiwaku and Cotakanwaxtedan, in 1870, captured two soldiers in the Fort Sisseton area who had deserted from Fort Ransom. Each scout was paid $30, the usual fee for capturing army deserters. A patrol escorted the deserters back to Fort Ransom.[29] In 1876, Private Benjamin F. Brown, Company B, Seventeenth United States Infantry, was absent from the morning roll call, and in a short time it was determined that he had deserted the post. Commanding Officer Captain Edward P. Pearson ordered two Indian scouts to pursue Brown and return him to the post. After a couple days, the scouts returned with the body of Private Brown. The scouts had found Brown and shot him in the line of duty. Brown was buried in the post cemetery.[30]

Enlisted Indian Scouts performed their duties well; however, discipline was a problem at times. The 1868 Post Returns show that each month there was at least one scout under arrest or in confinement because of some indiscretion. In May 1873, ten Indian scouts deserted and took their Spencer carbines with them. Two hours later, a mounted party of First Lieutenant William R. Maize, Dr. Will E. Turner, and thirty soldiers took pursuit. In a short time they found the deserters near Roy Lake, about six-and-one-half miles north of Fort Sisseton. Lieutenant Maize, after hearing no response to his request to surrender, gave orders to the soldiers to begin long-range fire. After twelve to fifteen shots, the deserters surrendered without returning fire. The soldiers took the scouts' Spencer carbines and escorted them to the post where they were placed in the guardhouse. After the deserters spent a few days in the guardhouse, the matter was dropped.[31]

One scout was tried at a garrison court-martial in June 1876 for refusal to obey orders. Indian scout Private Tamazakunduta, United

States Army, was ordered to clean the stable by Indian scout Sergeant Thomas Katate but refused to do so. Tamazakunduta then grabbed a crowbar and hit Sergeant Katate. He was arrested immediately and placed in the guardhouse. At the trial, Tamazakunduta, through his interpreter, pleaded guilty and said, "I am sorry for what I have done and hereafter I am going to obey all orders." He was fined $12 of his month's salary of $13 as punishment.[32]

One outstanding Enlisted Indian Scout was Sergeant Jim King, "Akicitana." He enlisted at Fort Sisseton in 1871 and served the post in various capacities. In June 1881, the post quartermaster officer, Akicitana, and several soldiers traveled to the south boundary of the military reservation. Some settlers had earlier stopped Fort Sisseton soldiers from cutting wood on the military reservation. The settlers thought they were on their own land, but the correct boundary line was pointed out to them by the officer. That same year, King was assigned the task of visiting nearby Lake Traverse Reservation to mark trees to be cut and used as telegraph poles. The poles, removed with the permission of Chief Gabriel Renville, were used to build the telegraph line between the post and Webster.

In April 1882, Jim King was promoted to sergeant. He then reenlisted after being assured of a pass, from time to time, to visit his wife and family who lived on his reservation farm. In December 1886, Jim King was given an honorable discharge from the detachment of Enlisted Indian Scouts with the United States Twenty-fifth Infantry. Major Frederick Mears, post commander, demonstrated

Sgt. James King, "Akicitana," Enlisted Indian Scout, served at Fort Sisseton, 1871-1886.

high praise for Akicitana by giving him a character rating of 'excellent' on his discharge. Following his discharge, King served for ten years as chief of Indian police on the Lake Traverse Reservation and then served for eleven years as deputy sheriff of Marshall County. He retired in Sisseton.

The Band

There were from five to seven musicians at the post between April 1865 and January 1868, enough to form a band. An 1867 invitation to Miss Ellen Brown, daughter of Joseph R. Brown of Browns Valley, forty miles east of the post, stated: "You are respectfully invited to attend a ball and supper to be given by Company C, Tenth Infantry their quarters, on Christmas evening December 25, 1867. Dancing commences at 8:00 p.m. Supper midnight."[33] Fort Sisseton temporarily lost its band in 1869 when it changed from a four-company post to a two-company post of about 100 men and six officers.

Army regulations permitted one band to a regiment, which was stationed where the regiment was headquartered. A military regiment consisted of ten companies of men, which was too large to be stationed at one frontier military post. For example, ten companies of the Seventeenth Infantry were spread among five army posts: Companies F and I at Fort Sisseton; E and K at Fort Pembina; C at Fort Totten; G at Fort Abraham Lincoln; and Companies A, B, D, H, and the regimental band and headquarters at Fort Yates.

The regimental headquarters and band were stationed only at a four-company post; therefore, Fort Sisseton, a two-company post, was never the location of the regimental band. Headquarters for the ten companies of the Seventeenth Infantry Regiment was first at Fort Abercrombie and later at Fort Yates. In 1874, the Seventeenth Infantry regimental band traveled seventy-six miles by team and army wagon from Fort Abercrombie to Fort Sisseton. They spent four weeks entertaining the members of the post. Commanding Officer Robert E. A. Crofton reported that the regimental band "has afforded great pleasure to the two companies serving at the post."[34]

Between 1870 and 1881, there were from one to four field musicians present for duty at Fort Sisseton, not enough for a band. The field musicians were generally fifers, trumpeters (buglers), or drummers. A trumpeter provided music for reveille, duty calls, retreat, and alarms. In 1876, Private John Ryan was the musician of the post guard. He blew the bugle for reveille, duty calls, and general alarms. On the night of 28 January 1876, between 9:00 p.m. and midnight, Ryan left his guard post without permission. He attended a ball given by the enlisted men of the post. During his absence, a fire started in the commanding officer's house. Another guard shouted "fire" and called Ryan to sound the alarm. Fortunately, the fire was not serious, but Commanding Officer Robert E. A. Crofton had Ryan arrested. At the garrison court-martial Private Ryan was fined $10 and sentenced to seven days of hard labor.[35] A trumpeter, fifer, and drummer could provide enough music for such ceremonial events as guard mount, retreat, and drill formations. In April 1879, the post's two field musicians were required to practice two hours daily with head trumpeter Mr. Ksyski. Trumpeter J. Flanagan arrived at the post and joined the other trumpeters in May.

There are six musicians listed in the post records for 1882, enough for a band. Commanding Officer C.E. Bennett reported forty-seven men in Company F and forty-eight men in Company I, which "takes into account the band."[36] The band kept busy playing at Fort Sisseton's military and social events.

On 25 May 1884, Companies E and G of the Twenty-fifth Infantry replaced the two companies of the Seventeenth Infantry and its band. The Twenty-fifth Infantry companies, however, brought with them a string band. The string band made its first appearance at a 4th of July celebration in Webster.

Post Commander Captain David Schooley advised the Department of Dakota that a military band had been organized at the post in 1885. He requested ten band instruments at no cost to the men. Band instruments cost from $20 to $60 each: B-flat cornet, $51.30; B-flat clarinet, $25.00; B-flat valve trombone, $62.50; bass drum, $10.40 and B-flat slide trombone, $44.34.[37] Generally, profits from the post fund were used to pay for sheet music and band instruments. With new band instruments, the band could perform both as a string band and a military band. The band went along when the two companies of the Twenty-fifth Infantry left the post in May 1888. Their replacement, Company G, Third Infantry, had no band except a trumpeter who provided the necessary bugle calls. However, the fort must have had some kind of band or musical group, because there was an 1889 New Year's eve military ball at the post. The eighteen-foot by thirty-eight-foot school room was used for the ball as well as the library and court-martial room.

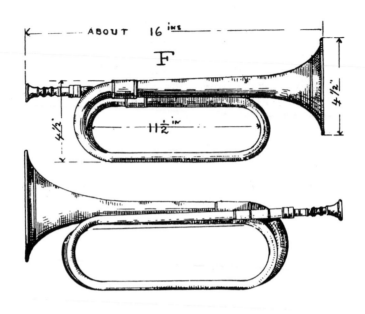

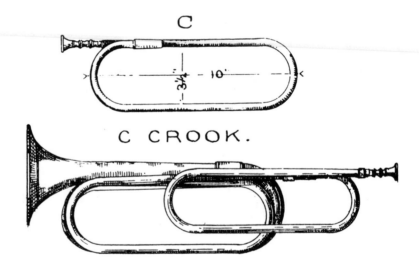

Army trumpet specifications.

Courtesy **U.S. Army Uniforms and Equipment,** *1889*

Headquarters of the Army,

(2333 acp 77

ADJUTANT GENERAL'S OFFICE,

Washington, May 26, 1877.

Sir:

You are hereby notified that the Secretary of War has appointed Mr. John Vander Horck a Post Trader at Fort Sisseton, D.T., under the provisions of Section 3 of the Act of July 24, 1876.

As soon as he shall be prepared to enter upon the discharge of his duties you will cause the removal from the Military Reservation at that post, upon the conditions set forth in War Department Circular of Dec. 13, 1876, of any trader not holding a letter of appointment from the Secretary of War under said Act.

E D Townsend
Adjutant General.

To the Commanding Officer
Fort Sisseton
Dakota Terry

Appointment of John Vander Horck as post trader, 1877.

Courtesy National Archives

When there was no military band at the post, trumpeters, fifers, or drummers were always available to play for the fort's military functions of guard mount, inspection, parade, or retreat. Soldiers who played guitars, violins, and other instruments entertained at post social events when there was no military band available.

Civilians

Post Sutler (Trader)

The sutler was a private businessman who sold food, tobacco, liquor, clothing, and other necessities to the post officers, enlisted men, and civilians. In 1866, the sutler's business, located on the east side of the post, consisted of three log buildings: a thirty-foot by sixteen-foot one-and-one-half-story house; a twenty-six-foot by twenty-nine-foot storehouse; and a thirty-six-foot by twenty-four-foot one-and-one-half-story store.[38] A later map of the post showed a horse barn and a stable for the sutler's cattle herd.

The council of administration and the post commander selected the sutler, subject to final approval and appointment by the secretary of war. It was a profitable enterprise because the sutler was given the exclusive right to do business at the post. For this right, the sutler paid $.10 per man per month to the Fort Sisseton post fund (about $10.00 a month.)[39] Library books, food items, and recreational equipment for the enlisted men were purchased from this fund. The commanding officer appointed an officer as post treasurer who managed the fund.

The following post sutlers, called post traders after 1876, did business at Fort Sisseton:

Mark Donnie	1 August 1864 to March 1865
J. N. Searles	March 1865 to July 1867
McWintermute	July 1867 to November 1870
T. W. Baldwin	November 1870 to February 1877
Charles H. Handy	February 1877 to May 1877
John Vander Horck	May 1877 to July 1886
Gustave Linder	July 1886 to 1 June 1889

Private George W. Doud in his diary refers to the post sutler on 27 September 1864, two months after Fort Sisseton was established: "Sut. *[sic]* store at fort. Shoulder straps [officers] of the drinking kind admitted in the house. No private soldier admitted in doors. They go to the window...for what they want."[40] Quartermaster Sergeant Andrew Fisk made reference to the social functions the post sutler often provided, in his diary of 27 January 1866: "I had considerable sport at the sutler store today playing the [card] trick called 'Turn Jack'. 25 February 1866- Sold Searles, post sutler 120 pound of company flour for $7.40. Bought hams with the same."[41]

John Vander Horck from Minneapolis was a well-known post trader. Vander Horck, born in Germany, migrated to Chicago in 1852 and then to St. Paul in 1855, where he operated a grocery store. During the 1862 Minnesota Sioux War, Governor Ramsey appointed him a captain. He and a company of eighty-two men were ordered to garrison Fort Abercrombie. They successfully defended the fort for four weeks against an Indian attack. After the war, he became a hardware dealer in Minneapolis. In 1877, the secretary of war appointed him post trader at Fort Sisseton. Because Vander Horck played a part in the development of Britton, as a member of the Britton Land and Trust Company, organized on 3 April 1885, the people of Britton named a street after him, Vander Horck Avenue.

The post commander appointed three officers to the council of administration who regulated the sutler's business and prices. Every six months, the council reviewed the sutler's cost of the goods purchased and set his prices, allowing for a reasonable profit. A copy of the price list was posted in the store.

The sutler's 1872 price list disclosed 243 different items for sale. At the time there were no settlers in the area, so the sutler depended upon the people of the post and transient freighting parties for business. Fort Sisseton customers included about 106 officers and men plus another twenty-five to thirty civilians consisting of wives, laundresses, and tradesmen. Enlisted men earned from $13 to $22 a month and civilians from $15 to $30 a month.

The various categories and some of the items listed for sale in 1872 were as follows:

Dry Goods—(fifty-six items)—towel $.35, shirt $2.50, ladies cotton hose $.50, men's shoes $3.00, cap $1.00;

Groceries—(seventy-three items)—tomatoes $.40 a can, jelly $.35 a jar, bacon $.20 a pound, butter $.30 a pound, eggs $.40 a dozen, lard $.30 a pound, broom $.50 each, walnuts $.40 a pound;

Notions—(114 items)—tooth brush $.25, razor $1.25, violin string $.35, coffee pot $.45, envelopes $.15 a bunch, lead pencil $.10, sweet oil $.25 a bottle, Graham's cocoa hair oil $.50 a bottle, rifle powder $.50 a pound, playing cards $.50 a deck, 22 different kinds of smoking pipes $.25 to $.50 each, cigars $.10 each, Sterling smoking tobacco $.50 a pound, matches $.10 a box.[42]

A similar 1878 price list included more items: cheese $.20 a pound, men's socks $.50 a pair, buffalo overcoat $15.00, candy $.25 a pound, wash board $.30, sardines $.25 a can, tobacco plug $.10, Durham tobacco $.80 a pound, Lager bottle of beer $.30, and a drink of whiskey $.15.[43]

Post Trader Vander Horck was frequently in disagreement with the commanding officer and the council of administration. Vander Horck was ordered to stop his cattle and horses from entering the parade ground for grazing in 1880. In 1881, he was told to keep his hogs one-half mile from any post building. The trader was asked to keep his stable clean in 1882. The council of administration, in a special order in 1883, called attention to "the present very uncleanly condition of the Post Trader's Store, aside from the men's bar makes it unfit for a lady to go in or near it."[44]

The post trader had considerable competition from the post commissary. The commissary sold food items at cost, plus ten percent for transportation, to the enlisted men and officers. But the trader did well on many other items not for sale in the commissary.

Crafts and Trades

During 1864 and 1865, the peak construction years of the post, an average of ten carpenters, brick layers, stone masons, and teamsters was employed monthly. They were paid from $60 to $70 a month. During the busy month of November 1864, however, the post quartermaster paid twenty-eight tradesmen and thirty-four Indian scouts $3,829.[45] Considerable soldier labor was also used for constructing the post.

In July 1867, after post construction was almost completed, civilians and their monthly salaries were listed as follows: one clerk, $125; one sawyer, $93; one wheelwright, $80; two blacksmiths, $80 and $50; one carpenter, $100; one mason, $75; and two interpreters, $100 and $50. Interpreters were needed because of a large Indian population nearby and for the post's Enlisted Indian Scouts. Post Commander Captain J. C. Bates, in 1870, rehired William Quinn as post interpreter and guide at a salary of $100 a month plus one food ration per day. Bates said, "Many Indians come to the post because 1,200 are in the vicinity and it is essential we have an interpreter. Mr. Quinn is an excellent interpreter and a very good guide."[46]

Another type of civilian employee, sometimes a Sisseton or Wahpeton, listed in the Fort Sisseton Post Returns, was a station keeper. The employee managed a station, generally a log building or two, which military personnel or civilians used for an overnight stay when traveling along a military road. A station was located on the seventy-six mile wagon road between Fort Sisseton and Fort Abercrombie. The station keeper was paid one ration a day plus $5.00 a month. In July 1877, there were three station keepers listed on the payroll. There were two station keepers between the post and Breckinridge, Minnesota, in 1880, and one between the Sisseton-Wahpeton Agency and Browns Valley. Mail haulers were frequent users of these stations.

The 1880 federal census listed twelve civilian workers at Fort Sisseton: one baker, wife, and son; one farmer, wife, son, and daughter; one storekeeper, wife, and three sons; one hospital matron; two brickmakers; one blacksmith; one painter; one engineer; one carpenter; and two tinsmiths.[47] At the time there were twenty-one civilians on the post plus six officers, eighty-three enlisted men, and one Indian scout.

Commanding Officer Captain David Schooley, reported on the importance of the carpenter trade at Fort Sisseton: "Of the several different kinds of mechanics at a military post, none is so important as a carpenter. There is considerable lumber...here which might be put to good use had we skilled workmen. In our present helpless condition should one of the command die, the quartermaster would be at a loss to furnish a coffin."[48]

The enlisted men at the post were skilled in many different trades and crafts. The January 1882 Post Returns enumerated enlisted men who performed a certain trade or craft at the post: two clerks, two carpenters, one blacksmith, three stonemasons, two machinists, one wheelwright, one harness maker, three farriers, one electrotyper (a plate used in printing, made by electroplating a wax impression), three butchers, one printer, two shoemakers, one baker, one cooper, one boilermaker, one plasterer, one embalmer, one telegraph operator, and two tailors.[49]

Enlisted men usually performed their trade in the line of duty. The tailors, however, charged for their services. In 1873, a private working as a tailor was allowed to have a light in his shop until midnight in order to finish his work. He abused the privilege one night by bringing in whiskey and partying with two other privates. At the garrison court-martial they were fined $10 each. Post regulations in 1883 limited the charge to $.25 for altering a coat and $.08 for a trouser. Post Commander Captain Clarence E. Bennett expressed disfavor when he found out the tailors were charging as high as $2.00 for altering a coat and $1.50 for a trouser. The tailors responded by saying they would not work for regulation prices. Eventually, a compromise was approved. Barber prices were as follows: shave for an officer, $.15, enlisted man, $.10; haircut for an officer, $1.25, enlisted man, $.75.[50]

Laundresses

Laundresses at Fort Sisseton lived in one or two of the nine one-story log buildings at the post. Laundresses were often the wives or relatives of enlisted men. Andrew Fisk, on 12 February 1866, noted in his diary that their laundress, Mrs. Ide, left on the stage for Sauk Centre, Minnesota, the day before his company left for the same place.[51] In April 1869, there were five laundresses at Fort Sisseton doing the laundry for 108 enlisted men of Companies B and H, Twentieth United States Infantry.[52] There were eight laundresses for 116 enlisted men of Companies B and C, Seventeenth Infantry, in 1874.[53] The laundresses charged for their work on a piece-by-piece basis. One laundress, Betty Rencer, died of consumption on 9 July 1868 and was buried in the post cemetery. No laundresses were listed at the post in the 1880 federal census. Post commander C. E. Bennett, however, refers to laundresses at the post in 1882.

Endnotes

1. Harold H. Schuler. *Fort Sully: Guns at Sunset.* Vermillion, South Dakota: University of South Dakota Press, 1992:72.
2. Unmarked newspaper clipping from the files of the Minnesota State Historical Society, St. Paul, Minnesota.
3. Francis B. Heitman. *Historical Register and Dictionary of the United States Army.* 2 vols. Washington: GPO, 1903. (Hereafter cited as Heitman: United States Army.)
4. Heitman: United States Army.
5. Heitman: United States Army.
6. Circular 12. RG 393. V. 16. vol. 1:6. National Archives, Washington, D.C.
7. C. E. Bennett to Edgar Howe, 11 and 15 July 1879. Letters Sent. RG 393. V. 2. vol. 7. National Archives, Washington, D.C.
8. Federal Census, 1880. South Dakota Archives, Pierre, South Dakota. (Hereafter cited as Census, 1880.)
9. *Dakota Daylight,* 28 July 1887.
10. David Schooley to Adjutant General, Fort Snelling. 5 September 1884. Letters Sent. National Archives, Washington, D.C.
11. Post Adjutant to A. E. Kilpatrick, 21 October 1878. Letters Sent. RG 393. V. 2. vol. 7. National Archives, Washington, D.C.
12. Census, 1880.
13. General Orders. RG 393. V. 15. vol. 1. National Archives, Washington, D.C.
14. *The Britton Sentinel,* 31 August 1888.
15. Adjutant General's Office. Oath of Enlistment and Allegiance, Form No. 73. South Dakota National Guard Museum, Pierre, South Dakota.
16. Dakota Territory Census, 1870.
17. *Report of the Secretary of War,* 1890, vol. 1:287.
18. Post Medical History, August 1870. RG 94. V. vol. 1:182. National Archives, Washington, D.C. (Hereafter cited as Medical History.)
19. Circular No. 7. C. E. Bennett, 27 March 1880. RG 393. V. 16. vol. 1:39. National Archives, Washington, D.C.
20. *Webster Reporter and Farmer,* 14 February 1884.
21. Andrew F. Fisk Diary. Roll 81. Minnesota Historical Society, St. Paul, Minnesota. (Hereafter cited as Fisk Diary.)
22. Fisk Diary.
23. Medical History, January 1874. RG 94. V. vol. 2:155.
24. Medical History, March 1875. RG 94. V. vol. 2:210.
25. Victor Biart report. RG 393. V. 19. Box 8. National Archives, Washington, D.C.
26. David Schooley to Adjutant General, Department of Dakota, 5 September 1884. 9W2 37/27/A. National Archives, Washington, D.C.
27. Census, 1880.
28. Indian Scouts. Microcopy 233. Roll 70 and 71. National Archives, Washington, D.C.
29. RG 393. V. vol. 2. 24 July 1870. Letters Sent. National Archives, Washington, D.C.

30. Edward P. Pearson to Adjutant General, Department of Dakota, 22 May 1876. Letters Sent. RG 393. V. 2. vol. 6. National Archives, Washington, D.C.

31. Medical History, RG 94. V. vol. 2:132.

32. Courts-Martial. RG 393. V. 18. vol. 1:68. National Archives, Washington, D. C.

33. Museum Display. Fort Sisseton Visitors' Center. Fort Sisseton, South Dakota.

34. Major Robert E. A. Crofton to Adjutant General, Fort Abercrombie, 12 September 1874. Letters Sent. RG 393. V. 2. vol. 5. National Archives, Washington, D.C.

35. Garrison Courts-Martial. RG 393. V. 18. vol.1:235. National Archives, Washington, D.C.

36. C. E. Bennett to Department of Dakota, 14 May 1881. Letters Sent. RG 393. V. 2. vol. 9. National Archives, Washington, D.C.

37. *Report of the Secretary of War*, 1889. vol. 1:718.

38. S. P. Folsom and H. Von Minden Fort Sisseton Map, 1866. File 2229A, South Dakota Archives, Pierre, South Dakota.

39. *Regulations of the United States Army*, 1881. Article XLV.

40. George W. Doud Diary. South Dakota Archives, Pierre, South Dakota.

41. Fisk Diary.

42. General Orders, 8 May 1872. RG 393. V. 11. vol. 1. National Archives, Washington, D.C.

43. Circular, 16 December 1878. RG 393. V. 16. vol. 1:20. National Archives, Washington, D.C.

44. Order 47. RG 393. V. 15. vol. 2. National Archives, Washington, D.C.

45. Post Returns of Fort Sisseton, November 1864. National Archives, Washingon, D.C. on microfilm roll 1179, South Dakota Archives, Pierre, South Dakota. (Hereafter cited as Post Returns.)

46. J. C. Bates to the Adjutant General, 26 June 1870. Letters Sent. RG 393. V. 2. vol. 2. National Archives, Washington, D.C.

47. Census, 1880.

48. David Schooley to Department of Dakota, 15 June 1884. Letters Sent. 9 W 2. 37/27/A. National Archives, Washington, D.C.

49. Post Returns, January 1882.

50. C.E. Bennett to Department of Dakota, 26 January 1883. Letters Sent. RG 393. V. 2. vol. 12. National Archives,Washington, D. C.

51. Fisk Diary.

52. Medical History, April 1869. RG 94. vol.1:119.

53. Medical History, January 1874. RG 94. vol.2:154.

Chapter 6
Misconduct and Punishment

It was not uncommon for Fort Sisseton soldiers to be bored, to dislike army discipline, and to miss family. Consequently some were involved in misconduct, sometimes serious misconduct. The army had 128 rules of conduct printed in the Articles of War. Any violation of the rules was punishable by either a general or garrison court-martial. A court-martial was similar to a civilian trial before a judge, except that, in the army, the case was judged by a panel of army officers.

Guardhouse and Prison

Any soldier arrested for misconduct was taken immediately to the guardhouse, where he remained in confinement awaiting a court-martial. Fort Sisseton's fifty-foot by twenty-foot brick guardhouse, with iron bars on its windows, was built in 1865. Early plans show two small cells, each four feet by eight feet. Next to the two cells was another confinement area of about sixteen feet by twenty feet. The two small cells were used for those accused of more serious crimes. The west room of the guardhouse was used by the officer of the day, corporal of the guard, and guards on duty. There was an eight-foot porch on the west side of the building. The guardhouse and prison were heated with wood-burning stoves. One officer inspecting the post in 1870 noted the guardhouse had poor ventilation and bad floors, and that the two small cells were "damp and dark."[1] Guard duty was rotated among the soldiers. Each day, twelve to fourteen enlisted men were picked for guard duty and served a twenty-four-hour period. Army regulations required a guard to stay at his post; carry his gun and ammunition belt at all times; stay fully dressed, even when resting during two-hour shifts; challenge all who approached and ask for the countersign; and repeat calls from distant guard posts.[2]

Placing armed guards at their posts around Fort Sisseton was a part of an elaborate ritual called "guard mount." Each morning at 9:00 a.m., the guard musician sounded his bugle to call the new guards in full-dress uniform to assemble on the parade ground in front of the guardhouse. After inspection by the corporal of the guard and the officer of the day, the new guards were marched to their posts to relieve the old guards coming off duty. When there was a band at the post, music was played during guard mount.

In April 1867, guard posts were as follows: one in front of the guardhouse; one at the stable; one on the north side of the haystack; and four outside of the ditch, one each on the north, east, west, and south sides. Commanding Officer Jesse A. P. Hampson issued Special Order No. 2 for the guards: "Sentinels will be instructed to prevent any Indians, except interpreters, entering the post after retreat and will give the alarm in the event of the approach of Indians after night."[3]

Guard posts in 1880 included post commissary, post quartermaster, officers' quarters, magazine, adjutant's office, laundresses' quarters, men's barracks, hospital, and stable. Their principal duty was to guard against fire, theft, and intruders.

In case of a fire or alarm at night, the drummer on duty at the guardhouse began beating his drum until the post was awakened. Fort Sisseton General Orders describe the procedure for responding to a threatening situation:

> In case of alarm at night, the assembly will be beaten by the drummer on duty at the guardhouse. In case of fire the long roll will be beaten. If assembly is beaten, all companies will parade under arms on their part of the parade ground. If the long roll is beaten, the men will assemble without arms. In both cases the men will await further orders from the Commanding Officer.[4]

Guard duty was serious business. Any violation of duty resulted in punishment. The following are examples of garrison courts-martial for those who violated the rules: a private who failed to attend guard mount was fined $2.00; a private who had taken two prisoners to the sink and stopped in the barracks on his return was fined $2.00;

Interior of restored Fort Sisseton guardhouse.

a corporal of the guard who failed to post a guard at his post was acquitted; a private who was drunk on guard duty was fined $5.00 and given seven days of labor; the officer of the day was ordered to explain to the commanding officer why a guard was in the guard-house having coffee rather than being at his post.

To restrain a prisoner, a ball and chain was attached to the leg of a prisoner. In 1869, Post Surgeon Major B. Knickerbocker asked permission to have the ball and chain removed from a prisoner's ankle while in the hospital under treatment for a debility.[5] Another example of placing prisoners in leg irons was reported in 1870 by Commanding Officer Captain John S. McNaught: "Sergeants Thompson and Callanan of Company B, Twentieth United States Infantry, who had been in irons since their capture, have been at work daily chopping wood under the charge of the guard. They succeeded on 6 June 1870 in inducing the guard to desert with them and thus made their escape. They were recaptured and sent to Fort Abercrombie for trial."[6] A prisoner escaped on 2 July 1873 and eluded the Indian scouts who were sent in pursuit.

In September 1871 Post Surgeon C. E. Munn treated several cases of colic among prisoners in the guardhouse. Believing it was due to exposure from the cold at night, Munn ordered a filled bed-sack and two woolen blankets for each of the prisoners.[7] The number of prisoners in the guardhouse varied. In March 1865 there were eight, compared to a monthly average of nine in 1868 when 201 men were stationed at the post. One a month was confined in 1872, but there were five in jail in the month of January 1873. The average monthly occupancy in the guardhouse in 1882 was two, but one month it was nine.[8] At the time, 104 men were stationed at the post.

General Court-Martial

A general court-martial was used to try men who had been charged with such capital crimes as larceny, murder, or desertion. The commanding officer of the Department of Dakota would appoint a panel of five or more officers to conduct the court-martial. Panel members were from Fort Sisseton and other military posts. Sometimes, the accused would be tried at a general court-martial in Fort Sisseton or at an another post. Punishment depended upon the severity of the offense and could consist of a fine, dishonorable discharge, prison, or death.

There were fewer general courts-martial than garrison courts-martial conducted at Fort Sisseton. In 1885, for example, two general courts-martial and thirteen garrison courts-martial were held.[9]

One twenty-three-day general courts-martial was conducted at the post, between 20 May 1868 and 12 June 1868, for soldiers from various posts who had been charged with capital crimes.[10] In 1875, a corporal who had been arrested for a shooting was sent to Fort Abercrombie, seventy-six miles northeast of the post, for a general court-martial. It was very expensive for Fort Sisseton because the fort had to send seven witnesses to testify at Fort Abercrombie.

Usually, a general court-martial was conducted for a soldier who had deserted and was captured. In 1873, six soldiers deserted, five in 1883, and two in 1887. Two privates deserted in 1889, six weeks before the post closed. The sheriff of Marshall County aided in the search for the two privates by sending telegrams containing their descriptions to nearby towns. Catching deserters was not easy, but the $30 reward for capture paid by the United States Army aided in the search.

On 7 September 1882, a post soldier was convicted for shooting at a fellow soldier with the intent to commit murder. He was sentenced to seven years at hard labor at the Minnesota State Prison, Stillwater. While forming an escort to deliver the convicted soldier to the prison, Commanding Officer Captain Clarence E. Bennett issued Post Order No. 158 to the sergeant of the guard: "He will be securely ironed by iron shackles on his ankles and handcuffs on his wrists to prevent his escaping the guard."[11] The next day, a detachment consisting of First Lieutenant George H. Roach and five armed soldiers escorted the prisoner, along with three others who had been convicted earlier, to Webster, where they all boarded the train for Fort Snelling.

Garrison Court-Martial

A garrison court-martial was held at the post by a panel of three officers appointed by the commanding officer. It was convened for enlisted men who had committed minor offenses. Punishment could be a fine, reduction in rank, imprisonment at the post prison, or hard labor on the post. An unusual type of punishment used at Fort Sisseton was to have a prisoner carry a thirty-pound log around the parade ground for a designated period of time.

Garrison courts-martial were at first held in any location suitable for the event. Following 1880, they were held in a special twenty-foot by twenty-foot court-martial room in the library and school building. The procedure for a garrison court-martial was typical of a civilian trial. When the panel of three officers convened, the defendant (called a prisoner during the proceedings) was brought from the guardhouse prison to appear before the court. The order was read to the defendant, after which he was asked if he had any objection to any member present named in the order. After swearing, the defendant was arraigned, charged, and the specifications were read. The defendant was then asked how he pleaded. If the accused had no testimony or statement, the court closed for deliberation. After review, the court would announce whether the accused was guilty or not guilty; if guilty, the sentence was announced also.[12]

In an 1874 trial, Sergeant Dan O'Grady was charged with beating Private Eugene LeRand with his gun. In this case, both the prosecution and the defense presented witnesses at the trial. It appears the accused could ask questions of the witnesses because there were no attorneys listed in the case. During the first day of the trial, the prosecution [Army] presented four witnesses: Corporal Joseph Marchand and Privates Eugene LeRand, Whipple, and Runes. Privates Whipple and Runes were cross-examined by Sergeant O'Grady. The next day the court heard the defense with Private Smith as the principal witness. During the proceedings, Sergeant O'Grady asked Smith seven questions and the court asked two. Sergeant Dan O'Grady was found not guilty.[13]

Fort Sisseton's garrison courts-martial records indicate the type of misconduct and punishment for post soldiers:

4 December 1865—"Billy and Sport refused to go on the water wagon and had to pack cord word;"[14]

1 July 1868—A soldier was drunk in the barracks and got into a fight with another soldier. He was found guilty and sentenced to ten days at hard labor;[15]

22 July 1868—A private missed reveille and roll call. He was fined $10 and given ten days of hard labor.[16] That same day another private, who had been ordered several times not to leave clothing under his bed, was caught again and fined $2.00 plus five days at hard labor;[17]

5 August 1868—A sergeant of Company E did assault, cut with a knife, strike and beat the bugler of Company E. The sergeant's rank was reduced to the grade of private.[18] That same day, a private was absent from drill. His punishment was to carry a log of wood around the parade ground, not to exceed thirty pounds, every alternate hour from reveille to retreat;[19]

4 February 1873—A private who had been ordered by his sergeant to fill the sergeant's bed sack with hay replied: "I will not do it, I will go to the guard house first." His sentence included a $10 fine and ten days at hard labor;[20]

11 March 1874—A private was found drunk in the kitchen while on kitchen police duty. He was fined $3.00.[21]

The number of garrison courts-martial at Fort Sisseton varied from year to year. Post garrison courts-martial records show that there were twelve in 1876, thirty-seven in 1877, seven in 1878, twelve in 1879, eighteen in 1880, and thirteen in 1885. Between 1880 and 1885, an average of fourteen per cent of the 106 soldiers at the post were involved in a garrison court-martial.

Endnotes

1. John S. Billings, Circular No. 4. 5 December 1870. Surgeon General's Office, Washington: GPO.

2. *Regulations of the United States Army*, 1881.

3. Special Orders, 9 April 1857. RG 393. V. 13. National Archives, Washington, D.C. (Hereafter cited as Special Orders.)

4. General Orders. 21 April 1870. RG 393. V. 11. vol. 1. National Archives, Washington, D.C. (Hereafter cited as General Orders.)

5. Post Medical History. 1869. RG 94. vol. 1:109. National Archives, Washington, D.C. (Hereafter cited as Medical History.)

6. J. S. McNaught to Adjutant General, 18 May 1870. Letters Sent. RG 393. V. 2. vol. 2. National Archives, Washington, D.C.

7. Medical History, 1871. RG 94. vol.1:234.

8. Medical History, 1882. RG 94. vol.3:199.

9. Frederick Mears' Annual Report, 1 September 1885. RG 393. V. 2. vol. 13. National Archives, Washington, D.C.

10. Special Order, 12 June 1868. RG 393. V. 2. vol. 1.

11. General Orders. RG 393. V. 15. vol. 2:78.

12. General Courts-Martial. RG 393. V. 18. vol. 1. National Archives, Washington, D.C. (Hereafter cited as General Courts-Martial.)

13. General Courts-Martial. RG 393. V. 18. vol. 1:71.

14. Andrew Fisk Diary. Roll 81, Minnesota Historical Society, St. Paul, Minnesota.

15. General Orders, 1 July 1868. RG 393. V. 11. vol. 1.

16. General Orders, 22 July 1868, RG 393. V. 11. vol. 1.

17. General Orders, 22 July 1868, RG 393. V. 11. vol. 1.

18. General Orders, 5 August, 1868, RG 393. V. 11. vol. 1.

19. General Orders, 5 August, 1868, RG 393. V. 11. vol. 1.

20. General Orders, 4 February, 1873. RG 393. V. 11. vol. 1

21. General Courts-Martial, 11 March 1874. RG 393. V. 18. vol. 1.

Chapter 7

Military Duty and Pageantry

Sounding Duty Calls

Fort Sisseton's commanding officer provided a daily schedule of activities for the soldiers, from reveille to retreat. The schedule followed army regulations. A post bugler sounded a bugle to call the men to the scheduled events. Post Commander Clarence E. Bennett's 1882 schedule is typical of the daily duty calls.

The day began at 5:45 a.m. when the musician of the guard blew reveille, the first call. The bugler was required to sound his bugle clearly and distinctly in front of the officers' quarters, in front and rear of the men's barracks and in the direction of the stone stable to the north. Officers and men had fifteen minutes to dress and be on the parade ground by 6:00 a.m. reveille. Following roll call, the men policed the grounds and barracks before heading to the company mess hall for a 6:30 a.m. breakfast.

At 7:00 a.m. the bugler sounded sick call for those who needed to see the post physician. One time the bugler failed to sound sick call and was reprimanded by his company commander. Fatigue (work) call was sounded at 7:30 a.m. Those answering work call had been placed on the fatigue roster the previous day. One work list included many jobs: whitewashing the insides of the barracks; cleaning the hospital and root cellar; repairing the cemetery fence; putting up wooden grave markers; and feeding the cattle and horses. Another job was emptying the slop and refuse barrels located at the hospital, officers' quarters, men's barracks, and laundresses' quarters. In the summer there was hay to cut, gardens to till, wood to haul, and cisterns to clean.

After the 7:30 a.m. work call, another bugler replaced the musician of the guard to sound the day's remaining calls. A daily function, rain or shine, was guard mount at 8:00 a.m. After the officer of the day placed the guards at their posts, the bugler sounded target practice at 9:00 a.m. This call did not include the men on fatigue whose turn on the range would be on another day.

Captain Bennett's 1882 schedule also required the bugler to begin sounding recall at 11:00 a.m. for those on the target range and 11:30 a.m. for those in the work details. This allowed the men time to relax before going to the company mess for their noon meal. In the afternoon most of the schedule was repeated beginning with fatigue at 1:00 p.m. A half-hour later, drill began on the parade ground. The drill detail was recalled at 3:00 p.m. and the work detail at 5:00 p.m.

Eating a light supper and preparing for retreat at sunset filled the rest of the afternoon. Preparations included cleaning rifles, polishing shoes, and donning full-dress uniforms. At sunset, the bugle was sounded for the command to assemble on the parade ground. The officers checked formations before ordering the two companies to parade around the ground and stop in front of the flag pole and cannon. After roll call, while the band played, the ten-foot by twenty-foot national flag was lowered. The bugler then sounded retreat, after which a blank cartridge in the cannon was fired by the gun crew. A twelve-pound mountain howitzer was used as the sunset gun before 1882. After that a three-inch rifled cannon was used.

At 9:00 p.m., tattoo was sounded by the bugler to signal the end of the working day. Everybody then returned to quarters with taps sounding at 9:30 p.m. The schedule on Sunday consisted of an 8:00 a.m. inspection followed by guard mount and church service.[1] Military patrols, visiting generals, local conditions, and the weather resulted in some schedule modifications. However, army regulations stated the retreat ceremony "will not be dispensed with except on urgent occasions."[2] In 1872 and 1873 post commanders changed the schedule five times but the changes were minor. The 1882 schedule was very similar to Post Commander J. C. Bates' 1869 schedule, except that it listed different hours for target practice. The 1884 schedule was the same as that in 1882.

Inspections

Inspections were a large part of a soldier's life at Fort Sisseton. Army regulations required a weekly inspection by the company commanders and a monthly inspection by the post commander. An inspector from the Department of Dakota also inspected the post once a year.

One of the inspections was described by Sergeant Andrew J. Fisk, who arrived at the post on 12 November 1865. At the time, the post was still under construction and the men and officers were living in log huts. He noted briefly in his diary for 3 December 1865: "Inspection. Snowed two inches. Wrote to Hettie." A few weeks later, after the men had moved into the new field-stone barracks, he again wrote, "Inspection of arms and quarters today. Cold and stormy. We have all our inspections indoors now. Roll call also. In fact, we don't have roll calls mornings anymore. The officers don't come around so they can't blame us."[3]

The practice of not having morning roll calls ended after First Lieutenant William L. Briley became the new commander of Company A. Fisk noted on 18 January 1866 that Lieutenant Briley "was over to roll call this morning but nobody was up. When Sergeant Knight politely told him that we hadn't any roll calls in the morning all winter, he ordered us up at reveille after this."[4] Three days later Lieutenant Briley inspected the company and called the roll in front of the barracks. It was not unusual, however, to perform inspections inside the barracks during bad weather.

Saturdays were busy times in the barracks, preparing for Sunday's weekly inspection, which was usually held at 8:00 a.m. The men shined shoes, arranged footlockers, and cleaned rifles. They also cleaned and scrubbed the barracks with the two brushes and three corn brooms issued monthly to the companies. The company commander, usually a captain, inspected the barracks, kitchen, and mess halls for cleanliness. He also inspected the men's footlockers, clothing, and rifles. The captain checked to see if the men had washed their hands and faces daily, bathed once a week, and trimmed their beard and hair, all regulation requirements.

Often, weather permitting, a parade was held in conjunction with an inspection. An 1870 special order asked that all troops assemble at 11:00 a.m. on 30 April for a parade, review, inspection, and muster. Indian scouts would parade dismounted. The order also

stated that fatigue duty would be suspended after 4:30 p.m. the previous day, before inspection.[5]

The post commander expected the officers to set the standard
for inspections. Post Commander Edward P. Pearson wrote a letter
to Company Commander Captain Malcolm McArthur and asked him
to explain "why a man in your company was wearing shoes at
inspection this morning different from regulation issue. Hereafter
you will cause every member of your company to wear the prescribed shoe."[6] In 1877, new Post Commander Major Robert E. A.
Crofton sent another letter to Captain McArthur asking him for a
written report explaining why he did not wear the full-dress uniform
at inspection that morning.[7] It might have been easier for Major
Crofton to walk across the parade ground and talk with Captain
McArthur, but often letters were written as evidence that action had
been taken on a matter.

Major Crofton was concerned enough to issue Circular No. 4
ordering officers to wear the prescribed uniform on all ceremonial
occasions. He also ordered the companies to parade at the next
Sunday inspection, Company B to assemble north of the flagstaff,
and Company C south of the flagstaff. His concern with inspections
shifted to footlockers in Circular No. 7 issued a week later:
"Hereinafter at inspections the footlockers will be placed on one
side of the bunks near the front and open."[8]

In April 1877, Major Crofton asked that the companies be
inspected in light marching order. The equipment included a rifle,
ammunition, canteen of water, blanket, and a couple days' rations.
He also ordered that the men need not wear their back-packs but
they would be inspected in the barracks.[9] Because of the cold weather on 27 November 1877, the troops paraded outside in their wool
great coats, but the inspection was held inside the barracks. The
Articles of War and guard duty regulations were read to the men
after inspection.

On Saturday, 28 February 1880, muster and drill were suspended
so that the companies could prepare for a Sunday inspection by the
post commander. His once-a-month inspection was similar to the
Sunday inspection, but it also included the condition of the animals,
buildings, and grounds. Each month the post commander sent weekly and monthly inspection reports to the Department of Dakota.

The inspector general of the Department of Dakota conducted
annual inspections of the post in October 1884 and July 1885. On 30

September and 1 October 1886, the Acting Inspector General of the
United States Army, from Washington, Lieutenant Colonel Edwin C.
Mason, inspected the post. His report provides an excellent review
of the military condition of Fort Sisseton:

> The police of the post was admirable; neatness, order and
> cleanliness characterized every part of it. The arrangement of
> the contents of the storehouses, the interiors of the barracks,
> the grounds surrounding the barracks, quarters, stables and out-
> buildings; walks, drives, fences and outlying grounds for two
> hundred yards were in perfect order. At 9:00 a.m.,Friday,
> October 1st, the troops were paraded in full dress for a review,
> inspection and drill. The ceremony of review was correctly per-
> formed. The "march past" in quick and double time was particu-
> larly well done, cadences and alignments well preserved. The
> subsequent inspection showed that the arms, belts and boxes,
> and the clothing [military dress] to be in excellent order. The
> appearance of the troops under arms, their carriage and bearing
> was military in a satisfactory degree. After the inspection the
> troops were drilled, first by company and afterwards by battal-
> ion.[10]

The last Department of Dakota inspection was made in October
1888 by Lieutenant William F. Drummer, Twelfth United States
Infantry. He arrived on 26 October and left on 27 October.

Drill and Training

Army regulations required that soldiers practice close-order drill
to learn to march in unison. Troops also practiced various movements with their rifles. Commanding Officer John Clowney post-
poned these practices during post construction. Major Rose also
deferred training while the men built the post. He was supported by
his superiors in the Department of Dakota who advised him in
November 1864 that "the labor of preparing quarters etc., will prevent for a time much attention to drill, but when time allows that
should be made a particular point, and the most stringent discipline
enforced among the troops under your immediate command."[11]
When the spring of 1865 arrived, however, Major Rose appointed
Captain Louis J. Patch to supervise all drill of the companies of the

Minnesota Second Cavalry. At the time there were 108 serviceable horses on the post. Fort Sisseton records did not specify the type of drill and training performed by the cavalry companies. However, the men's training consisted of close-order drill plus mounted formations with their horses. Each cavalryman was armed with either the Spencer or Sharps carbine. The army's muzzle-loading .58 caliber Springfield rifle was difficult to handle on horseback.

Fort Sisseton was changed to an infantry post in June 1866 when Major S. B. Hayman and several companies of the Tenth Infantry arrived. The infantry companies practiced close-order drill and training according to Lieutenant Colonel Emory Upton's manual *Infantry Tactics*, adopted by the army. The new manual offered a simpler method of training and drill which could be learned more quickly than the old method.[12] Close-order drill helped prepare soldiers for field marches and training. Responding to commands, keeping in step, and performing column movements had a good disciplinary effect as well. It also prepared the men for such post events as inspection, guard mount, dress parade, and retreat.

Close-order drill training was conducted on the parade ground. Usually, company drill was directed by the first sergeant, sometimes in the absence of the company commander. However, in 1869 Commanding Officer J. C. Bates required that company commanders be present on the parade ground when their companies were practicing drill.[13] Often a company of forty men was divided into four sections of ten men for close-order drill. After drill by sections, the men assembled in columns of four and drilled in what was called "school of the company." Both companies then paraded as a battalion before the critical eyes of the post's commanding officer.

The men were provided specific training with their rifles: the manual-of-arms, stacking of arms, and bayonet exercises. Rifle training included target practice. Commanding Officer Clarence E. Bennett in 1880 reported that proper attention was paid to drill, manual-of-arms, and discipline. He said the men "are drilled frequently. New recruits are drilled 12 times a week."[14] The following week, however, Bennett excused the men from drill on Mondays and Saturdays in order for them to distribute supplies and do other work.

Following an 1884 inspection of the post, the adjutant general of the Department of Dakota gave the following evaluation in his report:

The discipline and bearing of the troops are good. The instruction and efficiency in some portions of the drill are probably better than at any other post in the Department; but it was noticed in the review of quick time, that the musicians are entirely incorrect in time and gave the cadence of the step at 110; and the instruction in battalion drill is defective.[15]

Fort Sisseton's nine-mile-wide by fifteen-mile-long military reservation was ideal for field-training marches. Frequently, detachments of men made short overnight practice marches. They learned how to form a camp, pitch and strike a tent, cook in the field, manage latrines, load and unload supply wagons, guard the camp, dig rifle pits, and operate against an enemy. One practice march in 1887 was made to a distant point outside the military reservation. Post Commander Frederick Mears ordered both companies of the Twenty-fifth Infantry on a six-day practice march. The men were equipped for heavy marching order and conducted the march as if in a hostile country. A fully equipped Fort Sisseton infantry soldier carried a load of about forty pounds. The load included his 8.4-pound Springfield rifle and a back-pack loaded with extra ammunition, overcoat, wool and rubber blanket, half a shelter tent, tin mess kit, clothing, one-quart canteen, and five-days' rations. The rations usually consisted of salt pork, hardtack, salt, coffee, and sugar. Hardtack was a nutritious half-inch-thick and three-inch-square dried flour-and-water biscuit. Nine of the biscuits equaled the army bread ration of one baked loaf per day. Company G left the post on May 19 and returned on May 24. Company E left the post on May 25 and returned on May 30. The round-trip march for each company totaled fifty-six miles, about ten miles a day.[16]

Weapons

Rifles, Carbines, Revolvers

The first soldiers at Fort Sisseton in 1864 were armed with various types of carbines and the .58 caliber, single-shot, muzzle-loading Springfield rifle. Most of the weapons were army surplus that had been used during the Civil War. In 1866, after the war, the army converted many of its .58 caliber, single-shot, muzzle-loading Springfields into .50 caliber, single-shot, breech-loading Springfields. The converted rifle fired metallic cartridges that were inserted into the breech or rear of the gun. Captain Javan B. Irvine of Fort Sully II reported that a soldier could fire ten shots a minute with the breech-loader compared to two a minute with the muzzle-loader.[17]

However, the troops of the Second Minnesota Cavalry at the post were armed with Sharps carbines, Smith carbines, and .44 caliber Colt pistols. Some of the carbines were still on hand in 1868, according to Captain Jesse A. P. Hampson, Tenth Infantry. He advised the Department of Dakota: "The mounted infantry and scouts at this place are armed with Smith and Sharps carbines. They are old and really unfit for active service. The Spencer carbine...will be of infinitely more service for mounted troops than the .50 caliber Springfield breech-loader. The Springfield is too heavy and unwieldy to be handled with facility by the troops and it also requires more care in loading than can be at all times given on horseback."[18]

An 1871 Fort Sisseton inventory shows that the 117 enlisted men in Companies B and F, Twentieth Infantry, were armed with the .50 caliber, single-shot, breech-loading Springfield rifle, Model 1866. Each soldier was also equipped with a bayonet scabbard and cartridge box. A supply of 29,700 center-primed .50 caliber metallic cartridges were in stock. All the officers and nine non-commissioned officers carried swords.[19] That same year Captain J. C. Bates listed fifty Spencer carbines and 19,288 cartridges still at the post.[20] Although Fort Sisseton was an infantry post, horses were still maintained for the mounted infantry and Indian scouts. A shorter carbine was easier to handle on horseback than the long-barreled 1866 Springfield. An infantry officer usually rode horseback when on a patrol with his company; therefore, he also preferred the carbine.

The army in 1873 introduced three new regulation weapons: a single-shot, .45 caliber Springfield rifle; a single-shot, .45 caliber Springfield carbine; and a .45 caliber Colt revolver. The rifle weighed 8.4 pounds and was 51.9 inches long, whereas the carbine weighed only 6.87 pounds and was 41.3 inches long. A trained infantryman or cavalryman could load and fire the breech-loading rifle or carbine sixteen times per minute.[21]

A report by Major J. E. Yard in 1873 showed that the post needed new rifles and pistols. His inventory listed seventy-one of the old .50 caliber Springfields, fifty-one of which were unserviceable. At the time there were also twenty-five unserviceable .44 caliber Colt revolvers and fifty-nine unserviceable Spencer carbines on hand.[22]

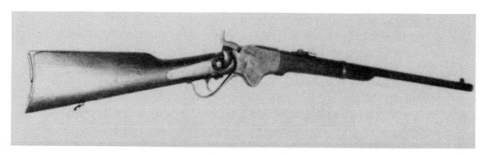

Spencer carbine owned by Captain David Schooley, who served at Fort Sisseton, 1884-1888.
Courtesy Edward J. Jarot

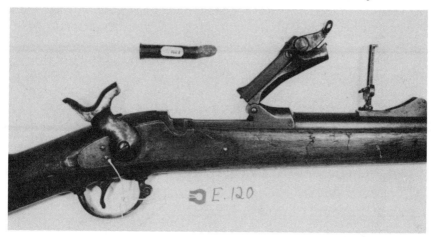

1873 breech-loading Springfield rifle.
Courtesy South Dakota State Historical Society

Springfield rifle bullets: left to right, .58 caliber, .50 caliber, and .45 caliber.

The new 1873 .45 caliber Springfield rifle and the Colt revolver were introduced to the post by the Seventeenth Infantry in about 1877. In time, all of the old .50 caliber Springfield rifles and Spencer carbines were returned to the United States Arsenal. Later the 1873 Springfield was improved with a better rear sight. Therefore, in 1879 Captain Clarence E. Bennett of the Seventeenth Infantry returned some of the old 1873 Springfields to the United States Arsenal in exchange for the newer models. By 1884, the remaining old 1873 Springfields were worn so badly, that Commanding Officer David Schooley asked that they too be replaced with the newest model of the 1873 Springfield.[23]

One of the post officers served as post ordnance officer. It was his job to see that all of the ammunition was properly stored in the magazine. He also completed inventory reports for the Department of Dakota. Training the men in the proper care and handling of their weapons was another of his duties. In 1883 Second Lieutenant Edward Chynowith was the post ordnance officer. Helping him were Sergeant George Bently and Private S. P. Lauffer.[24] Some of the army booklets on hand that were available for use by the ordnance officer were *Target Practice, McClellan's Bayonet Exercises, Casey's Rifle Tactics*, and *Laidley's Manual for Rifle Firing*. Also available were Post Ordnance Inventory forms.[25]

The 1873 Springfield and its later models continued in use at the post until it closed. May 1889 Post Returns state that because of the 1 June 1889 abandonment of the post, 34 rifles and 360 boxes of rifle ammunition were transferred to the Department of Dakota.

Target Shooting and Competition

Target practice spread rapidly in army posts after the introduction of the Model 1873 Springfield rifle. By 1875 the army held its first national rifle match in Creedmoor, Long Island, New York. Colonel *Laidley's Manual for Rifle Firing* gave shooting ability another boost in 1879. The manual explained how to clean and care for the rifle as well as how to disassemble and assemble it.[26]

Lieutenant General Philip H. Sheridan, commander of the military Division of Missouri in Chicago, asked Fort Sisseton's Major Clarence E. Bennett to send six crack shots to Fort Leavenworth by 1 August 1879. These men would compete with marksmen from other posts. The twelve best shooters from Leavenworth would then be sent to the rifle match at Creedmoor. Major Bennett was unable to provide the six men.[27]

It wasn't until 1880 that the post was ready for rifle competition. That year Major Bennett conducted ten days of rifle competition and sent in the names of the six best marksmen. He said, "The small scores for the 600-yard targets were due to the gusty wind."[28]

The men used their regulation Springfield rifles and cartridges for target practice at Fort Sisseton. There were two 600-yard rifle ranges. One was a half-mile north of the post and the other a half-mile south. Wooden frame targets six feet by six feet and six by twelve feet were used. A paper or canvas target was attached to the wooden frame. Apparently there was a large earth mound behind the targets because the men recovered the lead bullets and reloaded them in the spent metal cartridges.[29]

In 1881, Major Bennett reported a great increase in target practice at the post. Target practice was set from 9:30 to 11:00 a.m. on Tuesday and Wednesday. All soldiers were required to attend except cooks and the sick. After one practice, First Lieutenant George Ruhlen conducted a class on the general theory of projectile motion. The class also included information on the manufacture of gunpowder and metallic cartridges and on caring for the Springfield rifle.[30] At one post contest that summer, Sergeant George Bentley hit the 500-yard target, twenty-four out of twenty-five times.

In the same year, to create more interest Companies F and I of the Seventeenth Infantry challenged each other to a post rifle match. Each company picked seven of its best shots. During the contest each man fired seven times, firing seven shots each time at a 200-yard target. Company I beat Company F by a score of 169 to 166. No one could hit the target more than five times out of seven. Sergeant Jno. Massena had the best score: 3, 5, 3, 4, 5, 5, 4, a score of 29 of a total 49.[31]

In July of 1883, the post participated in three days of target shooting to decide the ten best marksmen. Targets were set at 200, 300, and 600 yards. Two lieutenants, two sergeants, one corporal, and five privates qualified as the ten-man team to attend the Department of Dakota rifle match at Fort Snelling, Minnesota. Shooters from twenty-two army posts attended. The best ten shots from that match were sent to the Military Division of Missouri contest in St. Louis. Ten men from the Military Division of Missouri were sent on to the army's national shooting match at Creedmoor.[32]

Qualifying for the team for the Department of Dakota match was only one part of target-practice competition. There were a number of individual honors as well. In 1883, for example, Major Bennett was pleased that all six post officers and eighty-seven of the enlisted men had qualified as marksmen. Bennett said, "Those not yet qualified will be kept shooting until the end of the target year."[33] Bennett also ordered a new set of reloading tools for each of the companies.

Each soldier was allowed a certain number of .45 caliber cartridges for target practice. Extra cartridges were created by reloading them. Unfortunately, Private James Conner, while reloading cartridges in the barracks, blew off a part of his left hand when a cartridge exploded. He was discharged from the army.[34] At all army rifle ranges in 1884, there were three deaths from shot wounds, and 47 soldiers were injured from exploding rifle cartridges.

When Commanding Officer David Schooley arrived at the post in 1884, he found two target ranges, each 600 yards long. One range had targets revolving on a horizontal axis. Schooley complained about poor barracks lighting for aiming during winter practice indoors. He was pleased, however, that the men had good reloading tools.[35]

Fort Sisseton's Sergeant G. Eppert received a Sharpshooter's Cross and a Silver Marksman's Pin in July 1885. In September, Second Lieutenant H. D. Reed and his team from the post's Twenty-fifth Infantry left Webster by train for Fort Snelling. They would be shooting for the Nevada Trophy, which was given for marksmen's skill in battlefield conditions. A Twenty-fifth Infantry team had won the Nevada Trophy in 1883 and 1884. The Post Returns did not show who won in 1885. However, Commanding Officer Major Frederick Mears was proud of the overall record of the two Twenty-fifth Infantry companies. Company E had twelve marksmen and twenty-seven first class shooters. Company G had one sharpshooter, fifteen marksmen, fourteen first class, three second class, and one third class shooters.[36]

Cannon

Major John Clowney and his military force had three cannon when he located Fort Wadsworth in August 1864. He placed the cannon in defensive positions at three corners of the fort site. One cannon was a brass six-pound smooth-bore field gun, Model 1841. Its barrel was sixty inches long with a bore of 3.67 inches.[37] It could hurl a six-pound ball about three-fourths of a mile.

The other two cannons were brass twelve-pound mountain how-itzers, Model 1841. Each of the muzzle-loading howitzers had a bar-rel 32.9 inches long with a smooth-bore of 4.62 inches.[38] It could throw a 8.9 pound projectile about a half mile. The limber, lightweight howitzer and the prairie carriage with thirty-eight-inch wheels were pulled by a team of horses. Supplies attached to the car-riage included two handspikes, two sponges and bucket, worm and rammer. The limber carried an ammunition chest, canvas water bucket, grease bucket, lanyard and friction primers. A trained gun crew could fire two rounds per minute with the mountain howitzer.

There is no evidence that Fort Sisseton was attacked or that can-non were used to defend it. The cannon, however, were a deterrent against an attack. Perhaps the Sioux leaders remembered the devas-tating effects of cannon fire when their attack on Fort Ridgely was repulsed in 1862. Indians of the Great Plains rarely attacked any of the army posts. Regardless, the cannons at the post were well main-tained and ready for action on short notice.

Fort Sisseton's mountain howitzers were often used on area patrols. When Major Clowney first arrived, he sent Captain Lewis S. Burton and 157 troops to explore the James River area. Burton and his command were armed with a mountain howitzer.[39]

A month later, in August 1864, Major Clowney sent Captain John T. Klatt and a detachment of fifty men and one mountain howitzer to the hay camp seventeen miles west of the post. Their mission was to protect a hay contractor and his party who were cutting hay for the post's 157 horses.[40] In early November, Major Rose was again warned of an impending attack on a few soldiers stationed at the hay camp. First Lieutenant Richard O. Hunt, twenty-five cavalrymen, and a mountain howitzer were rushed to the camp. Perhaps because of this show of force the attack never materialized.

Two more brass mountain howitzers were added to the post's inventory in 1865. Two years later a new sixteen-foot by twenty-two-foot field-stone and brick magazine replaced the log magazine. One feature of the new magazine was an arched brick ceiling. Suitable storage space for both rifle and cannon ammunition was provided in the magazine. Cannon were assigned to a section of the Third Minnesota Battery, commanded by First Lieutenant Horace H. Western and later by Captain John Jones.[41] In February 1866, the bat-tery returned to Minnesota, but the cannon apparently remained at the post because the cannon were a permanent fixture on the post inventory. When the two companies of the Twentieth Infantry replaced the three companies of the Tenth Infantry in 1869, the post cannon inventory of four mountain howitzers and one six-pound field piece remained the same.

Several kinds of cannon ammunition were provided by the army. A shot or ball was used against masses of troops. The shell was a hollow projectile filled with powder, which burst into four or five fragments when it exploded. It was used against buildings or troops hidden in woods. The spherical case or canister was a tin cylindrical can filled with small iron balls that showered on the enemy.

Storage and care of ammunition were the responsibility of the post ordnance officer. The magazine in 1871 was almost full of cannon ammunition: 423 strapped and fixed shells, 315 filled and fixed canisters for the mountain howitzers, and 219 strapped and fixed spherical case shot for the six-pound field gun.[42] It appears that none of the cannon ammunition was used during 1871-1873 because Major J. E. Yard's 1873 Annual Report lists the same amounts of cannon ammunition on hand.[43]

A number of blank cartridges for the mountain howitzers were also stored in the magazine. Blank cartridges were fired at retreat and for honoring visiting generals and national events. For example, thirty-seven blank cartridges were fired to celebrate the Fourth of July, one shot for each state. Commanding Officer Robert E. A. Crofton ordered 800 rounds of blank cartridges to replenish dwindling supplies in October 1873.[44]

The six-pound field gun was returned to the Rock Island Arsenal in 1877. Captain William Van Horn in an 1878 inventory listed the identifying marks on the remaining four mountain howitzers. All four of the howitzers were manufactured in 1863. Marked in the face of the muzzle of each cannon was Ario Co. ABr. Although two of the howitzers were received in 1864 and two in 1865, the numbers are similar: 218, 219, 224, and 227.[45]

Commanding Officer Captain Clarence E. Bennett in 1878 believed the howitzers were worn out. He advised the Chief of Ordnance in Washington, D. C.:

> After study I felt it was my duty to recommend the following ordnance be sent at once to Rock Island Arsenal: four 12-pound mountain howitzers and four prairie carriages, all unserviceable and 499 howitzer shells. The four cannon have their vents

enlarged and the carriages are rotting. This post is a guard to the Sisseton Indians and for the protection of the frontier. I will order two 3-inch rifled cannon and two Gatling guns. This post with the artillery I mention will have a strong influence in preserving the peace of this section.[46]

It wasn't until 21 June 1882, however, that one new three-inch rifled cannon and carriage and one new 1.5-inch caliber Hotchkiss revolving field gun and carriage arrived, half of Bennett's order. Three-inch rifled cannon had a longer range than the smooth-bore twelve-pound howitzer. That same day Captain Bennett ordered the four mountain howitzers and their prairie carriages dismantled and loaded onto wagons. The worn cannon and surplus ammunition filled ten wagons and were shipped to the Rock Island Arsenal.[47]

The Dakota National Guard in 1886 requested the use of the three-inch rifled cannon for their training encampment at Camp Hancock near Aberdeen, Dakota Territory. Major Frederick Mears informed them that the cannon was not available for such use. The Hotchkiss field gun was returned to the Department of Dakota in 1888 and was no longer listed in the post inventory.[48] In April 1889, two months before the post closed, Captain Joseph Hale arranged for the shipment of the three-inch rifled cannon, its ammunition and 911 blank cartridges to the Department of Dakota.[49]

In 1960, Robert J. Perry, president of the South Dakota Parks Association, and Jack Adams, publisher of the *Sisseton Courier*, obtained a surplus Model 1857 Napoleon cannon from the Pierre Independent School District. The *Pierre Capital Journal* in a 1911 issue reported that Congressman Charles H. Burke had obtained for Pierre four surplus Napoleon cannons from the War Department. One was placed in front of Central High School, two in front of the courthouse, and one in Riverside Cemetery. The Napoleon's tube was sixty-six inches long with a smooth bore of 4.62 inches and could throw a twelve-pound ball almost a mile. One of the Pierre school superintendents had the tube filled with cement to keep students from attempting to fire it. The cannon, without a carriage, was placed on a wooden stand in the center of Fort Sisseton's parade ground. It was dedicated by Governor Archie Gubbrud as a part of a 1961 celebration.

In 1990, members of the Volunteer South Dakota Telephone Pioneers of America, with the help of the students from the South

1857 Napoleon cannon, Fort Sisseton parade ground, 1965.

Inside Fort Sisseton magazine.

Dakota School for the Visually Handicapped of Aberdeen, raised money to have a carriage made for the cannon.[50] A part of the restoration process included the removal of the cement from the tube. Wendy Lewis, Naturalist at Fort Sisseton, said that removing the cement was a difficult job and took a long time.

The bronze cannon, Model 1857 Napoleon, and new carriage now stand guard in the center of Fort Sisseton's parade ground. The markings on the cannon show that it was made in 1862 by the Eagle Foundry, owned by Miles Greenwood in Cincinnati, Ohio. It was inspected by JRE (John Rufus Edie), Ordnance Officer, before it left the factory. The tube weighs 1,212 pounds and the serial number is 30.[51]

Cannon Salutes

The post's mountain howitzers were used for firing cannon salutes on the parade ground for the ceremonial functions of retreat, visiting generals, and national events. The magazine always contained a good supply of blank cartridges for such purposes. A trained gun crew fired the cannon.

During April 1865, First Lieutenant Horace H. Western and the Third Minnesota Battery mountain-howitzer gun crews fired 409 blank cartridges for salutes. On 17 April orders were received to fire 100 guns at noon in honor of the capture of Richmond. The term 100 guns meant that a cannon was fired 100 times. The smoke had barely cleared when the post was ordered to fire 200 guns on 19 April to celebrate General Robert E. Lee's surrender of the Confederate Army at Appomattox Court House, Virginia.[52] Following President Lincoln's assassination, the post was ordered to fire thirteen guns at daylight, one gun at intervals of every half hour throughout the day and thirty-six guns at sunset. During April the gun crew also fired a blank cartridge each night at retreat, totaling 409 salutes fired in April.

Army regulations required that a military post fire a thirty-seven gun salute on the Fourth of July, one shot for each state. In 1868, the celebration started with thirteen guns at daybreak, followed with a single shot every half hour throughout the day. All labor except the furnishing of water and ice was suspended for the day's festivities. At sunset a national salute of thirty-seven guns was fired.[53] Five days later a gun salute was fired upon notice of the death of former President James Buchanan.

National gun salutes at Fort Sisseton honoring deceased leaders included President Lincoln's Secretary of War Edwin M. Stanton in 1869 and former President Andrew Johnson in 1875. A salute was ordered on 5 October 1881 for President James A. Garfield following his assassination. Fort Sisseton General Orders for saluting President Garfield show that Second Lieutenant Edward I. Grumley and his gun crew were ordered to fire thirteen guns at dawn, one gun every half hour all day, and thirty-eight guns at sunset. During the day the post flag was flown at half mast and all labor had ceased.[54] After June 1882 a three-inch rifled cannon was used for saluting.[55]

On 8 August 1885 the post was again in mourning on the day of the funeral of Civil War General and former President Ulysses S. Grant. Britton's *Dakota Daylight* reported, "On the day of the funeral of General Grant, the troops will be paraded and the order read to them after which all labors of the day will cease."[56] On 30 April 1889, the post celebrated a day of national Thanksgiving, proclaimed by President Benjamin Harrison, by firing a national salute at noon.

Saluting Visiting Generals

Full military honors were given visiting generals when inspecting Fort Sisseton. When a general entered the parade ground, the colors were lowered as soldiers and officers saluted. The band played, followed by a gun salute. The number of guns per general, according to army regulations, were as follows: general in chief of the army seventeen, lieutenant general fifteen, major general thirteen, and brigadier general eleven.[57]

It was not unusual to arrange a little entertainment for a visiting general and his staff. Post Commander Robert H. Rose arranged a buffalo hunt in connection with Major General John M. Corse's visit in mid-October 1865. The hunting party consisted of about 100 officers, enlisted men, and Indian scouts. They traveled by horseback, ambulance, and wagons. Chief Scout Gabriel Renville led the group, which headed for "buffalo country about Buzzard's Roost (Hawk's Nest), a high peak on the western slope of Coteau des Prairie, about 40 miles nearly southwest from the fort and overlooking the James River flats. Near this point, about where the town of Groton is located, we struck an immense herd (a terror-inspiring one) from 25,000 to 30,000 strong."[58]

During the hunt one of the lieutenants on Corse's staff got so excited he dropped one of his revolvers and shot his horse in the back of the head with the other. Samuel J. Brown shot and injured a buffalo that turned on him and chased him back toward the hunting camp. Within 100 yards of the camp, Captain Arthur H. Mills shot the buffalo.[59]

The day after returning to the post, (21 October 1865), Major General John M. Corse was given a thirteen-gun salute before he made his inspection. At the time, the Third Minnesota Battery and three companies of the Second Minnesota Cavalry, totaling ten officers and 272 enlisted men were stationed at the post. Later, Major Rose ordered First Lieutenant Lyman B. Smith and fifteen men, fully armed, mounted, and equipped, to escort the general and his staff to Fort Ridgely.[60]

Major General Alfred H. Terry in April 1882 had ordered two companies of the Seventh Cavalry of Fort Meade to Fort Sisseton to help in handling some problems with the Indians. General Terry decided to make an inspection of the post and check the area's military situation. On 14 July Captain Bennett received word that Major General Terry would inspect the post on 17 July. Captain Bennett issued Post Order 124 listing the following events and duties: post escort to pick up the general at the Webster train station, cannon salute, and full dress parade and review. Private John Connolly of Company F, Seventeenth Infantry, would serve as an orderly for General Terry.[61]

Preparations for the inspection included practice firing of blank cartridges with the new three-inch rifled cannon that had arrived 21 June 1882. On the day of the parade, the six officers and ninety men of Companies F & I, Seventeenth Infantry, in full dress uniform were stationed on one side of the parade ground. The six officers and 109 men of Troop A and B, Seventh Cavalry, in campaign dress, were located on the other side. The command "attention" was given as Major General Terry entered the parade ground. The six-piece post band played two flourishes before the gun crew fired a thirteen-gun salute. On order the post band began playing as the units marched by the reviewing stand. General Terry then made his inspection. Commanding Officer Clarence E. Bennett later said, "General Terry had high praise for the soldiers and troops. At the parade they marched and drilled and went through the manual-of-arms splendidly."[62]

Endnotes

1. General Orders, 12 April 1882. RG 393. V. 15. vol. 1. National Archives, Washington, DC. (Hereafter cited as General Orders.)

2. *Regulations of the United States Army*, 1881. Par. 340:41,344. (Hereafter cited as *Regulations*.)

3. Andrew J. Fisk Diary, 14 January 1866. Roll 81. Minnesota Historical Society, St. Paul, Minnesota. (Hereafter cited as Fisk Diary.)

4. Fisk Diary, 18 January, 1866.

5. Special Orders, 27 April 1870. RG 393. V. 13. National Archives, Washington, D.C.

6. Edward P. Pearson to Malcolm McArthur, 29 February 1876. Letters Sent. RG 393. V. vol. 6. National Archives, Washington,D.C.

7. Robert E. A. Crofton to Malcolm McArthur, 18 February 1877. Letters Sent. RG 393. V. 7. Box 4. National Archives, Washington, D.C.

8. Circular No. 7, 1 March 1877. RG 393. V. 16. vol. 1:4. National Archives, Washington, D.C.

9. Circular No. 10, 9 April 1877. RG 393. V. 16. vol. 1:5. National Archives, Washington, D.C.

10. John H. Nankivell. *25th Infantry*. Reprint. Fort Collins, Colorado:Old Army Press, 1972.

11. George W. Prescott to Robert H. Rose, 1 November 1864. *South Dakota Historical Collections* 8:499. (Hereafter cited as *SDHC*.)

12. *American Military History*. Department of the Army, July 1959:288.

13. General Orders. RG 393. V. 15. vol. 1.

14. C. E. Bennett to Department of Dakota, 15 March 1882. Letters Sent. RG 393. V. 2. vol. 10. National Archives, Washington, D.C.

15. Adjutant General of Department of Dakota. RG 393. V. 7. Box 5. National Archives, Washington, D.C.

16. Post Returns of Fort Sisseton, 31 May 1887. National Archives, Washington, D.C. On microfilm roll 1179, South Dakota Archives, Pierre, South Dakota. (Hereafter cited as Post Returns.)

17. Javan B. Irvine, Letters to his wife, 15 June and 20 July 1867. South Dakota Archives, Pierre, South Dakota.

18. Jesse A. P. Hampson to Department of Dakota, 26 February 1868. Letters Sent. RG 393. V. 2. vol. 1. National Archives, Washington, D.C.

19. Ordnance. M 1281. Stock 32. Shelf 4. Roll 8. Room 400, National Archives, Washington, D.C.

20. Weapons Inventory, 8 November 1871. RG 393. V. 19. Box 8. National Archives,Washington, D.C.

21. Harold H. Schuler. *Fort Sully:Guns at Sunset*. Vermillion, South Dakota:University of South Dakota Press, 1992:119.

22. J. E. Yard's Annual Report, 31 August 1873. RG 393. V. 2. vol. 4. National Archives, Washington, D.C.

23. David Schooley to Department of Dakota, 5 November 1884. Letters Sent. RG 393. V. 7. Box 5. National Archives, Washington, D.C.

24. C. E. Bennett to Department of Dakota, 10 January 1883. Letters Sent. RG 393. 2. vol. 12:1-11. National Archives, Washington, D.C.

25. Book List, 14 June 1867. RG 393. V. 7. Box 1. National Archives, Washington, D.C.

26. George Ruhlen to Department of Dakota, 30 April 1881. Letters Sent. RG 393. V. 7. Box 4. National Archives, Washington, D.C.

27. Philip H. Sheridan to Post Commanders, 6 March 1879. RG 393. V. 7. Box 4. National Archives, Washington, D.C.

28. C.E. Bennett to Department of Dakota, 30 May 1880. Letters Sent. RG 393. V. 2. vol. 9. National Archives, Washington, D.C.

29. C.E. Bennett to Department of Dakota, 3 October 1882. Letters Sent. RG 393. V. 2. vol. 11. National Archives, Washington, D.C.

30. George Ruhlen to Department of Dakota, 30 April 1881. Letters Sent. RG 393. V. 7. Box 4. National Archives, Washington, D.C.

31. Letters Sent, 22 May 1881. RG 393. V. 2. vol. 9. National Archives, Washington, D.C.

32. C.E. Bennett to Department of Dakota, 19 July 1883. Letters Sent. RG 393. V. 2. vol. 12. National Archives, Washington, D.C.

33. C.E. Bennett to Department of Dakota, 15 September 1883. Letters Sent. RG 393. 2. vol. 12:131. National Archives, Washington, D.C.

34. C. E. Bennett to Department of Dakota, 15 September 1883. Letters Sent. RG 393. V. 2. vol. 12:131. National Archives, Washington, D.C.

35. David Schooley to Inspector of Rifle Practice, Department of Dakota, 18 October 1884. 9W2 37/27/A. National Archives, Washington, D. C.

36. Frederick Mears' Annual Report, 1 September 1885. RG 393. V. vol. 13. National Archives, Washington, D.C.

37. Post Returns, August 1864.

38. Post Returns, August 1864.

39. John Clowney to R. C. Olin. *SDHC* 8:407.

40. John Clowney to Assistant Adjutant General, District of Minnesota, 10 August 1864, *SDHC* 8:430.

41. Post Returns, June 1864.

42. Gun Inventory, 8 November 1871. RG 393. V. 19. Box 8. National Archives, Washington, D.C.

43. Annual Report, 31 August 1873. RG 393. V. 2. vol. 4. National Archives, Washington, D.C.

44. Robert E. A. Crofton to Department of Dakota, 21 October 1873. Letters Sent. RG 393. V. 2. vol. 4. National Archives, Washington, D.C.

45. William W. Van Horne to Department of Dakota, 5 April 1878. Letters Sent. RG 393. V. 2. vol. 6. National Archives, Washington, D.C.

46. C.E. Bennett to Chief of Ordnance, 12 November 1878. Letters Sent. RG 393. V. 2. vol. 7. National Archives, Washington, D.C.

47. C. E. Bennett to Department of Dakota, 21 June 1882. Letters Sent. RG 393. V. 2. vol. 11. National Archives, Washington, D.C.

48. Post Returns, May 1888.

49. Post Returns, April and May, 1889.

50. Robert J. Perry Papers, Aberdeen, South Dakota.

51. 1857 Napoleon cannon, Fort Sisseton parade ground.

52. Post Medical History. RG 94. vol. 1. National Archives, Washington, D.C.

53. General Orders, 3 July 1868. RG 393. V. 11. vol. 1.

54. General Orders, 5 October 1881. RG 393. V. 15. vol. 1.

55. C. E. Bennett to Department of Dakota, 21 June 1882. Letters Sent. RG 393. V. 2. vol. 11. National Archives, Washington, D.C.

56. *Dakota Daylight*, 24 July 1885.

57. *Regulations*, 1881:614.

58. Sisseton and Wahpeton Bands versus the United States. Washington: Court of Claims, page 72.

59. Samuel J. Brown, "Buffalo Republic", Senate Document 23, 56th Congress, Second Session. 5 December 1900.

60. Special Orders, 21 October 1865. RG 393. V. 13. National Archives, Washington, D.C.

61. Post Orders, 14 July 1882. RG 393. V. 15. vol. 1. National Archives, Washington, D.C.

62. C. E. Bennett to Department of Dakota, 16 October 1882. Letters Sent. RG 393. V. 2. vol. 11. National Archives, Washington, D.C.

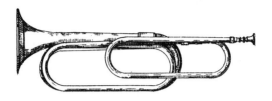

Chapter 8
Post Supplies

Food

The Army Ration

Food at Fort Sisseton was available from the following sources:

* Army ration—measured amounts of certain foods provided by the army. Army rations were prepared and served free in the company mess halls to the enlisted men.[1] Officers had to purchase army rations from the commissary;

* Non-ration food—food items other than those composing the army ration that the army provided to the post commissary. The commissary manager sold non-ration foods to company mess halls, enlisted men, officers, civilian employees, and Enlisted Indian Scouts;[2]

* Post Fund—profits from the sale of surplus bread, made with free flour provided by the army, and use fees from the post trader made up the post fund. The fund was used to buy extra army ration and non-ration food from the commissary for the company mess halls;[3]

* Post Garden—vegetables grown in the post garden were added to the food supply. Profits from the sale of extra vegetables were placed in the post fund;[4]

*Post Trader—enlisted men, officers, civilians, and scouts also purchased food items from the post trader.

The regulation army ration changed little between 1863 and 1889. An army ration was a soldier's one-day food supply of forty-six ounces. It consisted of one meat item daily: either twelve oz. pork, twelve oz. bacon, twenty oz. fresh beef, or twenty-two oz. salt beef. Also included was one of the following: eighteen oz. of soft bread (about one loaf), eighteen oz. flour, sixteen oz. of hard bread (hardtack), or twenty oz. of corn meal. Each day one of these food items was included: 2.4 oz. beans, 2.4 oz. peas, 1.6 oz. rice, or 1.6 oz. hominy. The ration also contained a portion of coffee, tea, vinegar, salt, and pepper. One portion of sugar, molasses, or syrup was also added.[5]

A day's army ration was not issued to each soldier individually but was a part of bulk supplies delivered to the post. The army ration was supplemented by other non-ration foods purchased from the post commissary with post funds. Vegetables grown in the post garden were also added.

Ordering and Administration

The commanding officer appointed a post officer to direct the commissary of subsistence. Helping the officer was a commissary sergeant who did the ordering, receiving, storing, selling, and accounting of all food items.

Once a year Fort Sisseton's commissary officer ordered an annual supply of the army ration and non-ration food from the Department of Dakota. A 1877 circular provided specific instructions for ordering food supplies. First, Fort Sisseton's commissary of subsistence sergeant inventoried and examined existing supplies. Then the sergeant completed the order and listed the amount on hand for each item ordered. The commissary officer reviewed the order before it was sent. One post commissary sergeant in 1878 listed this warning about the army ration food: "Do not send peas, rice or hominy as the troops will not eat these articles. Sufficient beans on hand to issue in lieu of. If you must send, send small quantities."[6].

There were special instructions to order non-ration food for sale to the enlisted men and officers. The commissary officer of the Department of Dakota recommended that the order state "what brand or kind of article is wanted, giving the kinds of soap, starch, soups, syrup, tobacco etc."[7] One Fort Sisseton commissary sergeant's 1881 order listed the following favorite brands: Aldens Dried Apples; Baker Chocolate; Dr. Prices Vanilla Extract, 2 oz. bottle; Fairbanks Lard, five pound cans; Colemans Mustard, 4 oz. can; Wilson Packing Beef Tongue, cans; Durham Tobacco; Winslows

Corn, canned; Imperial Soda Crackers; Eagle Brand Milk, canned; F. Schumachers Oatmeal; White Star Yeast; Colgates Cashmere Soap; Huckens Mock Turtle Soup; Golden Syrup, one gallon cans; and English Breakfast Tea.[8]

The annual food order was completed before February 1 each year and sent to the Department of Dakota. A lengthy process between the Department of Dakota and the army in Washington, D.C. was undertaken to fill the order. The process involved reviewing existing supplies, advertising for bids for new supplies, packing, and shipping. Food needed to be well packaged to survive shipping and post storage. Packaging included wooden cases and boxes, gunny sacks, cans, bottles, tins, and barrels.

Food articles were shipped by rail to the nearest railhead and then hauled to the post with team and wagon. Throughout the years the nearest railhead varied from seventy-two miles away at Herman, Minnesota, to twenty-two miles away at Webster, South Dakota. Food shipments from Herman were usually sent between late spring and autumn after the hot weather. Commanding Officer Robert E. Crofton, however, warned that shipments to the post must be shipped no later than 1 October because "9,313 pounds of potatoes last autumn froze on the way here." He also complained, "The pork received is put up in unsound barrels, they not having iron chine hoops as required by army regulations."[9] If bacon wasn't properly wrapped it got soft from the jolting wagon and the heat. The post preferred bacon and ham to be sewn in cotton sacks and packed in wooden boxes, 100 pounds per box. Most of the ham and bacon was provided by Chicago meat packers.[10]

Originally the commissary sergeant and family were provided quarters in one of the log huts. Benjamin Fillbrook lived in one of them, 1873-1880. In 1882, a cut field-stone house was completed for the commissary sergeant and his family. The eighteen-foot by thirty-five-foot building contained two rooms and a kitchen and porch. Commissary sergeants living in the new quarters were Edwin F. Ambrose, 1882-1884; David B. Jeffers, 1884-1885; David F. Driscoll, his wife and two children, ages one and three, 1885-1888.

Managing the post commissary required the full time work of the commissary sergeant and one or two soldiers. When Sergeant Edwin F. Ambrose headed the commissary, Private Thomas P. Drew helped handle and weigh stores. Not only was there the work of receiving, storing, issuing, selling, and accounting of food, but there was administrative work as well. A review of the hand-written Fort Sisseton commissary records for 1880 shows that eighteen different forms were used for reporting to the Commissary of Subsistence, Department of Dakota. Some of the forms were Invoice Stores Received, Return of Provisions, Beef Cattle Slaughtered, Receipts of Subsistence Stores, Beef Cattle on Forage, Abstract of Food Sales to Auction, and Issue of Tobacco to Post Trader.[11]

Non-ration foods were sold to soldiers, Enlisted Indian Scouts, civilian employees, officers, company messes, and the hospital. A book was maintained noting the sales. Each month a separate form was completed showing the amount of sales to each of those categories. The sergeant placed the money from such sales in an office safe. At the end of the month, the reports and monies were sent to the Commissary of Subsistence Officer, Fort Snelling.

Food Storage Facilities

Major Clowney had 200 wagonloads of supplies with him when he located Fort Wadsworth on 1 August 1864. His food supply included an adequate supply of army rations: salt pork, salt beef, hardtack, beans, flour, sugar, coffee, and some vegetables. Two-and-a-half months later, on 15 October, Brackett's train of 200 wagons arrived carrying enough supplies and food for 800 men for one year. At first, food supplies were stored in tents or stacked in the open.

Much of the food supply, however, was transferred to a new commissary and quartermaster building completed in late October. The building of eight-inch-square sawed oak, was 145 feet long and twenty-four feet wide with a shingle roof. There was a cellar under a third of the building. It was described as a fair building, "but strong winds drive snow through the sides and roof, doing great damage to stores."[12]

Because of limited storage space, Major Robert E. Rose in 1865 recommended to General Sibley that a larger brick or stone warehouse be built for the year's food supply. Rose said, "we are now obliged to pile up out of doors our pork and part of our flour."[13] His request was denied.

Enormous supplies of food were stored in the sawed-oak commissary. Some of it ended in poor condition. In the winter of 1865-1866, for example, 218 barrels of flour turned sour and caked. Six hundred pounds of green coffee also spoiled. In 1867 Commanding Officer S. B. Hayman reported that stores were in good condition except that the following items were in only fair condition: 141 barrels salt pork, 218 barrels flour, and thirty barrels salt beef. Hayman issued it to the Sisseton and Wahpeton Indians before spoilage.[14]

In 1869, Fort Sisseton was changed from a four-company post of 200 men to a two-company post of 100 men. The south field-stone barracks was no longer needed for quarters; therefore it was converted into a commissary and a quartermaster storehouse. To discourage theft, wooden doors were changed to iron. Bars were installed over the windows. Barrels of water were placed inside and outside the building for fire protection. As a further protection against fire or theft, an armed guard was stationed nightly at Guard Post No. 1, which was located near the warehouse.

There was usually an ample food supply on hand. For example, in July 1888 there were 20,000 rations on hand, a 200-day food supply for the 106 soldiers.[15] The south stone barracks, old sawed-oak commissary, and root cellars provided adequate storage space.

Commissary Store and Sales

The south half of the converted barracks was used for the commissary. The ninety-one-foot-long by forty-five-foot-wide food storage space totaled 4,095 square feet. Inside, a small office was built for the commissary sergeant. Next to it was an issuing room where a twenty-eight-foot-long, four-foot-wide and three-foot-high counter was built. The counter contained drawers for storage of sugar, coffee, and other items.

Most of the food containers were stored in orderly rows with aisles between. This arrangement made it easy to locate and inventory food items. Shelving was built where needed. An ice box, large enough to hold a ton of ice, was located in the meat room. It was used to store a seven-day supply of fresh beef plus bacon slabs hung on racks. In hot weather, a ton of ice lasted one day only. Each morning it took an hour to haul out the melted water.[16] Presumably some barrels of salt pork, flour, corn meal, and sugar were stored in the 1864 sawed-oak commissary.

The commissary was like a grocery store. Its hours of operation were set by the commanding officer. In 1877 Post Commander Major Robert E. A. Crofton set the business hours between 8:00 a.m. and noon daily except Sunday, when it was closed. It was also closed the last two working days of the month for inventory. During the temporary absence of Commissary Sergeant Ambrose in 1881, the business hours were changed to one hour in the morning and one in the afternoon.

A typical day at the commissary included issuing army ration supplies, at no cost, to company cooks. Company cooks would also buy non-ration foods with company post funds to enhance the menu. Soldiers also stopped by from time to time to purchase items. Food items were priced at the army's cost plus ten percent for transportation.

Post officers were frequent customers at the commissary, where they purchased their food. They dined with their families, or if single, at the officers' mess. Officers were eligible to buy both army-ration and non-ration food. Some July 1869 purchases by Post Surgeon B. Knickerbocker included eleven pounds flour, two pounds pickled mackerel, five pounds lard, one can peas, one pound corn starch, one pound candles, one pound clams, two pounds crackers, one pound butter, one can tomatoes, and one pound Java coffee.

A typical customer was married officer Captain John S. McNaught. Some of his March 1871 food purchases and prices paid were one case tomatoes $.75; twenty pounds corn meal $.40; one can preserves $.59; ten pounds white sugar $1.45; five pounds Java coffee, $.29 a pound; four pounds soap $.34; nineteen pounds fresh beef, $.14 a pound; three pounds prunes $.51; three pound box of crackers $.21; three pounds butter $1.08, $.36 a pound; one pound candles $.19; 1/4 pound pepper $.13; and two cans pineapple, $.28 a can. His total food purchases for the month were $25.95.[17]

Married officers in 1871 each spent an average of $292 per year at the commissary for food. In 1879, most officers paid their bill once a month, using a check on either the First National Bank or the Second National Bank of St. Paul.

Sales were also made to enlisted men. During the first seven months of 1874, 109 enlisted men spent an average of $2.30 a month each for food at the commissary. Sales to Dr. C. E. Munn for the hospital mess for the first five months of 1871 totaled $164. The commissary in 1884 sold a monthly average of 477 pounds of fresh beef at ten cents a pound.

Keeping records and handling money were the responsibility of the commissary sergeant. His safe in the commissary office on 7 November 1882 contained $807 in the following denominations: $163 currency, $283 checks, $340 gold, and $21 silver.

OFFICE A. C. S.

FORT SISSETON, D. T.   *March 31st*   1886

The

Chief C. S., Dept of Dakota,
Fort Snelling, Minn.

Sir:

I have the honor to transmit herewith for payment, certified voucher, in favor
of Schaeble and Palmer, for 44.44, which has
not been paid by me for want of funds.

Very respectfully,

Your obdt servant,

J. O. Green

2nd Lieut. 25th Infty,

/ enclosures /   O. C. S.

Letterhead from Acting Commissary of Subsistence, Second Lieutenant James O. Green, Fort Sisseton, 1886.

Courtesy National Archives

Monitoring the condition of food supplies was one of the principal duties of the commissary sergeant. The commissary was inspected weekly by the post surgeon, monthly by the commanding officer, and yearly by the Department of Dakota. Some food stocks were damaged or spoiled in storage. An 1873 inspection report listed many unfit stores: fifty-one pounds of flour, musty; 1,632 pounds of peas, wormy; two cartons soda crackers, mice; eighteen pounds of ham, wormy; forty-nine pounds smoked herring, wormy; 801 cans peas, old age; ninety-six cans cranberry sauce, frozen; fifty cans lima beans, old; eighty-five pounds Java coffee, musty; two cans peaches, damaged; and 198 pounds sugar, damaged.[18]

Some items were not used or sold but carried on the inventory. An 1875 inventory listed 275 gallons of molasses on hand that had been received in 1869. Also on hand were eighty-eight cans pear preserves and 295 cans of pineapple preserves received in 1870. In 1877, 2,104 pounds of bacon were found wormy. The commissary sergeant in 1879 listed sixteen cartons Edam cheese, 120 cans oysters, 168 cans assorted soup, twenty-four bottles of raspberry syrup, eighty-four cans beef tongue, and sixteen pounds cream of tartar as surplus. Commissary Officer Lieutenant Edward I. Grumley in 1880 found it was necessary to issue 1,017 pounds of hardtack in tin boxes which had been received two years earlier. He noted in his report the hardtack was "in an excellent state of preservation and gave satisfaction to the command. It lasts longer in tin boxes than wooden cases."[19]

Spoiled food was generally destroyed. However, fit surplus foods were sold at public auction. One such auction was held in 1885, after public notice was given by posters in all of the adjacent towns, Webster, Britton, Aberdeen and Browns Valley. Sometimes advertisements were placed in area daily newspapers. However the food was disposed, proper notation was always made to the Commissary of Subsistence, Department of Dakota.

The post commissary was strong competition for the post trader. The commissary sold its food items at cost plus ten percent for transportation. A post trader therefore stocked some food items not listed in the commissary. A trader's principal business was beer, whiskey, and tobacco.

Beef-on-the-Hoof and Beef-on-the-Block

Beef was the principle meat item in the army ration. It was served as the main part of a meal four or five times a week. Salt pork, delivered in barrels or boxes, was served other times. Canned cod or mackerel was served each Friday. Beef-on-the-hoof was delivered to the post by beef contractors. The cattle were placed in a corral and butchered as needed. Sometimes beef-on-the-block (butchered) was made available to the post.

Post Trader T. W. Baldwin maintained a beef herd of about sixty head. He was the successful bidder in 1873 and provided beef-on-the-block at $.14 a pound. Fort Sisseton's Commanding Officer Captain John S. McNaught questioned the quality of Baldwin's beef: "The beef was very thin. There was not sufficient quantity of fat on the issue of beef to cook it—from two to three pounds of grease being used in each company to cook it for dinner. I learned that the last issue consisted of one steer and one heifer, the heifer very heavy with calf when she was killed. Your cattle are running around in the post eating government hay. You must herd them."[20] McNaught in August ordered Baldwin to keep his cattle out of the government hay yard.

In 1877, the Department of Dakota decided to supply beef-on-the-block. Post Commander Robert E. A. Crofton was ordered to reduce the size of his beef herd. Crofton objected to the new policy because the nearest place of purchase was Breckinridge, Minnesota, sixty-five miles away. Crofton maintained that Fort Sisseton had good cattle stables and plenty of grass and hay to maintain its government beef herd. Major Crofton said that between 1 June 1876 and 31 May 1877 the post butchered fifty-two head, producing 25,012 pounds of beef. Including the cost of the herders and hay, it cost only $.11 a pound.[21]

To further its beef-on-the-block policy, the Department's commissary officer instructed Crofton to experiment with freezing butchered beef in the snow for later use. Major Crofton later reported: "As per your instructions an experiment in freezing beef was made by killing two steers, freezing and packing the meat in snow. The meat was kept below freezing. The meat, when used, had lost its flavor and could not be recognized as the same beef that had been frozen two months before."[22] For the time being, beef-on-the-block delivery was stopped.

In 1878, Commanding Officer Clarence E. Bennett began a new program to improve the quality of the post's government beef herd. The herd consisted of fifty or sixty beeves delivered to the post each year by a contractor. Bennett's program consisted of better care, feeding, watering, and sheltering the beef cattle. Specifically he wanted the cattle watered in the morning and evening at a nearby lake. The covered stable had hay racks and feed troughs. The stable was kept clean, and salt was provided once a week. During nice weather, the cattle would be grazed from sunrise to sunset and then returned to the corral and counted. In good weather, with no grazing available, the cattle were turned loose in the yard and fed. During bad weather the cattle would be tied in the stable, fed twice a day, and watered. Corn-fed beef were kept tied in the stable.[23]

A slaughterhouse was completed in 1879. Five beef were butchered each month. The butcher, with help, killed a beef and brought it to the commissary, where it was weighed and hung in the meat room. It was cut up the next morning. Between 1 May 1879 and 1 May 1880, the commissary issued 22,949 pounds of fresh beef to the mess halls. The commissary also sold 6,284 pounds of fresh beef at $.10 a pound to other buyers. On 15 July 1880 a St. Paul beef contractor delivered sixty head of beef to the post corral. His bid was $.08 a pound. In 1883 fresh beef was issued to the company messes four days out of seven.

In 1883, Sergeant Rudolph Gaief was in charge of the beef herd. Three herders and a butcher helped him. A herder's log barracks was located about three-fourths of a mile from the post near the stable and corral. The wood-frame stable was eighty-two feet long and thirty-one feet wide. A slaughterhouse was located beyond the stable. Herders guarded the cattle and fed and watered them. They also cleaned the stable and hauled hay from the stacks. Sometimes hay was cut and stacked by a contractor and other times by soldier help. The post maintained a horse-powered corn mill operated by Private Charles Smurr. Sacks of corn were delivered to the post and ground into corn meal and fed to the cattle.

Palmer and Baker's meat market of Webster was the successful bidder for providing beef-on-the-block in 1887. Their bid was $.095 a pound delivered. It was only a twenty-two-mile wagon trip to the post that took less than a day with team and wagon.

Post Fund

The army provided several financing methods to help support a post fund. The fund was used to enhance the life of enlisted men. One method required the post trader to pay $.10 per month to the post fund for each enlisted man on duty. This payment was for the exclusive right-to-do-business at the post. The trader's payment to the post fund totaled about $10 a month at Fort Sisseton. In addition, profits from the sale of surplus garden products were placed in the post fund.

Another financing method was for the quartermaster to provide extra flour to the bakery, flour that exceeded the eighteen ounces per day allowed each soldier. The flour was used to bake extra bread that was sold to the enlisted men for $.10 a loaf. Profit, less baking expenses, from the sale of this extra bread also went into the post fund. Baking expenses included hops, malt, salt, potatoes, lard, and $.35 a day for the baker. Bread-sale profits in October, November, and December 1873 totaled $67.26.

An officer was designated as treasurer of the post fund. This officer and a committee of enlisted men purchased items to benefit the soldiers. Items purchased included food, band instruments, recreational equipment, books, and newspapers for the post library. One purchase in 1873 was a marine clock for the guardhouse. In 1880, apples were purchased for the company messes, especially after the army agreed to pay the transportation.[24]

Some post-fund profits were distributed to the company fund of each company. In 1873, Company B, Twentieth United States Infantry, had $120 in its post fund, and Company F had $76. The companies often used the fund to buy non-ration food from the commissary to increase the variety of food served at the company messes.

First Lieutenant George Ruhlen was treasurer of the post fund in 1879 and accidentally misplaced the combination to the safe. He had to write to the manufacturer to obtain the correct combination in order to open the safe, which contained $347 of public and post funds.

Post Garden

Each army post was required to grow a vegetable garden if suitable land was available. Seed potatoes, garden seeds, and tools were provided at cost by the army's subsistence department. The post fund was used to buy these items. Vegetables not needed for the garrison were sold and the profits placed in the post fund.

In 1872, Company B, Twentieth Infantry, was sent north to guard and protect the Northern Pacific Railroad employees who were building a bridge across the James River. Company B left two men at the post to cultivate the company's garden. At the time there were three gardens within a half mile of the post.

At first, the post had two root cellars. One was sixty-one feet long, twelve feet wide and eight feet high. The other smaller one was twenty-two feet long, sixteen feet wide and eight feet high. The partially exposed cellars had basement windows with iron grating used for ventilation. In summer, pork, cheese, pickles, canned goods, and vegetables were stored in the cellar. In the winter, stoves were used in the cellar to keep food from freezing.[25] The root houses in December 1879 were open between 12:30 p.m. and 1:00 p.m. for the issue of vegetables. At the time, Second Lieutenant Robert W. Dowdy was the officer responsible for the condition and operation of the root houses.[26]

In 1880, the post garden consisted of twenty acres. Many vegetables were included in the 1881 seed order: beans, beets, cabbage, parsnip, parsley, peas, peppers, radishes, squash, turnips, tomatoes, dill, sage, clover, carrots, watermelon, cucumbers, lettuce, onions, and mustard. It also included a large supply of wild rice seed that was planted around the nearby lakes.[27]

The production of vegetables in the post garden was very bountiful. Post commissary officer Second Lieutenant Edward I. Grumley in 1882 said, "The commissary has not purchased any vegetables since 1874. The company gardens have since that time abundantly supplied the garrison with all classes of garden vegetables."[28]

The soldiers built a new root house in 1882. Captain Clarence E. Bennett proudly reported,

> Root house for two companies built; finished in December 1882 in winter weather, ground freezing rapidly and driving snow storms. Two cellars 44 feet long by 22 feet wide. Roof rests on heavy oak posts and wall planked over and covered with clay. [Stove] chimney in center between the two cellars so stores can be put in each cellar if necessary. At the west end a cellar is dug, 14 x 22 feet for use of officers. These are very fine cellars, well made, in fact, the best root and vegetable cellars for use of troops I have ever seen in the Army. They will hold all the vegetables the companies can raise.[29]

In January 1883 Bennett reported that all the vegetables were transferred to the new root house and securely locked.[30] Some of the produce harvested in 1883 included 1,100 bushels of potatoes and 146 bushels of onions.[31]

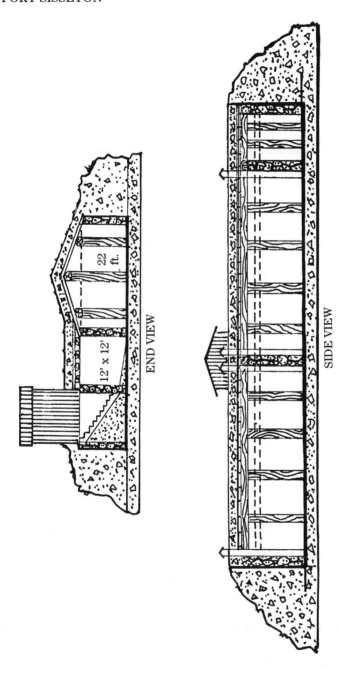

END VIEW

22 ft.

12' x 12'

SIDE VIEW

Drawing by Bob Child

Root cellar, side and ground view, 1882.

The Menus and the Mess

Army field rations were served to enlisted men during the first few months of post construction. These rations included salt pork, salt beef, flour, hardtack, beans, some vegetables, coffee, and sugar. Four hundred wagon-loads of food and supplies were delivered to the post between August and October 1864. Food supplies, however, did not include beef-on-the-hoof.

Despite large supplies of food on hand that first winter, there was a shortage of vegetables, which caused an outbreak of scurvy. Cemetery records show that Private Peter Gulbranson, Company B, Second Minnesota Cavalry, died of scurvy on 3 December 1864. A month later Post Surgeon Charles J. Farley advised the Department of the Northwest that the post needed larger quantities of potatoes, onions, and pickles, or else two-thirds of the men would have scurvy by spring. A detachment of men went to Fort Abercrombie for vegetables but obtained only a barrel each of potatoes and onions. However, extra vegetables were received from Fort Snelling in time to curb the outbreak. Because of a shortage of vegetables in 1867, there was another outbreak of scurvy. Sauerkraut, pickles, and vegetables arrived before the illness became serious.

It is not known what mess facilities were available before 9 December 1865 when the men moved into the new stone barracks. Presumably each company used one of its tents or log huts for a mess facility. Sergeant Andrew Fisk noted in his diary on Thanksgiving Day 1865 that there was "nothing extra on our tables." Fisk's reference to tables suggests that one of the log huts may have been used for mess purposes.[32]

After Fisk's company moved into the new stone barracks, he said that the 1866 New Year's menu included "Baked Beans for breakfast, soup for dinner, molasses and bread for supper. A good many of the boys and myself took a few glasses for my health. Cold." A few days later Fisk wrote "the boys had a high old time last night. Peach brandy, cherry brandy and canned peaches and tomatoes in great abundance. Had canned peaches and tomatoes at supper." On 10 January Fisk went fishing with "some of the boys. I caught a good little perch. They were first-rate eating." Later in the month of January Fisk visited the wood chopper's camp two miles from the fort. "They made me spend the night with them. Splendid grub. Flap jacks, fried potatoes and onions, coffee and sugar." On 7 February, he said, "The boys made a raise [baked dish] of pork and flour tonight."[33]

About that same time a thirty-foot by nineteen-foot log bakery, equipped with two ovens, was finished. The baker could bake 470 loaves of bread a day, despite poor lighting and ventilation. New quarters and freshly baked bread helped boost the morale of the men immensely.

Each of the two cut field-stone barracks was large enough to house two companies of about forty men each. Each half of a barracks contained an orderly room, wash room, sleeping room, mess hall, and kitchen. One inspector visiting the post said the barracks' kitchen was twenty-three feet wide and nineteen feet long. He did not indicate the size of the mess hall, but drawings show it was larger. Army regulations required that a company kitchen contain a wood-burning cooking range, bake pans, round boilers, four dish pans, four butcher knives, one scale, two meat choppers, two meat saws, six meat forks, four frying pans, six can openers, coffee boiler, and other typical kitchen items used in food preparation. The mess hall required enough dishes and utensils for forty-eight place settings.

Post Surgeon Charles E. McChesny in 1873 said that he and the officer of the day made daily inspections of the kitchens and messes and found, "There has been little variety in the diet of the troops."[34] Dr. McChesny in an 1875 inspection report said, "Cooking has been well performed with the exception of the bread which part of the time has been sour and heavy—evidently imperfectly breaded [kneaded]."[35] His report prompted the commanding officer to order the adjutant to find out why the bread was sour. A new wooden bake house with a hip roof was built in 1877 at a cost of $362. The twenty-foot-wide by twenty-eight-foot-long bakery contained two large ovens, store room, kneading table, and water sink. A later inspection prompted Commanding Officer Clarence E. Bennett, a West Pointer, to write, "Sergeant Joseph Snyder of Company F, Seventeenth Infantry, is one of the best post bakers in the service. When the Department Inspector inspected the post bakery, he said the bread he then saw was as fine as any he had ever seen in a post bakery."[36]

At first, the cook's job was rotated among the men of the company. This was supposed to help teach men to cook their food when in the field. It also produced some poorly cooked food. Later two cooks and an orderly were designated from each company. Companies F and I, Seventeenth Infantry, each had two privates as cooks in 1881. Other kitchen help was obtained from the companies on a rotation basis. A non-commissioned officer, usually a corporal, was placed in charge of the company kitchen.

The corporal and the two cooks decided the menu according to the requirements of the army ration. To enhance the menu, they often included non-ration food. The corporal or a cook walked next door to the commissary to pick up the army-ration food. At the same time, he purchased the non-ration food with money from the company's post fund. Some of the basic food items were stored in the kitchen, but most of the food was stored and issued at the commissary.

An 1881 regulation listed menus for one week based on the army ration. A typical regulation breakfast menu for one week included a third of a loaf of bread, coffee, and sugar each morning. Pancakes were served four times a week and beef and potatoes (beef hash) three times a week. Rice and hominy were served twice a week on different days.

The main meal was served at noon, according to the 1881 regulation. Beef was served as the main dish five days. Pork was served one day and cod or mackerel on Friday. Baked beans were served on Wednesday. Bread and potatoes were served each day. A serving of either onions, turnips, beets, carrots, or cabbage was served separately or mixed with a main dish each day. A little vinegar was used each day in main dishes. No coffee or tea was served at noon.

A very light meal was served at supper. It consisted of tea, sugar, milk, and a third of a loaf of bread. During the week, dried fruit was served three nights and cheese three nights with a serving of beef on Saturday. Smoked herring was served on Friday.[37]

Post Commander Clarence E. Bennett in 1882 ordered three shotguns for each of the two companies, "to encourage the men in hunting and use of fire arms and to benefit the company messes by the game thus procured."[38] Post Surgeon James B. Ferguson that same year said, "The enlisted men have no cause to complain of their rations as they are ample in quantity and nutritious. Fresh vegetables in abundance—potatoes, cabbage, beets, carrots and onions."[39]

Except for a shortage of vegetables during that first winter that led to a scurvy outbreak, there was always plenty of food at Fort Sisseton. If a soldier didn't like a meal, he perhaps complained and then walked to the commissary or post trader to buy something to his liking, if he had the money. Fresh turkey must not have been on hand in the post commissary in 1886 because Commanding Officer

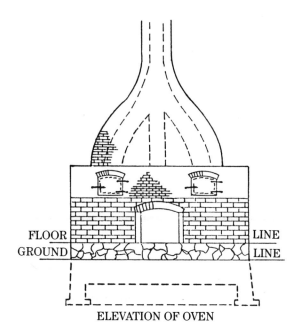

ELEVATION OF OVEN

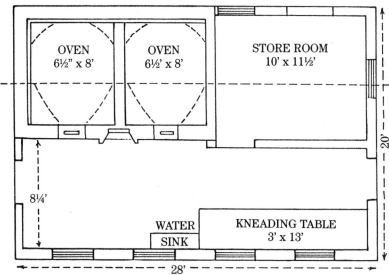

Original plan for new bakery, 1877.

Drawing by Bob Child

Major Frederick Mears ordered a twelve-pound Thanksgiving turkey from a Webster meat market.

Supplies

Post Quartermaster

A first lieutenant served as post quartermaster. Helping him was a quartermaster sergeant. The post quartermaster was responsible for all livestock, supplies, and equipment other than food: such things as furniture, tools, wagons, clothing, kitchen utensils, wood, coal, hay, and grain. He also arranged for the transportation of supplies, food, and troops.

The quartermaster officer and the sergeant were responsible for ordering, storing, and issuing supplies. They had a small office in the storage building. There were forty-four separate forms used for requisitioning supplies. Annual inventories were sent to the Department of Dakota. George Eppert was the last quartermaster sergeant, serving at the post from 1885 to 1889.

Quartermaster supplies and food supplies were stored in the same sawed-oak warehouse until 1869, when the south field-stone barracks was converted to storage. Food supplies were stored in the south half of the barracks and quartermaster supplies in the north half.

A large supply of clothing was kept on hand. A free clothing allowance was available to each enlisted man. Some clothing was also available for officers to purchase. Fort Sisseton's Commanding Officer Edward P. Pearson in 1875 questioned the army's selection of winter clothing. Winter duty outside included watering and feeding livestock, putting up ice, cutting and hauling extra wood, and guarding the post. Pearson recommended that the soles of buffalo shoes be lined with buffalo skin the same as the uppers. He believed buckskin mittens would be better than two pairs of wool mittens. He wanted buffalo coats issued to the post and furnished to the men each winter. Winter headgear didn't properly cover the ears.[40] By 1881, buffalo coats were issued to the post rather than to the soldiers. Each spring the buffalo overcoats, fur caps, and gauntlets were returned to the quartermaster sergeant for storage until the next winter.[41]

Managing existing supplies was a constant problem at the post; often there was a surplus of certain items in the inventory. There were so many surplus army blankets on hand in 1870 that they were used to cover unplastered walls in the bakery and other buildings. A few years later, First Lieutenant George H. Roach asked the Department of Dakota how to dispose of excess infantry clothing stored in the warehouse: twenty-five uniform coats and caps, 160 lined blouses, 300 flannel shirts, 126 pairs of shoes, and ten pairs of boots. At the time, there were about 104 enlisted men at the post.

Surplus supplies continued to be a problem in 1884. The Inspector General of the Department of Dakota filed this report: "There are a good many surplus stores at the post. The following articles are undoubtedly in excess of the requirements of the garrison: twenty canvas lined great coats; 131 campaign hats; sixty mosquito bars; forty buffalo overcoats; 100 bedsacks; six dozen No. 9 white Berlin gloves; seventeen pair buffalo overshoes; 175 pair of different sized trousers; forty pair shoes; thirty uniform coats; seven company clothing books; five company morning report books; 120 axes; one set of small ambulance wheels, which are too small for hilly country but might be serviceable about Fort Snelling; one box ambulance harness for four mules; and two letter presses."[42] Some surplus supplies were returned to Fort Snelling, and some were sold at public auction.

The post quartermaster officer was also in charge of the blacksmith, carpenter, and wheelwright. A brick blacksmith-and-carpenter shop with a covered space between was built in 1880, replacing old log structures. There was also a shop used by the wheelwright to repair wagon wheels.

Board of Survey

The commanding officer had the authority to appoint three officers as a board of survey. Board duties included investigating and fixing responsibility for damage or loss of food or supplies. Whenever a contractor delivered any shipment of food, beef on the hoof, hay, or other supplies, the board met to find out the quantity and quality of the items received. Some items had to be weighed, such as hay and coal, before acceptance.

In July 1868, the board met to pass on the condition of 800 sacks of flour and nineteen sacks of potatoes received. One meeting of the board was held in 1869 to decide if the following canned food items should be condemned: four cases peas, thirteen cases of oysters, four cases currant jelly, four boxes of chocolate, and ten boxes of

OFFICE

POST QUARTERMASTER

FORT SISSETON, D. T., *May 24* 188*6*

To the

 Post Adjutant

  Fort Sisseton. D. T.

Sir:

  In compliance with A. R. # 1832. I have the honor to forward herewith the following report

No. 1. Building occupied by the Commanding Officer is in fair condition it needs ceiling for Porch and painting. This building has a small room on the south side, a wing is necessary on the north side 20 feet long by u feet wide to complete the building, also a new kitchen and servants room 28'X16' under one roof. 16'X16' for kitchen 12'X16' for servants room, also a coal shed to be built, there being none.

No. 2. Building known as the Comdg. Officers Quarters at present, occupied by 2 Officers is in fair repair, the hall and stairs needs rebuilding 2 kitchens are needed, also one servants room. The Material to construct new stairs, 2 kitchens & servants room, are asked for on annual Estimate of 1886. The Porch needs ceiling, flooring & columns, and the house needs painting.

Fort Sisseton original letterhead, post quartermaster, 1886.

Courtesy of National Archives

pineapple.[43] The board met five times in July 1879. Other board actions in later years included:

* Investigated the death of a mule
* Figured out the value of property taken by a deserter
* Examined subsistence stores not fit for sale
* Ascertained why the inventory was short a half-barrel of sugar
* Decided what to do with 364 pounds of Java coffee that was musty and wormy.

Fuel

Wood was the primary fuel burned in stoves and fireplaces. Troops or wood contractors cut trees on the military reservation and in nearby areas. Wood was purchased by the cord, a pile of wood four feet wide, eight feet long and four feet high. A horse-powered wood-sawing machine was used at the post to cut cordwood into firewood. Sergeant James Frick was in charge of the wood-sawing machine in 1872. He caught his forearm in the driving wheel once, breaking his third finger.

Post Trader T. W. Baldwin was the successful bidder for providing wood in 1873. He apparently had cut his wood too near the boundary of the Lake Traverse Reservation and was ordered by the post commander "not to remove your wood which you have cut near the Indian Reservation, near the Ransom trail, until it is definitely settled whether you have been cutting on the reservation or not."[44] Apparently the matter was resolved because Baldwin later delivered 1,128 cords of oak wood at $10.50 a cord.

In advertising for bids for the 1874 wood supply, Commanding Officer Crofton reminded the bidders that wood would have to be cut near the James or Elm River, forty miles away. The supply of trees on the military reservation was dwindling. The bid that year was $19.50 a cord for 1,128 cords. Cutting and hauling wood forty miles had increased the contractor's cost. Post Commander Clarence E. Bennett in 1881 said, "During the past 16 years (1864-1881) the post used up the best timber of all kinds on the military reservation for fuel."[45]

When the railroad arrived at Webster, the post began using hard coal for fuel. Preparations for the use of Scranton anthracite hard coal were made during the spring and summer of 1883. A 188-foot-long by fifteen-foot-wide coal shed was built. It had a number of windows so wagon haulers could shovel the coal into the shed. Coal stoves were placed throughout the garrison. Garland Hard Coal Heaters were placed in the officers' quarters.

Six hundred tons of coal arrived at the Webster train station in late autumn 1883. Twenty Sisseton and Wahpeton men and their teams and wagons were hired to haul the coal to the post. After the twenty-two-mile trip, each wagon was examined and weighed on the quartermaster scale before unloading. During the winter of 1883-1884, the post used 100 tons of coal a month. One cold spell between 2 February and 21 February averaged eight degrees below zero.

A large platform was built between the two grain bins at the Webster train yard to handle 500 tons of coal for the next winter. Coal was unloaded on the platform and stored until it was hauled to the post. The *Webster Reporter and Farmer* in its 25 September 1886 issue noted that twenty tepees were located a mile east of Webster. Indian haulers and their families lived at the camp while hauling coal.

A cut field-stone oil house was built in 1888. It was about twenty feet square and stored kerosene used for lamps and lanterns. It was the last building constructed at the post.

Horses, Hay, and Wagons

Fort Sisseton was primarily a cavalry post until June 1866. The Second Minnesota Cavalry had 210 horses and mules on hand for the first winter of 1864-1865. Because of a shortage of feed, Captain James M. Paine was ordered to take 100 horses back to Fort Snelling in December. That left thirty-two horses and seventy-eight mules to feed that cold winter.

A log horse barn replaced a pole barn in late 1864. A new fifty-stall stone stable was completed in 1865. During 1865 and up to June 1866, the Second Minnesota Cavalry maintained an average of 100 horses and mules at the post. In June of 1866 the Tenth United States Infantry replaced the Second Minnesota Cavalry. The Tenth Infantry fed and watered 115 horses in 1867, of which twenty were used for the mounted Enlisted Indian Scouts and sixty for the mounted infantry. The number of horses on hand was reduced to sixty-seven in 1868.

Various infantry units stationed at the post between 1868 and 1883 maintained a herd of about forty mules and horses. Post Returns for 1874 show twenty-six horses and twenty mules on hand,

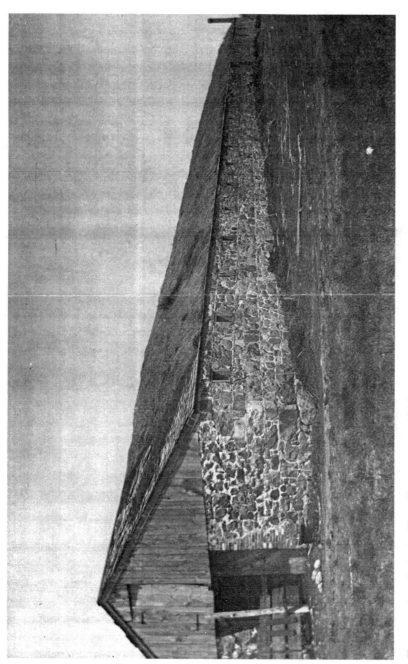

Courtesy Larry F. Ness

Horse and mule barn, Fort Sisseton, ca. 1930.

including two private horses owned by Post Commander Major Robert E. A. Crofton. Numbers in 1883 were similar, with twenty-six mules and ten horses on hand. Animals that year were used as follows: four mules for the ambulance, four four-mule teams (sixteen) for draught, one two-mule team in use for the beef herd, one two-mule team for hauling manure, and two on a standby basis. Six horses were used for riding, two horses for herding the cattle, and two horses were used to operate a horse-powered sawmill and horse-powered corn grinder.

In 1883 "Corporal Michael Duggan, Company F, Seventeeth United States Infantry, was in charge of the post stable, stock, and property in use at the stables....He had a room in one end of the stable....He and the teamsters sleep in the stable, the better to guard against loss of animals, harness and saddles."[46]

One enlisted man was designated as the farrier, often the same person as the blacksmith. He reshod the horses and mules each month. Lacking a veterinarian, the farrier usually took care of ill horses and mules. The farrier had access to the Army's Standard Supply Table. The table listed various horse medicines, many of which were on hand. Another enlisted man acted as post saddler, repairing harnesses and saddles.

There were areas of good hayland on Fort Sisseton's 82,112-acre military reservation. The hay was cut by either a hay contractor or by the soldiers. The post needed about 200 tons of hay each year for its horses, mules, and cattle. A hay contractor charged $5.00 a ton to cut and haul the hay. It was stacked in five-ton stacks near the cattle herd and horse barn.

In 1883 a new wagon shed large enough to house twenty-six wagons was built. However, by 1887 the shed was too large for the wagon inventory. Post Returns for 1887 list on hand only two army wagons, three escort wagons, two spring wagons, one ambulance, two water wagons, two hand carts, and two mule carts.

Transportation

Transportation during the Fort Sisseton era consisted of team and wagon, stagecoach, railroad, and steamboat. Although Fort Sisseton was distant from navigable rivers, sometimes all forms of travel were used in troop movements or hauling supplies to the post. In 1873, for example, all forms of travel were used to transfer Companies B and C, Seventeenth United States Infantry, from Fort

Rice to Fort Sisseton. On 6 October the six officers and 105 enlisted men boarded the steamboat *Peninah* at Fort Rice and headed north on the Missouri River to Bismarck, arriving the same day. The next day they traveled on the Northern Pacific Railroad to Moorhead, Minnesota. October 8 and 9 they marched thirty-one miles south to Fort Abercrombie. On 11 October the party began the seventy-five mile march on the Abercrombie Road to Fort Sisseton. After marching twenty-one miles, they camped that night at Wild Rice Creek. They marched sixteen miles to the Twin Lakes Station 12 October. They arrived at the slope of the Coteau the night of 13 October after marching twenty-one miles. The next day they marched seventeen miles to the post. The two companies of the Seventeenth Infantry replaced Companies D and F, Twentieth Infantry, who were transferred to Fort Pembina, North Dakota.[47]

There were a number of trails or roads to the post. The route generally depended on the location of the railhead. In 1864 and 1865 supplies were hauled by team and wagon from the railhead at Sauk Centre, Minnesota, 123 miles east. Later Minnesota railheads closer to the post were Breckinridge, sixty-five miles; Herman, seventy-two miles; Morris, seventy-five miles; Lake Kampeska, sixty miles; and Browns Valley, forty miles. For example, in 1872 the post was using the St. Paul and Pacific railhead at Morris, Minnesota. It took four days by stage to travel the seventy-five-mile trip to Morris. The route crossed the Lake Traverse Reservation, through Browns Valley, and east to Morris. Much of the freight was hauled by contract teams. Regardless of the route, it was a three- or four-days' ride with team and wagon. The dirt road was either dusty, muddy, or frozen.

It was a military requirement to mark prairie roads with poles, bushes, piles of stone, or sod mounds to keep travelers from wandering off course. Road markings, however, were often hard to follow in a blinding blizzard. That was the case in the winter of 1866 when Captain Albert R. Field and Company A, Second Minnesota Cavalry, were ordered to transfer from Fort Sisseton to Sauk Centre for duty. It is not known why the company headed north, considering Sauk Centre was 123 miles to the east. Captain Albert R. Field with his company of about forty men left the post on 13 February. The party arrived at the foot of the Coteau at 9:00 a.m. At 11:00 a.m. Captain Field, C. Smith, P.J.C. Walker, and C. L. Fertile left the party to go ahead to Twin Lake. Sergeant Fisk tells what happened to the remaining men of the company and their encounter with a blizzard that took the lives of Captain Field and three men.

February 13—We then got out about 10 miles and were caught in a terrible snow storm—lost the road—had to turn back. Lieutenant and 12 of us managed to get into the foot of the Coteau about dark. The rest of the boys on the prairie I expect. Bitter cold. 35 degrees below zero. Clothes all froze stiff to us—nothing to eat. Terrible long night. All we could do to keep from freezing to death.

February 14—The rest of the boys on the prairie all night-about 2 miles from here. Harkness froze to death and a good many badly frozen. We were all day getting them and our teams into the Coteau. Austin Maxwell acted like a hero last night on the prairie—used his mule whip and kept the boys from freezing to death. Had some coffee and frozen bread. Have got the tents up and frozen boys as well taken care of as possible.

February 15—[At Fort Wadsworth]—Thank God we are once again by a warm fire. We put all the badly frozen boys in one sleigh this morning. Lieutenant and I started ahead to hurry out help for the boys. We came in at 11 o'clock. Captain Peter B. Davy with several teams started out immediately and met the team about six miles out and brought them in all right. Five men in the hospital. Have not heard a word from Captain Field and the [3] boys. We have got 28 horses left out of 55 that we started with.

February 18—Teams got in from foot of Coteau with all our baggage and Corporal L. G. Harkness body. One of the boys that left with Captain Field got in this evening. Nearly dead. It is thought the Captain and the boys froze to death.

February 19—They found Captain Field's horse and one belonging to one of the boys. No hope for them. They must be all dead."[48]

On 25 February the company left the post again for Sauk Centre.

The seventy-five-mile road to Breckinridge and Fort Abercrombie was a route well marked and used by the post. In 1869 the route was described as being marked with a twelve-foot pole every quarter-mile to half-mile. Mounds of sod, with the grass side down, were stacked four feet square and four feet high around each pole. The south forty miles of the route, from Twin Lake Station to the post, was marked with 130 poles. Twin Lake Station consisted of a couple log buildings and a stable with a caretaker in charge.[49]

Commanding Officer Clarence E. Bennett complained in 1878 that he couldn't tell the approach of a storm because there was no barometer at the post. He requested a signal station be established at the post to avoid another disaster like the loss of Captain Field and three men in 1866.

Commanding Officer Bennett was authorized in 1879 to survey for a new dirt road to the Twin Lake Station enroute to Breckinridge. A plow and scraper were used to fix the road and place four-foot mounds around poles located every half mile or in sight of each other. If water or timber were located a short way off the road, a mound was placed on the side of the road, showing the direction.[50]

In 1881 the Chicago, Milwaukee and St. Paul Railroad began serving Webster, South Dakota, twenty-two miles south of Fort Sisseton. The same railroad in 1886 began serving Britton, eighteen miles northwest. Passenger trains in 1884 left Webster daily, except Sunday, at 9:20 a.m. and 4:40 p.m. Freight rates to Minneapolis were $1.00 a hundred pounds, first class. Area settlers and their teams were hired to haul freight from Webster and Britton.

Stagecoaches, primarily hauling the mail and passengers, ran between the post and various railheads. Different vehicles were used: open or covered spring wagon, covered army ambulance, or stagecoach. Sergeant Andrew Fisk noted in his diary in 1866 that the company's laundress (Mrs. Ide) traveled by stage to Sauk Centre. A mail stage ran between the post and the railhead at Morris, Minnesota, two times a week in 1872. In 1880 a mail stage ran three times a week between the post and Herman, Minnesota.

The Webster and Britton Stage Line began operating between the two towns via Fort Sisseton in 1885. The fee was $2.00 a person between Webster and the post, and $1.75 from there to Britton. Each passenger was allowed to carry twenty-five pounds of luggage free. A *Dakota Daylight* advertisement on 20 February 1885 was as follows: "Daily stage line Webster to Fort Sisseton and return. U. S. Mail Stage. Leaves Webster at 7:00 a.m. and arrives at Fort Sisseton at noon. (Makes a close connection with the stage to Britton). The Britton stage leaves the Fort at 1:00 p.m. and back in Britton at 6:00

p.m. W. M. Paul, proprietor." Later in 1885 W. M. Paul sold his stage business to the Atchison Brothers. The brothers also rented out horses and rigs during holiday seasons.[51]

Webster-Fort Sisseton-Britton stage coach. Note armed soldier on left, 1885.
Courtesy of South Dakota Archives

Endnotes

1. *Regulations of the United States Army*, 1881:1084. (Hereafter cited as *Regulations.*)

2. George D. Hughes, Assistant Adjutant General, Department of Dakota. Circular, 23 October 1877. RG 393. Commissary Files, National Archives, Washington, D.C. (Hereafter cited as Hughes, Circular.)

3. *Regulations*, 1881.

4. *Regulations*, 1881:571-575.

5. *Regulations*, 1881:1084.

6. Post Commissary Officer to Department of Dakota, 23 August 1878. Letters Sent. RG 393. V. 20. vol. 1:80. National Archives, Washington, D. C.

7. Hughes, Circular.

8. Commissary Order, 1 February 1881. RG 393. V. 20. vol. 4:262. National Archives, Washington, D.C.

9. Robert E. Crofton to Department of Dakota, 5 December 1873. Letters Sent. RG 393. V. 2. vol. 4. National Archives, Washington, D.C.

10. RG 393. V. 20. vol. 4. National Archives, Washington, D. C.

11. Commissary Record, 1880. RG 393. V. 20. vol. 1. National Archives, Washington, D.C.

12. S. B. Hayman to Department of Dakota, 22 November 1867. Letters Sent. RG 393. V. 2. vol. 1. National Archives, Washington, D.C.

13. Robert H. Rose to Henry H. Sibley, 9 December 1865. Letters Sent. National Archives, Washington, D.C.

14. S. B. Hayman to Department of Dakota, 22 November 1867. Letters Sent. RG 393. V. 2. vol. 1. National Archives, Washington, D.C.

15. Post Returns of Fort Sisseton, July 1888. National Archives, Washington, D.C. On microfilm roll 1179, South Dakota Archives, Pierre, South Dakota. (Hereafter cited as Post Returns.)

16. RG 393. V. 20. vol. 5. National Archives, Washington, D.C.

17. Commissary Sales. RG 393. V. 20. vol. 1. National Archives, Washington, D.C.

18. Robert E. A. Crofton to Department of Dakota, 5 December 1873. Letters Sent. RG 393. V. 2. vol. 4. National Archives, Washington, D.C.

19. Edward I. Grumley report, 20 October, 1880. RG 393. V. 20. vol. 4:287. National Archives, Washington, D.C.

20. John S. McNaught to T. W. Baldwin, 3 April 1873. Letters Sent. RG 393. V. 2. vol. 4. National Archives, Washington, D.C.

21. Robert E. A. Crofton to Department of Dakota, 29 June 1877. Letters Sent. RG 393. V. 2. vol. 6. National Archives, Washington, D.C.

22. Robert E. A. Crofton to Department of Dakota, 9 April 1877. Letters Sent. RG 393. V. 2. vol. 6. National Archives, Washington, D.C.

23. Post Commissary of Subsistence, 19 October 1878. RG 393. V. 20. vol. 4. National Archives, Washington, D.C.

24. Circular, 24 October 1880. RG 393. V. 16. vol. 1:44. National Archives, Washington, D.C.

25. George Ruhlen report, 6 September 1880. RG 393. V. 20. vol. 4:214. National Archives, Washington, D.C.

26. Circular, 6 December 1879. RG 393. V. 16. vol. 1:33. National Archives, Washington, D.C.

27. Clarence E. Bennett to Department of Dakota, 31 January 1881. Letters Sent. RG 393. V. 2. vol. 9. National Archives, Washington, D.C.

28. Edward I. Grumley report, 25 November 1882. RG 393. V. 20. vol. 5:29. National Archives, Washington, D.C.

29. *Fort Sisseton.* Schumcker, Paul, Nohr and Associates. Mitchell, South Dakota, 1974:89.

30. Orders, 18 November 1882. RG 393. V. 15. vol. 2. National Archives, Washington, D.C.

31. Post Garden, 10 October 1883. RG 393. V. 2. vol. 12. National Archives, Washington, D.C.

32. Andrew J. Fisk Diary, 7 December 1865. Roll 81. Minnesota Historical Society, St. Paul, Minnesota. (Hereafter cited as Fisk Diary.)

33. Fisk Diary, 7 February 1866.

34. Post Medical History, December 1873. RG 94. vol. 2:150. National Archives, Washington, D.C. (Hereafter cited as Medical History.)

35. Medical History, July 1875. vol. 2:227.

36. Clarence E. Bennett to Department of Dakota, 10 January 1883. Letters Sent. RG 393. 2. vol. 12:1. National Archives, Washington, D.C.

37. *Regulations,* 1881:1084.

38. Clarence E. Bennett to Chief of Ordnance, 6 April 1882. Letters Sent. RG 393. V. 2. vol. 10. National Archives, Washington, D.C.

39. Medical History, November 1882. vol. 3:192.

40. Edward P. Pearson to Department of Dakota, 4 March 1875. Letters Sent. RG 393. V. 2. vol. 5. National Archives, Washington, D.C.

41. General Orders, 16 May 1881. RG 393. V. 15. vol. 1. National Archives, Washington, D.C.

42. Inspector General to Commanding Officer, Fort Sisseton, 5 November 1884. Letters Received. RG 393. V. 7. Box 5. National Archives, Washington, D.C.

43. Quartermaster. RG 393. V. 20. vol. 1:94. National Archives, Washington, D.C.

44. Post Adjutant to T. W. Baldwin, 6 October 1873. Letters Sent. RG 393. V. 2. vol. 4. National Archives, Washington, D.C.

45. C. E. Bennett to Department of Dakota, 20 November 1881. Letters Sent. RG 393. V. 2. vol. 10. National Archives, Washington, D.C.

46. Clarence E. Bennett to Department of Dakota. 10 January 1883, Letters Sent. RG 393. 2. vol. 12:1-11. National Archives, Washington, D.C.

47. Post Returns, October 1873.

48. Fisk Diary, 13 February through 19 February, 1866.

49. Circular, 6 November 1869. RG 393. V. 7. Box 1. National Archives, Washington, D.C.

50. Clarence E. Bennett to Department of Dakota, 31 July 1879. Letters Sent. RG 393. V. 2. vol. 8. National Archives, Washington, D.C.

51. *Dakota Daylight,* 17 December 1885.

Chapter 9

Entertainment and Social Life

Enlisted Men

Fort Sisseton was an isolated military post, like many others on the frontier. It was a three- or four-day wagon or stage ride to the nearest town with a railhead: Breckinridge, Herman, or Morris, Minnesota. Later, small settlements were started at Browns Valley, forty miles east, and Lake Kampeska, sixty miles southeast. Few people lived in the Fort Sisseton area. In 1880, only ninety-seven people lived in Day County. The railroad arrived at a new station point, Webster, twenty-two miles south, in 1881. However, it still took most of the day to drive a team from Webster to the post.

Because of these distances, the soldiers' social life was centered at the post. Military and post duties occupied much of the soldiers' time. There was free time, however, to buy beer, whiskey, tobacco, and food from the sutler to break the routine. The sutler also had a room for playing billiards. Card playing, riding, picnicking, target shooting, letter writing, dancing, ice skating, schooling, hunting, fishing, and reading also helped eliminate boredom. Most of the soldiers were young and needed some respite. According to the 1870 Federal Census, the average age of the post's soldiers was twenty-six.

After nearby towns were established (Webster 1881, Britton 1884), soldiers participated in some of the towns' public events. When Day County held its first election in 1882, six voting districts were established. One of the polling places was Fort Sisseton, where soldiers and settlers voted. The post lent its cannon and crew to Webster for the 1884 and 1885 Fourth of July celebrations. At the

1884 Fourth of July celebration, fifty-four blank charges were fired at sunrise to begin the day's activities.

First Lieutenant Henry P. Ritzius, of the post's Twenty-fifth Infantry, was placed in charge of an 1885 Grand Army of the Republic encampment in Aberdeen. Webster sponsored a South Dakota statehood celebration shortly after President Cleveland signed the Enabling Act, 22 February 1889. *The Webster Reporter and Farmer* noted that "Sergeant Dubbs of Fort Sisseton was in town last Monday and took in the [Statehood] jubilation meeting that evening."[1]

An Early Glimpse

Sergeant Andrew Fisk's diary, 1865-1866, provides an excellent record of early entertainment and social life at the post. His first entry about Fort Wadsworth attests to the post's remoteness. Before leaving Fort Snelling in late October for Fort Wadsworth, he noted: "Our company is ordered to Fort Wadsworth—bad luck. Men feel badly about being ordered to Fort Wadsworth. It seems as though I was going out of the world again—but it is a soldier's duty to obey orders."[2] He arrived 12 November 1865 with Company A, Second Minnesota Cavalry, consisting of three officers and ninety men. This brought the total to ten officers and 272 enlisted men from the Second Minnesota Cavalry and Third Minnesota Battery stationed at the post.

Fisk and his men lived in log huts until the new barracks were finished 9 December 1865. On 14 November, Fisk took his first bath in three weeks and put on clean clothes. That night "we indulged in a stag dance. Weather warm."[3] Fisk's social life during the remainder of November and December is described in his diary:

"Paid today and after debts paid had $20 left. Commenced drinking with Doc.

"Two men each made $25 tonight playing 'Honest John'.

"Four of Co. H men put in the guard house for refusing to drive a mule team.

"Doc off playing poker tonight.

"Boys are having a great sport skating on the ice. Doc, Dad, Shep and Spillman playing poker all day. Shep is ahead.

"This evening skated over to the Indian camp. Ice slick and clear from snow.

"Considerable peach brandy circulating tonight. Sergeant Jim Walker, Corporal Homer Hills and I have two bottles.

"First Lt. Wm. L. Briley gave me a song with music, Wake Nicodemus the Slave.

"Seven men turned over their ordnance to me preparatory to going on a furlough."[4]

On 10 December, the day after the men moved into the new barracks, he wrote, "We washed and changed our clothes. Our boys caught many fish. They cut holes in the ice and the fish bite greedily."[5] During a bitter cold spell in mid-December, the men were able to leave the barracks only twice a day. Fisk's pony broke through the ice while being watered at the lake, but freed itself.

There was a special party the night of 16 December 1865: "Men had a big time in the quarters last night. Beat drums and fired guns. Kept up the racket until eleven o'clock. All the non-commissioned officers were called over to the captain's office today and lectured."[6] On Christmas the men were served roast pig. Later they celebrated by "getting full of whiskey." On Christmas day Fisk played cards and read novels.

Just before Christmas, C. French had started a writing school with twenty men enrolled. Sergeant Fisk, who attended the school, said, "C. French's writing school in full blast tonight in the kitchen. About forty of the boys are attending. It is a good thing—it makes the evenings pass away pleasantly and profitably. The boys have all improved at least 100 percent since the school commenced."[7] On 11 January French started the second term of his writing school: "A good attendance. What a change there has been in our evenings. Before all was an unknown—some dancing—some playing cards, now everything is still and quiet."[8]

January 1866 was another bitter cold month. Fisk described the following events:

"7 January—Artemus Ward Jr. (my pony) threw me off in a big snow drift coming from water. Nobody hurt. A stormy cold day.

"8 January—Wrote a letter to Jack Wilner—consisting of eight pages of letter paper.

"17 January—Was down to Co. K quarters, (south barracks) to a 'stag dance' this evening. Quite a pleasant time. Cotillions and fancy dances. Do most anything to pass away time.

"20 January—Colder now by a good deal than yesterday. Thank the Lord we have got good warm quarters and have the chance to stay in them.

"21 January—No mail. Copied some songs this evening.

"25 January—Lieutenants Briley and Stevens took a ride to the foot of the Coteau and back today. Lt. Stevens slightly tight. I am reading, to pass time away, a novel titled 'Love Me, Leave Me Not.'

"29 January—Took a sleigh ride this evening.

"2 February—Long dull day and longer evening. Read a novel and learnt [sic] some songs to pass away these long—long evenings.

"9 February—Warm, took a ride to wood camp. Splendid sleighing on the lakes.

"10 February—Whoop, Whoop, Hurrah. Received orders today to proceed without delay to Sauk Centre and report for duty. Great rejoicing and jubilee. Hurrah. All excitement."[9]

Sergeant Fisk and Company A, Second Minnesota Cavalry left the post on 13 February 1866. They encountered a severe blizzard at the foot of the Couteau, which is described in Chapter 8.

Whiskey and Beer

The Fort Sisseton trader operated separate bars for enlisted men and officers. Officers could buy whiskey by the bottle, but enlisted men were limited to buying it by the drink. Business hours of the bars, as well as the amounts of whiskey and beer that could be sold to the enlisted men, were regulated by the post commander. There were many changes through the years pertaining to these quantities that could be sold. Post Commander Captain John S. McNaught admonished Post Sutler T. W. Baldwin about this in 1872: "It has been brought to my knowledge that in one or more cases, you allowed more than two glasses of beer to EM [enlisted men] yesterday PM, notwithstanding my instructions to you to allow no EM to have more than two glasses of beer during the forenoon, nor more than the same quantity in the afternoon. Should this occur again I shall be compelled to stop further sale of beer."[10]

In 1875, civilians and teamsters traveling with a twenty-five-wagon train to Fort Sully stopped at the post. Trader Baldwin was authorized to sell each of them two drinks of whiskey per day. Baldwin was directed not to sell or give any intoxicating liquor to Caleb Clark of Company B, Seventeenth Infantry, in 1876. New post trader John Vander Horck was ordered in 1877 not to sell more than four glasses of beer a day to enlisted men: two between 11:00 a.m. and 1:00 a.m. and two between 5:00 p.m. and 6:00 p.m. He could not sell any beer, liquor, or wine in quantity. Enlisted men on duty could not visit the trader's store or bar.

During the summer of 1878, Post Commander Captain William W. Van Horne reversed his orders three times. On 2 June, he advised Post Trader Vander Horck that no whiskey, brandy, or wine could be sold to the enlisted men without his written order. Two days later Captain Van Horne authorized the sale to enlisted men of one drink of whiskey in the morning and one in the evening. In early October, however, the commander revoked his order and declared that no whiskey could be sold to enlisted men except with his personal order. New Post Commander Captain Clarence E. Bennett, however, on 5 November amended the prior order and permitted the post trader to sell whiskey to enlisted men in moderate quantities.[11]

In May 1879, Captain Bennett and the council of administration believed that Vander Horck was selling good whiskey to officers and poor whiskey to enlisted men. The council of administration set the price of keg beer at $.10 per drink and extra fine whiskey at $.15 a drink. They warned the trader "that none but good whiskey will be sold at this post and no distinction made in the quality of that sold to officers and that sold to the enlisted men."[12]

Later that same month, Post Surgeon Charles E. McChesny reported, "The liquor kept by the post trader is not of such a quality as should be permitted to be sold at a military post, as its effects indicate that it is a vile compound."[13] Vander Horck, however, maintained that the liquor vended at his place was purchased from a responsible firm. He requested that]the post surgeon make an analysis of the whiskey. Later the post surgeon reported that since the trader had obtained a new barrel of whiskey, it was of a better quality.

During the first nine months of 1881 John Vander Horck sold 1,550 cigars at $.10 each. The favorite brands were Don Carlos, F'ler-de-alma, and Fine Taste that cost the trader $.04 each. The favorite smoking tobaccos were Durham, Lone Jack, and Vanity Fair. The sutler was required to sell tobacco at cost to enlisted men, not to exceed sixteen ounces per month. He charged them regular price for additional tobacco. Trader Vander Horck also operated a billiard room for the enlisted men.

There is no evidence that Fort Sisseton soldiers drank more whiskey and beer than soldiers at other frontier forts. According to post records, however, there were three tragic deaths because of excessive drinking.

November 1882—Private Patrick Sheehan, Company I, Seventeenth Infantry, was found dead on his bunk in the company quarters. He had been drinking in the evening, and his companions related that he had a pint flask of whiskey from which he drank repeatedly. He fell across his bed with his face down. Post Surgeon James B. Ferguson did a post-mortem and filed this report: "The stomach contained 25 fluid ounces of liquid of a strong berry odor mixed with the debris of digestion. I believe the man died from accidental suffocation while helplessly intoxicated."[14]

July 1883—Post Surgeon Victor Biart listed in his journal that a "private in a fit of insanity carried on by excessive drinking, committed suicide by cutting the superior thyroid artery and the internal jugular vein."[15]

March 1887—A *Webster Reporter and Farmer* news story reported: "A soldier at Fort Sisseton by the name of Marshall Phillips, while under the influence of liquor, strayed away from the fort, about two months ago, during a severe storm. Every effort to find him unavailing till last Saturday when he was discovered in a snow drift. He had wandered out on the prairie and got lost and unable to find his way back."[16]

The three privates were buried in the post cemetery.[17]

Gambling

Playing cards was the favorite form of gambling at Fort Sisseton. A deck of cards cost only fifty cents at the post sutler. A court-martial in 1877 involved a case of insubordination between a private and his sergeant during a card game. A private in the north barracks had joined a card game called "twenty-one," commonly known as "blackjack." His sergeant walked in and asked him to do the dishes. However, the private said he had made a bet and preferred to finish the game. "Either wash dishes or go to the guardhouse," was the sergeant's reply. Again the private refused and was then arrested. At the court-martial the private was fined $5.00.

Another time that year a corporal was running a little game in the north barracks called "shoo fly." During the game a private deliberately knocked over a candle on the card table. In the commotion, he picked fifty cents off the table. Another player saw the indiscretion and began a fight with the private. At the court-martial, one witness said the players had a total of $25 on the table. The private was fined $3.00.

The *Dakota Daylight* in an 1885 story reported a gambling incident at the post: "The lads at the fort fixed up a little sporting headquarters to indulge in a little game of chance. The fact fell to the ears of the commanding officer, whereupon he proceeded to corral the delinquents. It is said that had his honor made the raid an hour before, there would not have been enough troops remaining to guard the transgressors who were shut up for punishment."[18]

Outdoor Activity

Fort Sisseton's military reservation (nine miles wide by fifteen miles long) was a paradise for hunting and fishing. Picnics were held in its groves or near one of its many lakes during the summer. In the winter there was ice skating.

Hunting and fishing were the favored outdoor sports. Buffalo were very common in the region in the 1860s. Post Surgeon Charles J. Farley wrote about an 1865 hunt: "On 4 July, Commanding Officer Robert H. Rose detailed a small party of men to go buffalo hunting. So numerous were the buffalo in the vicinity of the post that fully 300 were slaughtered in four days."[19]

Shotguns were available for hunting prairie chickens and grouse on the military reservation. Soldiers were permitted to buy shotgun shells and encouraged to hunt. Fishing was a frequent sport, according to an 1885 story in the *Dakota Daylight:* "The boys are having fine sport these days fishing in the lakes in the military reservation. Pickerel, weighing from two to twenty pounds each, are easily speared or shot in the clear pure water. The fish are of excellent flavor."[20] People from Britton, Webster, and the area also picnicked and fished on the military reservation.

There was an island in one nearby lake. When the lake froze, soldiers liked to skate over to the island and back. In 1870 Corporal Francis Hubner, Company F, Twentieth Infantry, drowned while ice skating on this lake. He was buried with full military honors at the post cemetery.

Dancing

Fort Sisseton soldiers liked to dance. Sergeant Fisk referred to stag dances in the post's barracks in 1865 and 1866. After spouses of enlisted men and laundresses arrived, mixed company dances were often held. An invitation to Miss Ellen Brown, Browns Valley was sent by Company C, Tenth United States Infantry, to attend an 1867 Christmas eve ball and supper in its barracks. Browns Valley, Minnesota, was only forty miles to the east, about a day-and-a-half ride by team and wagon.

Post Surgeon Major B. Knickerbocker in 1868 had praise for the enlisted men's interest in music and their ability to keep occupied: "Many of the enlisted men have a good ear for music, and during the long winter evenings their instruments, of which they possess a number, and their adaptability to tune them, make pleasant many a passing hour. Music, dancing, singing, reading and fishing seem to be their most favorite amusements."[21]

In early April 1879, the men of Company F, Seventeenth United States Infantry, were given permission by Commanding Officer Clarence E. Bennett to hold an "entertainment" in the mess hall of its barracks. Dance music was provided by men of the post. The mess hall was about twenty-two feet wide and thirty-six feet long. No doubt the adjacent kitchen was also used. It is not known how many of the forty-four men of Company F were excused to attend the dance. Men who were excused from duty did not need to attend the 9:00 p.m. tattoo roll call held in front of the barracks. After 1880, some evening dances were held in the eighteen-foot by thirty-eight-foot schoolroom.

Webster and Britton had public dance halls. Presumably some soldiers attended dances in the two towns. Some of Webster's places of entertainment included the Opera House and the Prior House Hotel. Horses and carriages could be rented from the livery stable for Sunday drives. Britton's dance halls were Hindman's Hall and the Dwight House [Arlington House after 1888]. Charles Vander Horck, son of Post Trader John Vander Horck, and wife attended an 1885 masquerade ball in Hindman's Hall in honor of Washington's birthday. The ball was referred to as "rich, rare and racy" by the local paper.

When the Twenty-fifth Infantry, and its two companies of seventy-four Black soldiers, came to the post in May 1884, it brought along a string band. The string band played at Webster's 1884 Fourth of

July celebration. On 3 July the local paper reported that "The Fort Sisseton string band will discourse music the afternoon and evening at Webster on the 4th." On 10 July 1884 the paper said, "The largest ball ever given in Day County was held at the courthouse the evening of the 4th. Eighty couples participated in the different changes of a lively dance."[22] The Black soldiers left in June 1888.

A news story in the *Webster Reporter and Farmer* about the post's 1889 New Year's eve military ball sponsored by Company G, Third United States Infantry, read: "O. T. Nelson of the West Hotel represented the City at Fort Sisseton's New Year's, and reports there is nothing too good for outsiders at the post. Grand parade in the afternoon and military ball in the evening and a royal time all round. Quite a number of our boys were invited but lost a good thing by failing to attend."[23]

The post celebrated Washington's birthday with a party and ball in February 1889. A part of the entertainment included a matinee by the Webster Rifles Dramatic Company. The Webster Rifles, a local South Dakota National Guard unit, presented the drama *Above the Clouds*.

Baseball

Fort Sisseton soldiers organized baseball teams and played against each other. Baseball equipment and uniforms were purchased with proceeds from the post fund. The best players made up a post team to play teams from area towns.

In July 1888, the "Webster Ball Tossers" played a game against the Third Infantry soldiers at Fort Sisseton. The Webster paper in reporting the game told about post life also:

> If the day had been ordered for the occasion, it could not have given greater satisfaction. A shower had laid the dust and left the air cool, and the sun shone up a world refreshed and beautiful. Quite a party of ladies and gentlemen accompanied the Webster club, all of whom were welcomed cordially and entertained royally by the soldiers. An excellent dinner was given us at the soldiers' dining table and everything was as neat and orderly as though prepared by women. After dinner we were shown about the library, school room, hospital, stables, and armory until the game was called. The score was 12 to 15 in

favor of the Webster club. Time of game was two hours—including orations by Morris. Thos. Lawler was the umpire.

After the game concluded, some of our ladies presided at the organ and all joined in a rousing sing of Gospel hymns. A soldier accompanied his comrades in several songs with his guitar. A company exhibited its perfection in military drill, for the benefit of the members present of the Webster militia. A fine lunch was spread for those of our party who remained until tea time. We shall remember our visit to Fort Sisseton with unsullied satisfaction, and the company of soldiers stationed there as intelligent, civil gentlemen.

The only calamity of the day to record, was the falling in love of one of our young ladies with the Fort schoolmaster; and perhaps that may not be considered a calamity, for the fine looking young pedagogue fell as deeply into the tender sentiment as did the young lady and who can tell all the happy results that may arise from seeming calamity.[24]

The post team lost a seven-inning game at Britton by a score of 12 to 3 in July 1888. In August the team traveled to Webster for a game, again reviewed by the newspaper:

The game started at two o'clock. Each club got square down to business and played ball for all the game was worth. The fort boys did some splendid fielding, our pitchers were too much for them, and they came to the bat only to fan the atmosphere—this was especially the case during the last six innings pitched by Fred Harris. The game was witnessed by a large crowd of people. The visiting club won a host of friends among our citizens, not only for their gentlemanly and courteous conduct during the game, but also during the entire time of their stay in the city. That the soldier boys reflected credit on the troop to which they belong, is the generally expressed opinion of our citizens.[25]

Pet Dogs

Indian scouts, enlisted men, and officers all owned dogs. Managing the pet dog population was a continuous problem. In May 1876, Commanding Officer Captain Edward P. Pearson ordered Second Lieutenant William A. Mann, in charge of the Enlisted Indian Scouts, to stop the scouts' dogs from howling: "You will direct your scouts to observe and note the dogs that have a habit of howling at the sounding by the bugler of reveille and retreat. After the 23rd, the scouts, after first driving them out of the garrison, will follow and shoot dogs guilty of the nuisance above described."[26]

In February 1877, Major Robert E. A. Crofton issued an order requiring all dog owners to obtain a certificate of ownership. All unauthorized dogs would be destroyed. After compliance, the captain posted a list of seventeen authorized dog owners and the names of their dogs. Four officers, post surgeon, post trader, and eleven enlisted men owned dogs. Among the dog population were German shepherds, cocker spaniels, and retrievers. Some dog's names and their owners were "Hunter," Captain Edward P. Pearson; "Pincher," Captain Malcolm McArthur; "Nero," Postmaster Dan P. Shilton; "Prince," Sergeant Grady; "Nelly," Sergeant Madigan; and "Poncho," Private Kelly. Posted with the list was this warning: "These dogs must be kept under control and not allowed to roam at large."[27]

A commanding officer in 1882 had similar problems with pet dogs. In Post Circular 1, Captain Clarence E.Bennett stated: "A complaint is made that the Greyhounds at the post chase the mules and stock. The owners will see that it is stopped at once. All dogs bark at ladies, children, laundresses and servants passing about the garrison. This must be stopped. Also the dogs are worrying company, hospital and private cows. All such dogs should be whipped until they stop the acts complained of."[28]

On 30 April 1882, Captain Bennett gave permission to First Sergeant Timothy Spillane to let his greyhound run loose for exercise. Spillane was responsible for seeing that the dog did not chase stock or otherwise bark at people. But the permission was revoked eight days later.

Library

A log building, containing ninety-four books, was used as a library in 1869. Library books and magazines were purchased from the post fund and army funds. In 1876 the Post Council of Administration approved $20.00 for the purchase of books and periodicals. The commanding officer disapproved two of the purchases because they were "indecent": a magazine subscription to *Days Doings* for $4.00 and a book *DeCameron* for $2.00.[29]

Magazines and newspapers ordered in 1879 included *North American Review, United Service Quarterly, Atlantic Monthly,*

Washington Sunday Herald, fifty volumes of *Half Hour Series,* and twenty numbers of *Franklin Square.* St. Paul's daily newspaper *Pioneer Press* was received by mail. Officers could check out books with the librarian any time. Enlisted men could check out books only between 5:30 p.m. and 6:00 p.m. Both officers and enlisted men were allowed to keep a book one week. Patrons were advised not to soil the books or turn down pages.

Magazines ordered in 1880 included *Harpers Illustrated Weekly, Harpers Illustrated Monthly, Scribners Monthly, Atlantic Monthly, Army and Navy Journal, Daily New York Herald, Philadelphia Sunday Times, Alta California-Weekly,* and *Waverly Magazine.*

In October 1880 a new library was opened on the north side of the parade ground. The one-story cross-shaped brick building consisted of an eighteen-foot by thirty-eight-foot school room, a twenty-foot by eighteen-foot library wing, and a twenty-foot by eighteen-foot court-martial wing.

Commanding Officer Clarence E. Bennett issued rules for the new library. All newspapers, pamphlets, and magazines were to be kept in the reading room from 8:00 a. m. until 9:00 p.m. Officers, however, were permitted to check them out overnight. On enlisted men's dance nights, officers had to have the items checked out before the dance started.

The library had grown to 475 books by 1882. More newspapers and magazines were added, including the *Chicago Sunday Times, New York Herald, New York Times, Washington Evening Star,* and *Forest and Stream.* The subscription prices ranged from $1.00 to $3.00 per year. Private Joseph Clarkson served as the librarian. His duties included checking out books and papers, sweeping and scrubbing the floor, and keeping the fires and lights burning.

Books ordered in 1885 consisted of *Boots and Saddles* by Elizabeth Custer, *Uncle Tom's Cabin,* and *The Leavenworth Case.* Britton's *Dakota Daylight* and the Webster *Reporter and Farmer,* each costing $2.00 a year, were included on the newspaper rack. The principal books circulated were about United States history. In 1888, Post Surgeon John L. Philips was appointed librarian, but the daily management of the library was performed by one of the privates.

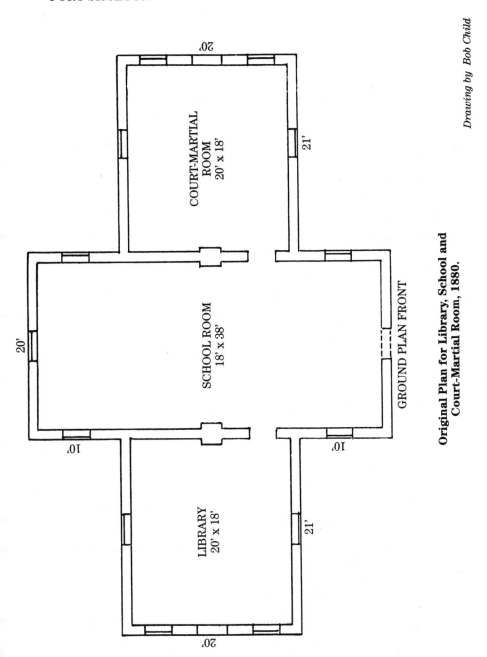

Drawing by Bob Child

COURT-MARTIAL
ROOM
20' x 18'

20'

21'

SCHOOL ROOM
18' x 38'

20'

10'

10'

GROUND PLAN FRONT

LIBRARY
20' x 18'

21'

20'

Original Plan for Library, School and
Court-Martial Room, 1880.

School

An 1866 Act of Congress required a military post to maintain a school for the enlisted men. It was not mandatory that enlisted men attend the school, however. The same building used as a school for enlisted men was used as a school for children living at the post.

A day school for the benefit of children living at the post was started 24 July 1868. It was located in the log chapel, formerly used as the officers' quarters. Post Chaplain George D. Crocker was the teacher and manager of the school. Classes were taught from 8:30 a.m. until noon and 1:00 p.m. until 4:30 p.m. Chaplain Hiram Stone succeeded Crocker as the teacher in 1870. Sergeant Charles Perry, Company F, Twentieth Infantry, helped Stone various times in 1872 and 1873. Perry was paid thirty cents a day for serving as the assistant school teacher.

Post Records show there was no school for enlisted men in 1871. By 1874 the children's school was also closed. New Commanding Officer Clarence E. Bennett took immediate steps to open the school for both groups in 1878. He ordered desks, chairs, tables, blackboards, books, and lamps. Bennett also ordered five quires of paper, twenty-five sheets of blotting paper, three lead pencils, thirty pen holders, one bottle of ink, sixty steel pens, two bottles of glue, and one blank book. The school, held in an old log building, opened 3 February 1879 with twenty-two enlisted men. Lieutenant Andrew E. Kilpatrick was in charge of the school.

A new school was opened 31 October 1880 in the joint-use building located between the hospital and the north corner of the barracks. The new brick building housed a school, library, and court-martial room. Privates Charles Cook and William I. Cook were teachers in 1883.

Army regulations permitted a teacher to inflict slight punishment on school children who misbehaved. Punishment included sitting or standing in a corner facing the wall. Occasionally students were punished by having to wear a "dunce-cap." Misbehavior by an officer's child could result in expulsion from school. Expulsion occurred only after failure of parental correction, suspension for one week, and a recurrence of bad conduct. The children of enlisted men could not be expelled from school; however, both parents and teacher had to take corrective steps until good behavior was secured.[30] Enlisted men who attended school during the evening were excused from retreat and tattoo.

Regulations were different for soldiers who attended the school:

> The hours of the school vary with the seasons of the year. Half hour after retreat the school-call for enlisted men may be sounded, when the scholars repair to their respective rooms for study and recitation, until first call for tattoo. They are allowed to take their text-books to their quarters, for study during any spare hour they may have during the day. The post commander should visit these schools daily, and note progress of the children and soldiers and make suggestions to the teachers when necessary.[31]

Following an 1884 post inspection, the Adjutant General of the Department of Dakota made the following point: "There is a school teacher at the post by the name of Crawford, a private of Company F, Seventeenth Infantry. The pupils are ready and willing to learn, but this teacher is so intemperate that he is totally unfitted for such a post, and I submit that he should be ordered to join his company and effort made to secure another teacher in his stead."[32]

Captain David Schooley replied to the Adjutant General two weeks later:

> Among the enlisted men at this post, none can be found competent to teach in the post school here. Many are ready and willing to go to school, but the principle source of information will have to be supplied from elsewhere. First Lieutenant Henry P. Ritzius will have general charge of the school but with his other duties will not be able to teach himself, except a little at night as the attendance of school in the army is not compulsory. I would respectfully request that a suitable man be sent us, if possible to assist in this work.[33]

However, an 1885 annual post report indicated Lieutenant Ritzius was still in charge of the school and library. Of fifteen children available for school, fourteen attended regularly. Average evening attendance for the soldiers was twenty-three. At the time there were eighty soldiers stationed at the post. Evening classes were cancelled one night because of a lack of attendance. The report also stated the supply of school books was ample. The problem of obtaining and keeping a teacher continued. Using one of the enlisted men for the job was common in the last years of the post. Private Frank H. Thomas was listed as the teacher in 1885, followed by Privates John O'Shea and William C. Henry from 1886 through 1888.

Chapel and Chaplain

A chaplain accompanied General Sully's 1864 military expedition into the Dakota Territory. Private George W. Doud, Eighth Minnesota Infantry, recalled in his diary that there was preaching by the chaplain on Sunday when the expedition camped. At one Sunday camp, near the Missouri River on 4 September 1864, he wrote, "Lay over. Boys hunting buffalo and kill many. Preaching and gambling only 20 rods apart."[34] A chapel and chaplain were a part of soldier life at Fort Sisseton also. Chapel was held in various buildings. In 1871, the chapel was located in a part of the former officers' quarters. When the new joint-use building was completed in 1880, the schoolroom in the middle portion was used as a chapel on Sunday.

The army required a chaplain to be an ordained minister of some denomination. He was assigned the rank of captain and lived in the officers' quarters. An early chaplain at the post was Isaiah Sweet, who served until 1867. Sweet was paid $100 a month and two free rations a day and fuel. George D. Crocker served as chaplain between 1867 and 1870. He was succeeded by Hiram Stone, who served until 1876. Both Crocker and Stone also served as superintendent of the post's school. Post records are incomplete as to later chaplains.

In 1876, one of the six churches on the Lake Traverse Reservation was located east of the post. Enlisted Indian Scouts serving at Fort Sisseton attended that church. In 1881, Commanding Officer Clarence E. Bennett advised the American Bible Society of Minnesota and Dakota that sixty-five free Bibles would amply supply the post's needs.

Ministers from Webster and Britton also preached at the post's chapel. One Sunday in 1885, Reverend W. G. Dickson of the Congregational Church of Webster preached at the post. Reverend Joseph C. Johnson, who homesteaded on the Northeast Quarter of Section Two, Sisseton Township, also preached at the post other times. Reverend Johnson carried a folding organ with him that he used for the service. The folding organ is now on display at the Day County Museum in Webster.

Officers' Social Affairs

After 1869, there was a monthly average of eight officers, including the surgeon and chaplain, living at the post. Officers lived, dined, and socialized separately from the enlisted men. They may have attended some enlisted men's social events in a supervisory capacity only.

The officers, married or single, entertained each other with card games, meals, visits, and holiday festivities. Some officers brought their upright pianos to the post: for example, Lieutenant Daniel Brush in 1878-1879 and Major Frederick Mears in 1885-1887. Group singing around these pianos in one of the officers' quarters was also popular. Spouses, children, and servants enjoyed watching the ceremonial events of guard mount, parades, and retreat. At times the post band played a concert. Summer picnics or ice skating were common family events. Some officers had a horse or two and enjoyed horseback riding. Hunting and fishing were also popular pastimes.

Officers could buy whiskey by the bottle from the post trader. The trader maintained a separate bar or club for the use of officers and their guests only. A billiard table was also provided for their entertainment. Overnight stays of an army paymaster, Department of Dakota inspector, or other visiting officers often resulted in social gatherings. The commanding officer was usually the host for such gatherings. Because of distance and difficult travel, outside visitors at officers' social events were limited. After the railroad arrived in Webster in 1881, followed by a stage line to the post, it was easier for visitors to attend social affairs.

Two companies of the Seventeenth United States Infantry were stationed at the post for eleven years, 1873-1884. At different times during that period, twenty-five Seventeenth Infantry officers served at the post. A glimpse into their backgrounds will help explain their social interests. The officers were from the following eastern states: Ohio, four; Illinois, three; two each New York, Delaware, Iowa, Pennsylvania, Connecticut, and Kentucky; and one each Wisconsin, Arkansas, Mississippi, Maine, and Michigan. The home state of one officer was not listed in the record. Four of the twenty-five officers were foreign born: Ireland three, and Germany one. Ten officers were graduates of West Point, seven worked their way up the ranks, and seven received their commissions by appointment. Eight of the officers had served in the Civil War, one of whom had been awarded the Congressional Medal of Honor for gallantry in action.[35] The Seventeenth Infantry officers were a diversified group representing a cross-section of America.

Six Seventeenth Infantry officers were stationed at the post in June 1880. Four of the officers, including the commanding officer, were married. Two couples had two sons each, and two couples had one son each. Each of the married couples had a servant. Two of the officers were single and shared one of the quarters. First Lieutenant George Ruhlen and Second Lieutenants Edward Chynowith and Robert W. Dowdy were graduates of West Point and acquainted with the social life of the United States Military Academy. Army officers generally were accustomed to party niceties and social functions and understood what it meant to be an "officer and gentleman."

After 1881, couples from Webster, Britton, and the area were invited to some of the parties hosted by officers. Parties were held either in the commanding officer's house or in one of the smaller officers' quarters. If a large social event, it was held in the eighteen-foot by thirty-eight-foot school room. The adjoining library or the court-martial room was used for the overflow. Officers brought their own furnishings to the post, which may well have included a silver service for party use. The Army did not issue a silver service to a frontier army post. Hors d'oeuvres and party food were made from supplies purchased from the post sutler or post commissary. Sometimes special items were purchased in Webster, Britton, or distant supply houses. Delivery was by stage or wagon from the nearest railhead.

The six to eight officers at the post at one time, were generally a closely knit group. They had to work together to make the post run smoothly.

Endnotes

1. *Webster Reporter and Farmer*, 7 March 1889.
2. Andrew J. Fisk Diary, 25 October 1865. Roll 81. Minnesota Historical Society, St. Paul, Minnesota. (Hereafter cited as Fisk Diary.)
3. Fisk Diary, 14 November 1865.
4. Fisk Diary, 25 November—8 December 1865.
5. Fisk Diary, 10 December 1865.
6. Fisk Diary, 16 December 1865.

7. Fisk Diary, 2 January 1866.

8. Fisk Diary, 11 January 1866

9. Fisk Diary, 5 January—10 February 1866

10. John S. McNaught to T. W. Baldwin, 5 June 1872. Letters Sent. RG 393. V. 2. vol. 3. National Archives, Washington, D.C.

11. Circular, RG 393. V. 16. vol. 1:17-19. National Archives, Washington, D.C.

12. Circular, 10 May 1879. RG 393. V. 16. vol. 1:25. National Archives, Washington, D.C.

13. Charles E. McChesny to John Vander Horck, 28 May 1879. Letters Sent. RG 393. V. 7. Box 4. National Archives, Washington, D.C.

14. Post Medical History, November 1882. RG 94. vol. 3:192. National Archives, Washington, D.C. (Hereafter cited as Medical History.)

15. Medical History, July 1883. RG 94. vol. 3:216.

16. *Webster Reporter and Farmer*, 24 March 1887.

17. *Fort Sisseton*. Schmucker, Paul, Nohr & Associates. Mitchell, South Dakota. 1974:43.

18. *Dakota Daylight*, 7 August 1885.

19. Medical History, 4 July 1865. RG 94. vol. 1:2.

20. *Dakota Daylight*, 17 April 1885.

21. Medical History, December 1868. RG 94. vol. 1:103.

22. *Webster Reporter and Farmer*, 3 and 10 July 1884.

23. *Webster Reporter and Farmer*, 3 January 1889.

24. *Webster Reporter and Farmer*, 26 July 1888.

25. *Webster Reporter and Farmer*, 16 August 1888.

26. Order, 20 May 1876. RG 393. 2. V. 6. National Archives, Washington, D.C.

27. Circular, 23 February 1877. RG 393. V. 16. vol. 1. National Archives, Washington, D.C.

28. Circular 1. RG 393. V. 16. vol. 1. National Archives, Washington, D.C.

29. Letter Sent, 10 March 1876. RG 393. V. 2. vol. 6. National Archives, Washington, D.C.

30. *Regulations of the United States Army*, 1881:58.

31. *Regulations of the United States Army*, 1881:58.

32. Inspection Report, 5 November 1884. RG 393. V. 7. Box 5. National Archives, Washington, D.C.

33. Captain David Schooley to Adjutant General, Department of Dakota, 18 November 1884. Letters Sent. 9W2 37/27/A. National Archives, Washington, D.C.

34. George W. Doud diary. South Dakota Archives, Pierre, South Dakota.

35. Francis B. Heitman. *Historical Register and Dictionary of the United States Army*. 2 vols. Washington: GPO, 1903.

Chapter 10

Health Care

Hospital

Hospital and medical services began when Fort Wadsworth was established. The first Post Surgeon, Dr. Lamberton, Thirtieth Wisconsin Infantry, supervised the unloading of the ambulance wagon, which contained a hospital field tent and medical supplies. The large temporary tent was erected near the construction area of the new post. Assistant Surgeon Second Lieutenant Edwin O. Baker, Company I, Second Minnesota Cavalry, helped Lamberton. In October 1864, a new forty-foot by forty-foot squared-timber hospital was built in the northwest corner of the parade ground.

In 1868, a new one-and-a-half-story brick hospital was opened. The sixty-foot-long by thirty-two-foot-wide building was also located in the northwest corner of the parade ground. A sixty-foot front porch faced the parade ground. Entering from the south side, two four-bed wards were located on the right of a six-foot-wide center hall. A small cellar was accessible by a trap-door in the floor.

On the left side of the center hall was a small office, kitchen, dining room, wash room, and a fifteen-foot by fifteen-foot dispensary. The dispensary was used as the surgeon's pharmacy, clinic, and operating room. Medical books, medicines, and instruments were on hand in the dispensary. Wash basins, bath tub, and other facilities for cleanliness were located in the wash room. All of the plastered rooms were ten feet high and warmed by radiating stoves. Three fireplaces supplemented the wood-burning stoves. Kerosene oil lamps were used for lighting. The lathed and plastered attic contained storage space and one room for the hospital steward's quarters.

Water was supplied from an adjoining 100-barrel-capacity galvanized sheet-iron cistern. Sick patients used bed pans and chamber pots; ambulatory patients and staff used an outside sink or toilet. An 1870 Department of Dakota inspection report called the hospital "primitive and unfit for proper care of the sick during the winter."[1] Later that year, new roof shingles were added before winter.

In 1872, the attic above the ward was remodeled to provide six more patient beds. Following a department medical inspection that same year, the report stated, "On the whole the condition of the hospital is as satisfactory as could be expected, taking its radical defects of construction into account."[2]

A storm caused considerable damage to the hospital in 1873, including the breakage of 118 window panes. Repair included the remodeling of two small wards on the east side into one large twenty-four-foot by thirty-foot ward. New windows with double sashes were installed on three sides of the enlarged ward. A new Pendergrast stove was placed in the ward. A three-inch-square wooden tube, connecting the ward, dispensary, and kitchen, provided better air circulation. The change resulted in six-hundred cubic feet of air space for each patient in the new twelve-bed ward. The upstairs was changed to storage space and two sleeping rooms for hospital attendants.

In 1883, two cut-stone buttresses were placed on the outside of the weakened east wall to strengthen it. After eighteen years of use, the old hospital became worn and obsolete. Funds were approved by the War Department in 1886 for repairing and remodeling the 1868 hospital. Post Surgeon First Lieutenant John L. Philips said that they vacated the hospital during remodeling and that the hospital furnishings were stored in two nearby log houses. A cooking range was moved into another log house that was used for a kitchen. Two hospital tents were erected in front, one for the three hospital attendants and the other for a dispensary and office.[3]

The old sixty-foot by thirty-two-foot hospital was remodeled as follows: the east-side ward was lowered to one story; the west side was raised to two stories; and an addition was built on the north side. A new sixty-foot porch was built on the south side fronting the parade ground. The first floor of the newly remodeled hospital included an enlarged ward on the east side, office and dispensary on the west side, and a kitchen and washroom in the north side addition. Four rooms upstairs were used for various purposes.

Looking towards the east, Fort Sisseton Hospital, ca. 1930.

Courtesy Larry F. Ness

1868 Fort Sisseton hospital.

Courtesy National Archives

Restored Fort Sisseton hospital, south front. Built in 1868, remodeled in 1886.

Restored Fort Sisseton hospital, east side.

A small library was available for use by the patients. Using the hospital's share of the post fund, Post Surgeon James B. Ferguson in 1881 purchased a subscription to the *St. Paul Daily Press* for the library. The fund was also used to buy extra food from the commissary to enhance the hospital menu. Garden produce from the hospital garden was also used to supplement the menu.

Hospital Staff

Post Surgeon

Twenty-six post surgeons served at Fort Sisseton; sixteen were contracted civilian surgeons, and ten were commissioned army officers. (See Appendix D for list of army and citizen surgeons.) Contracted surgeons enjoyed the same post privileges as army surgeons, such as living in the officers' quarters. A post surgeon was expected to handle any kind of medical illness or emergency.

Should a surgeon face an unexpected medical problem, he depended upon his medical books for more information. There wasn't time for a four- or five-day horseback ride to consult with another post surgeon. There were forty-one medical books listed in the 1881 Army Regulations. Some medical books in Fort Sisseton's hospital library were *Gray's Anatomy, Vogel's Diseases of Children, Dunglison's Medical Dictionary, Thomas' Diseases of Women, Wood's Practice of Medicine, Gross' Surgery, Wood's Library of Standard Medical Authors*, and *Bermingham's Medical Library.*

A post surgeon's main duty was treating the sick. His day began with the 7:00 a.m. or 8:00 a.m. sick call for soldiers. Some soldiers were treated and sent back to work or to the barracks; others were admitted to the hospital. In addition, emergencies were handled throughout the day.

There were many other administrative duties pertaining to the health and sanitation of the post. Each week the surgeon inspected the mess hall, barracks, and food and water supply. Other tasks included keeping the medical records and submitting monthly and annual reports to the Department of Dakota. One post surgeon said that the medical records "were kept with rigid exactness." An examination of the post's medical history showed the following records were kept by the post surgeon:

1. Morning Record—listed all men on sick call and their illness
2. Hospital register
3. Statement of hospital post fund
4. Account of hospital purchases
5. Medical history of post
6. Prescription book
7. Liquor issued
8. Surgical operations
9. Deaths and burials
10. Meteorological register
11. Ration account of hospital and companies
12. Letter book
13. Inspection reports of mess, quarters, food and water
14. Hospital payroll
15. Post sanitary report.[4]

An 1880 inspection stated the "Medical Department is in excellent condition. One of the best in the army."[5]

The hospital was the surgeon's domain, and he ruled it with confidence and authority. At times the surgeon felt that his authority was equal to or beyond that of the commanding officer. The commanding officer, however, had the final authority and occasionally had to discipline a medical officer. One example of a surgeon's indiscretion occurred in the squared-timber hospital in 1867. Commanding Officer S. B. Hayman wrote Post Surgeon William P. Lambert for an explanation: "It has been brought to my attention that while under the influence of intoxicating liquor you exposed yourself to the ridicule of the enlisted men by sleeping during the night on one of the beds in the ward of the hospital and at a late hour disturbing the rest of the sick by remarks of a frivolous nature."[6] Hayman wanted Lambert's civilian physician contract annulled, but all differences were resolved.[7]

Commanding Officer J. C. Bates had both praise and criticism for Surgeon B. Knickerbocker in 1870: "He is one of the most attentive and efficient medical officers that I have met in the service, with the exception of his quarrelsome and fault finding disposition."[8]

In the summer of 1873, Commanding Officer Robert E. A. Crofton had a continuous battle with Post Surgeon W. E. Turner. In June, Turner was advised, "On yesterday's morning report you returned Private Smith of Company D to duty and directed he be excused from inspection. I remind you only the post commander can excuse a soldier from inspection. This is the second time and I do not wish to be compelled to call your attention to it a third time."[9] In July, Turner was asked to explain why one of the two hospital attendants was absent from drill. Turner was reprimanded again in August for excusing the hospital cook from a morning inspection.[10]

Other Hospital Helpers

The commanding officer appointed a soldier or non-commissioned officer as hospital steward. Ten stewards worked in the Fort Sisseton hospital during its twenty-five years. (See Appendix D for list of hospital stewards.) A steward was an army hospital employee. Steward Augustus Gecks served seven years in this position. Quarters were provided in the upstairs of the hospital for the steward. The surgeon trained him to help with hospital duties, perform administrative tasks, and manage the employees of the hospital. For example, in 1867 the post provided a company of men to escort a herd of beef cattle to Fort Ransom. The post surgeon was unable to go along so he authorized Hospital Steward D. A. Graven to accompany the escort with an ambulance.

One important duty of a steward was to dispense the medicine. In the absence of a steward in 1882, Dr. James B. Furgeson dispensed all drugs and medicines because he felt it was unwise to trust that important duty to one of the untrained enlisted men. Despite the trustworthy status of stewards, they too had problems. One steward appeared at inspection in improper uniform, to the dismay of Surgeon Charles E. McChesny. Steward Frederick H. Russell in 1885 was placed under house arrest in the hospital for an unauthorized leave of absence.

Other hospital staff included a nurse, cook, and matron. Often enlisted men filled these staff positions. In 1883, Private Charles Seeshally was the cook; Privates Richard Morgan and Daniel Farrant were nurses. In 1872, Dr. C. E. Munn appointed a Dakota woman to serve as a hospital matron. The staff helped patients, cooked food, cleaned the hospital, and maintained the hospital garden.

Hospital Supplies

Fort Sisseton, like other remote army posts, maintained a year's medical supplies in its hospital. Medical supplies, according to army regulations, consisted of medicines, instruments, books, bedding, hospital clothing, furniture, equipment, and hospital stores. Ordering, handling, and accounting for medical supplies was the responsibility of the surgeon, helped by the steward. An inspection of the hospital in 1870 showed an abundant supply of drugs, stores, and instruments on hand. In 1872, the hospital received a new four-wheel ambulance. Form 18, Requisition for Medical Supplies, in the 1881 army regulations, listed 393 items that could be ordered.

The hospital ward contained iron bedsteads with mattresses. Each bed had sheets, blankets, and a pillow. Other equipment for the ward included bed screens, mosquito bars, bedside tables, chairs, trays, wash basins, and bed pans. Extra clothing, in wall cupboards, consisted of drawers, gowns, shirts, socks, and slippers.

Some of the thirty-two instruments that could be ordered for the Fort Sisseton hospital were steam atomizer, irrigator, spray apparatus, scissors, stethoscope, stomach pump and tube, syringe, thermometer, urinometer, and tourniquet. Also available was a field case, pocket case, obstetrical case, and tooth-extracting case. The field case contained a variety of instruments, including a surgeon's saw, amputating knife, scalpel, and forceps. Bandages, cotton

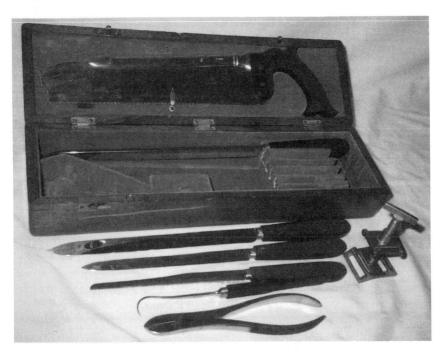

Surgeon's field case.

Courtesy Fort Lowell Museum, Tucson, Arizona

wadding, unbleached muslin, needles, plaster of Paris, binder
boards, splints, sponges, tape, and towels were available.[11] A skeleton was stored in a cabinet at the post hospital.

The 1881 Army Regulations listed 114 different medicines available for use at an army hospital. Most of the medicines were packaged in bottles, a few in tins and boxes. Included in the surgeon's
dispensary was a wedgewood mortar and pestle for compounding
drugs and medicines. Some of the medicines available to the hospital, according to army regulations, were carbolic acid, in one lb. bottle, for disinfecting; alcohol in thirty-two oz. bottle; camphor, in eight
oz. bottle, sedative; chloroform, in eight oz. bottle, anaesthesia; cod
liver oil, in pint bottle; powdered colocynth, in eight oz. bottle,
cathartic; tincture of digitalis, in two oz. bottle, cardiac stimulant
and diuretic; ether, in one lb. tin, anaesthesia; magnesia, antacid, lax-
ative; mild chloride of mercury (calomel), in two oz. bottle, cathartic
or purge; tincture of opium (laudanum), in eight oz. bottle, narcotic

for pain; zinc oxide, in one oz. bottle, ointment; whiskey, in thirty-two oz. bottle; and brandy in thirty-two oz. bottle.[12]

Post Surgeon C. Macauley in 1885 said, "The medical supplies at this post hospital are sufficient to meet any demand that may be made upon them.[13]

Sickness, Illness, and Injuries

It was a difficult challenge for the post surgeon during the post's first four months. There were seventeen soldiers ill in the field tent hospital in August 1864 and six in September. Private H. S. Benedict died from fever 24 September. Following the opening of the squared-timber hospital, there were twenty-five men sick in November and twenty-four in December. During those months, Lieutenant Robert Wood and six men died from typhoid fever. One man died of scurvy and two from other causes.[14]

Surgeon B. Knickerbocker listed the following hospital cases in November 1868: inflammatory, eleven; boils and ulcers, five; duty wounds, twelve; diarrhea, three; nervousness, three; constipation, one; and other, four. During 1870, there was an average of nineteen soldiers treated each month; this figure rose to twenty-six in 1873.[15]

A consolidated sick report for Fort Sisseton's brick hospital between 1870 and 1874 showed that there were a total of 669 sick patients in the hospital, 564 with diseases and 105 with accidents or injuries. The principal diseases were catarrh and bronchitis, 172; diarrhea and dysentery, sixty-five; rheumatism, thirty-nine; and fever, thirty-six. There were five cases of syphilis and five of gonorrhea. The report's 105 accident cases listed two gunshot wounds, and 103 wounds from accidents and injuries. Four men died during the period, one of them from drowning. There was an average of five officers and 102 enlisted men stationed at the post during those four years.[16]

Throughout all the army in 1885, forty percent of the soldiers reporting at sick call were committed to the hospital for treatment. Sixty percent were treated and returned to duty or to their quarters to convalesce.[17] The average hospital stay at Fort Sisseton's hospital was ten to twelve days. In 1886, 122 men were committed to the post hospital, an average of ten each month.[18]

Of the forty-four persons who died while living at Fort Sisseton, the cause of death was listed for thirty-six: fever, two; typhoid fever, nine; scurvy, one; drowned, two; frozen, three; consumption, four;

bronchitis, two; pneumonia, two; gunshot wound, two; gastrocide, one; inflammation of brain, one; spinal meningitis, one; debility, three; heat, one; intoxication, one; and suicide, one.[19]

The hospital also provided care for non-military men, women, and children connected with the post.

Treatment

Post soldiers were exposed to many of the diseases and injuries known today. Treatment, however, was provided according to the medical knowledge of the time by the post surgeon. A sick soldier reported to the hospital at sick call, usually at 7:00 a.m. or 8:00 a.m., depending upon the season. A soldier was admitted immediately if he became ill or injured while on duty. After notation in the hospital register of patients, the soldier waited to see the doctor until called by the hospital steward. About sixty percent of the time, the surgeon provided treatment in the dispensary and sent the soldier back to duty or to his barracks to convalesce. Dispensary treatment included the oral administration of medicine for pain, colds, fever, dysentery, constipation, etc. Ointments were applied for skin abrasions, or insect bites. About forty percent of the time, the disease, illness, or injury was serious enough to require hospitalization.

An early report of field medical treatment was made by Dr. J. W. Daniels with the Minnesota Second Cavalry. During the 1864 Sully campaign, he used sulphate of quinine to treat mountain fever or dysentery. It was given in doses of fifteen to thirty grains in a twenty-four-hour period. Beef tea was given at the same time. Post Surgeon Charles E. McChesny provided a simple remedy in March of 1879 when more men than usual were catching colds. He ordered the men to wear overcoats when it was cold outdoors.

An amputation performed by Surgeon James B. Ferguson illustrates that complicated surgery was performed at the post. Hospital Steward Augustus Gecks got caught in a 20 March 1882 snow storm on his way to Webster. The next day soldiers found him frozen but alive and brought him to the Fort Sisseton hospital. After a week of treatment, Dr. Ferguson decided that both lower limbs would have to be amputated. Dr. Ferguson described the operation:

> Yesterday I amputated both lower limbs of Steward Gecks in their middle third by the bilateral flap operation. Dr. Graves of

Webster administered the anesthesia and Dr. Harris of Webster assisted me in the operation. Four ligates were required in each stump. There was no hemorrhaging except by nervous oozing. The carbolic spray was used throughout the operation by means of a spray apparatus. Considering the low condition of the patient, both physically and mentally, he stood the operation as well as could be expected.[20]

A month later, after Geck's lower limbs were healed, Dr. Ferguson amputated his left hand two inches above the wrist. In June, Gecks was admitted to the Soldier's Home in Washington, D.C., and later he was discharged from the service. In 1884, there were 179 surgical operations throughout the army. Fifty-six (thirty-one percent) of those operations were amputations of arms, legs, feet, toes, or fingers. Of 236 cases of frostbite that year, nine resulted in amputation of the affected parts. Artificial limbs were provided by the army and replaced once every five years.

Dr. James B. Ferguson in November 1882 asked Surgeon O. W. Archibald of Fort Abraham Lincoln to come to Fort Sisseton and operate on his hemorrhoids. Archibald described the operation in the post's medical history:

> Surgeon James B. Ferguson today underwent an operation for the radical cure of internal hemorrhoids from which he had long been a severe sufferer. Five tumors, nearly the size of walnuts were ligated. Surgeon O. W. Archibald, Fort Abraham Lincoln, performed the operation. Anesthesia was not induced but chloroform was inhaled to deaden pain.[21]

Apparently recovered, Surgeon Ferguson treated a scarlet fever case in May 1883. Private Benjamin F. Morrow, Company F, Seventeenth Infantry, was admitted and diagnosed as having scarlet fever, a contagious disease. Ferguson applied the following treatment: "Firstly, cathartic; dicephoretic during fever, highest temperature 104. Very free use of gargle and vapor spray (iron and chloride potassa), a few gentle laxatives. Diet: light and nourishing milk, eggs and broth."[22] No other cases resulted.

As listed in the Fort Sisseton cemetery records, two soldiers died of accidental gun-shot wounds. After 1876, Fort Sisseton soldiers were armed with new .45 caliber Springfield rifles. A .45 caliber

Springfield rifle cartridge contained seventy grains of black powder and a 405-grain bullet. When fired, the bullet carried enough velocity to penetrate eight inches into a pine tree at 500 yards.

An accidental gun shot wound in July 1883 happened to Private James Conner, Company F, Seventeenth Infantry. Surgeon Victor Biart described the emergency: "Private Conner while unloading cartridges, accidentally exploded one, the ball passing through his left hand and necessitating the amputation of two fingers."[23]

Non-warfare gun-shot wounds were common in the army. In 1884 there were 142 cases of shot wounds in the United States Army. One hundred and seven men were treated and returned to duty, twenty-seven were discharged, and eight died. The causes of the shot wounds were as follows: bird shot, thirteen; explosion of cartridge, thirty-one; pistol ball, thirty; rifle ball, forty-nine; and other, twenty. The wounds affected all parts of the body: scalp, face, chest, abdomen, genitals, back, hands, legs, and toes.[24]

Post Surgeon First Lieutenant C. Macauley in February 1885 noted that fourteen soldiers had severe pain in the bowels, rendering them unfit for duty. After review, Macauley decided the bowel pain was caused by unfit cistern water. He recommended that melted ice be used year around for cooking and drinking, if possible.

The surgeon's medical duties also included delivering babies. Captain C.E.Munn, between 1870 and 1872, delivered a boy to Private and Mrs. Reef; a girl to Private and Mrs. George Van Horn; a son to Private and Mrs. Thomas Brown; and three boys to three privates and their spouses. He also delivered a boy to Captain and Mrs. John S. McNaught. The medical history shows that Post Surgeon C. C. Miller delivered an illegitimate baby in September 1878.

Post civilians were also admitted to the hospital. In July 1872, Martha Nash, who worked for one of the officers, was admitted for treatment and care. Post Surgeon C. E. Munn was so concerned about her condition that he wrote to her mother in Morris, Minnesota: "Your daughter is quite sick in the hospital and it was thought best that you should be with her, so commanding officer is sending a spring wagon down to bring you here."[25]

Although the post surgeon had a tooth-extracting case in his office, he preferred that the hospital steward do that work. In 1882, however, Commanding Officer C.E. Bennett asked Dr. T. S. Calkins, a Minneapolis dentist, to temporarily assist at the post. He asked the dentist to do some dental work at both Webster and the post.

Bennett offered a team and wagon to haul Dr. Calkins and his dental chair from Webster to the post.

Sometimes the surgeon's duties included care of Indians on the nearby Lake Traverse Reservation. In 1869, the celebrated Indian Chief John Otherday was admitted to the Fort Sisseton hospital for chronic bronchitis. After nine days of care, he died of hemorrhage. Although there was a doctor at the nearby Lake Traverse Reservation, the Fort Sisseton surgeon was called to help a few times. In 1881, the commanding officer ordered Surgeon James Ferguson to go to the Sisseton Agency and amputate a man's arm. Apparently the patient did not like the agency doctor. Later that year, the Sisseton Agency Indian Agent asked Dr. Ferguson to help again because the agency doctor was on leave. The agent said, "I have another serious case. Smiley Shepherd was thrown from a horse, fracturing his thigh. Twenty-two hours later, symptoms of violent concussion of the brain supervened. Gabriel Renville, his father-in-law wishes you to see him. Can you come forthwith?"[26] Commanding Officer C. E. Bennett agreed and sent Ferguson to treat Shepherd.

Sanitary Condition

Each month, sometimes weekly, the post surgeon inspected the overall sanitary condition of the post. His food and water inspection included food storage, company kitchens and mess halls, bakery, ice house, and cisterns. He also inspected for cleanliness in the hospital, guardhouse, barracks, married soldiers' and officers' quarters, sinks, and bathhouse. Also on his inspection list were the mule barn, cattle corral, and fortification ditch. Once a year a Department of Dakota medical officer made a sanitary inspection of the post.

The post's commanding officer took a leading role to assure proper sanitary conditions. Captain C. E. Bennett ordered the command in April 1879 to do the following: "Garbage, slops, dirt from policing, horse manure and filth of every kind will be hauled by the police party, under supervision of the officer of the day, to a place designated about three-fourths mile from the post and unloaded. It is positively prohibited to unload it in any other place. Slops will be collected in barrels, ashes in barrels and hauled off daily. It is positively prohibited to throw slops, soap suds or any kind of dirt in the fortification ditch."[27] Commanding Officer Bennett in 1884 not only repeated his order but said it would be enforced.

Endnotes

1. Post Medical History, RG 94. vol. 1:173. National Archives, Washington, D.C. (Hereafter cited as Medical History.)

2. Medical History, RG 94. vol. 1:287.

3. Medical History, RG 94. vol. 3:311.

4. Medical History, RG 94. vol. 1:117.

5. C. E. Bennett to James B. Ferguson, 2 September 1880. Letters Sent. RG393. V. 19. Box 8. National Archives, Washington, D.C.

6. S. B. Hayman to W. Lambert, 23 July 1867. Letters Sent. RG 393. V. 2. vol.1. National Archives, Washington, D.C.

7. S. B. Hayman to Department of Dakota, 27 July 1867. Letters Sent. RG 393. V. 2. vol. 1. National Archives, Washington, D.C.

8. J. C. Bates to Department of Dakota, 16 February 1870. Letters Sent. RG 393. V. 3. vol. 3. National Archives, Washington, D.C.

9. Robert E. A. Crofton to W. E. Turner, 2 June 1873. Letters Sent. RG 393. V. 2. vol. 4. National Archives, Washington, D.C.

10. Robert E. A. Crofton to W. E. Turner, 10 August 1873. Letters Sent. RG 393. V. 2. vol. 4. National Archives, Washington, D.C.

11. *Regulations of the United States Army*, 1881:1010. (Hereafter cited as *Regulations*.)

12. *Regulations*, 1881:1010

13. Post Surgeon Report, 24 February 1885. RG393. V. 7. Box 5. National Archives, Washington, D.C.

14. Post Returns of Fort Sisseton, August—December, 1864. National Archives, Washington, D.C. On microfilm roll 1179, South Dakota Archives, Pierre, South Dakota.

15. Medical History, RC 94. vol. 1:100.

16. John S. Billings. "Report on the Hygiene of the United States Army." Circular 8, Surgeon's General Office, 1 May 1875. Washington: GPO.

17. *Report of the Secretary of War*, 1885. vol. 1:712.

18. Medical History, RG 94. vol. 3:320.

19. *Fort Sisseton.* Cemetery Record. Schumucker, Paul, Nohr & Associates. Mitchell, South Dakota:1974:43.

20. Medical History, RG 94. vol. 3:174.

21. Medical History, RG 94. vol. 3:190.

22. Medical History, RG 94. vol. 3:210.

23. Medical History, RG 94. vol. 3:216.

24. *Report of the Secretary of War*, 1885. vol. 1:726.

25. C. E. Munn to Mrs. Nash, 31 July 1872. Letters Sent. RG 393. V. 2. vol. 3. National Archives, Washington, D.C.

26. Sisseton Agency Agent to James B. Ferguson, 3 May 1881. Letters Received. RG 393. V. 7. Box 4. National Archives, Washington, D.C.

27. Medical History, RG 94. vol. 3: 17.

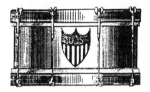

Chapter 11
Communications

United States Mail

United States mail was delivered to the post even while it was under construction. Mail routes to the post were generally from the nearest railhead. One early delivery was on 15 October 1864 when Brackett's wagon train brought mail and supplies from Fort Ridgely, Minnesota. The first scheduled mail service was from Fort Snelling via Fort Abercrombie, seventy-six miles northeast. Major Robert H. Rose used four scouts to deliver and pick up mail at Fort Abercrombie. In October, Rose built a temporary building at Lightning's Nest, about half way between the forts, to provide rest and overnight shelter for the scouts and their horses. In November, the Department of Dakota ordered Major Rose to build a small garrison midway between Abercrombie and Wadsworth. The garrison, for one officer and thirty men, consisted of several buildings and a stockade. The purpose of the garrison was for "the convenience of communications during the winter." It took four days to carry the mail from Fort Wadsworth to Fort Abercrombie.

Fort Abercrombie mail was then taken to Fargo and on to St. Paul. In August 1865, four men carried the mail between Forts Ridgely and Wadsworth. The first post office was opened in Fort Wadsworth 14 September 1865, with Jasper M. Searls as postmaster.

In 1866 mail arrived from both Forts Abercrombie and Ridgely, according to Sergeant Andrew Fisk:

> 3 January—B. Kline and R. MacConnell have taken the mail to Abercrombie once a week. It is about five weeks since we got a mail from Ridgely and two weeks since we got one from

Abercrombie. We are mighty anxious to get a mail once more. I tell you, nothing will make soldiers homesick so quick as not receiving letters from families or friends.

7 January—Mail from Ridgely. I only got one letter from Jack Wilner dated 2 December 1865.

12 January—an awful stormy day. Mail left for Fort Abercrombie. I pity the poor driver. Don't believe he can get more than a few miles and will have to turn back.

16 January—Bitter cold. A sort of mail got in from Abercrombie. Not a single letter for this company.[1]

Mail delivery improved in 1867. In April the post received forty official letters. One corporal and seven privates were on duty carrying mail between Wadsworth and Abercrombie. Mail service that year was expanded to Fort Rice, near the Missouri River, twenty miles south of Bismarck. Major S. B. Hayman employed three Indian scouts to take the mail west to "wooded coolies" at Coteau du Missouri. Here mail pouches were exchanged with mail carriers from Fort Rice. Mail arrived each Thursday from the Fort Rice route.

A weekly stage in 1870 hauled mail from the post to Sauk Centre, where it was placed on a train for St. Paul. That total trip took five days, much longer in poor weather. Fort Sisseton's post office closed in mid 1873 because the post commander couldn't find a postmaster. Two Indian scouts carried the mail twenty-eight miles to the Sisseton Agency, the nearest post office. A halfway house was established at Buffalo Lake. Sakatanshica was the first station keeper, followed by Thomas Katate. Katate, a former Indian scout at the post, was paid $5.00 a month and a daily ration for providing overnight lodging and stabling for the two mail carriers and their horses.

In 1875 the post office reopened, with Daniel P. Shilton as postmaster. On Sundays and Thursdays during 1877, mail and telegrams left the post by stage for Morris, Minnesota. Telegrams were then sent from the Morris telegraph station. When the Chicago, Milwaukee and Saint Paul Railway reached Webster in 1881, the post began sending their mail to that city. One eastbound and one westbound train left Webster daily. It took about five hours for the two-horse light wagon to make the twenty-two-mile trip to Webster. The mail wagon, with room for two passengers, left the post daily. During winter a sleigh with room for one passenger was used. George Ringer in 1884 ran a daily stage between Webster, Fort Sisseton, and

Britton, hauling mail and passengers. Charley Jones carried the mail between Britton and Fort Sisseton.

Carrying the mail between Webster and the post was not without difficulty, especially during winter. One carrier, Page Howe, froze to death during a snow storm in March 1882. His passenger, Hospital Steward Augustus Gecks, was found badly frozen, resulting in the necessity to amputate his lower limbs and left arm. Charles Davis had a narrow escape in the winter of 1888, according to the *Webster Reporter and Farmer:*

> The driver of the mail stage, Charles Davis, was caught [in a snow storm] at four-mile hill, this side of the fort. At once he got out, unhitched his team from the sleigh, took off their harness and turned them loose. He then turned his sleigh upside down in the snow and wrapping the blankets and buffalo robes around him, quietly laid himself down to weather the storm, with the howling, shrieking winds and eddying snow holding high carnival around him. During the night, wolves came to the sleigh and commenced munching and fighting over a quarter of beef in the sleigh, he was taking to the fort. Think what a trial it must have been to a man's nerves to hear these beasts fighting and snarling over the beef not three feet away from him. When the storm let up on Friday, he crawled out and taking the mail sack on his shoulder struck out for the fort where he arrived safe and sound about noon. The boys at the post, as evidence of his bravery...presented him with a fur cap and a pair of gloves.[2]

Telephone and Telegraph

In 1880 there were 1,650 miles of telegraph wire in the Department of Dakota. Money was requested for two more sections, one between Jamestown, North Dakota, and Fort Totten and the other between Morris, Minnesota, and Fort Sisseton. The request for money was denied. However, Fort Sisseton's Commanding Officer Clarence E. Bennett convinced the Department of Dakota that it would be inexpensive to build a telephone and telegraph line connecting Fort Sisseton and the Webster telegraph station. Captain Bennett had obtained prior approval from Chief Gabriel Renville to cut oak trees on the Lake Traverse Reservation. Soldiers, earning extra duty pay, would be used to cut the trees and erect the line.

Captain Bennett received authorization 12 July 1881 to build the telephone and telegraph line. Indian Scout Akicitana was sent to the reservation to mark trees for cutting. While the route was being surveyed and marked, thirteen soldiers began cutting five-inch diameter oak poles. Some men from the Lake Traverse Reservation were employed to help the soldiers. Storms of mosquitos and grayish brown flies were an annoyance to both men and mules. Some of the men became sick with poison oak and poison ivy. One private injured the top of his foot with an ax.

After half the poles were cut, another crew of soldiers began erecting the poles. Two four-mule teams were used to haul the poles to the surveyed route. Holes were dug with twenty-four long-handled shovels. A pole was erected every 165 feet, thirty-two to the mile. Dirt was stacked in a mound around the pole, providing fire protection. A lighting rod was placed on every fifth pole. A mile marker number was painted in black on the east side of every thirty-second pole to help provide direction in a storm. After 704 poles were erected, the men began stringing No. 14 steel wire to the insulators that were mounted to the poles with brackets. They finished 7 November during a snow storm. Thirty battery cells were installed in connection with the line.

Although the telephone and telegraph were on the same wire, each could be operated separately by use of a switch. It was a joint-use line by the military and by Northwestern Telephone Exchange Company. Telegraph instruments and telephone equipment were installed in the Western Union office and railroad telegraph office in Webster. Similar equipment was placed in the commanding officer's house and the adjutant's office at the post.

Two Le Clanche batteries, a Blake transmitter, and a Gilliland telephone were installed at each end of the line. The first telephone call was made from Webster to the post on 28 December 1881. A magneto call bell rang in Captain Bennett's office, and he answered the phone. Conversation included a warning that a blizzard was headed toward the fort. Later, Bennett sent a telegram to the Department of Dakota, advising them that the military telegraph line was also open for business. Captain Bennett said, "It was one of the best constructed lines in the United States."[3]

In March 1882, C. E. Bennett was ordered by the Department of Dakota to discontinue the use of the telephone despite the fact that it worked well. A legal problem prevented the Signal Service from operating a military telegraph on the same line with a private telephone company. The telephone equipment was returned to the Northwestern Telephone Exchange Company.

Maintenance of the telegraph line was a continuous problem. In 1882, lightning struck a pole about ten miles south of the post. It split the pole, burned the line, and broke both the insulator and bracket. Men were sent out to repair the damage. Following a break in the line in 1883, Bennett advised the Department of Dakota:

> The telegraph line has been repaired and I now have a sergeant and five privates watching the telegraph poles along the entire line, to keep the prairie fires from burning them down. I have sent out the mowing machines and scythes to mow the grass around the telegraph poles where it grew tall. Mounds that were covered with weeds are now covered with fresh dirt. Some of the farmers along this line are nailing barbed wire fencing to the poles making it dangerous for the repairman, if he should slip.[4]

In January 1883, Private John C. Rourke, Company F, Seventeenth Infantry filled in as telegrapher. Private C.J. Raymond, United States Signal Service, became the new telegrapher in July 1883. Some of the official telegrams sent from the Department of Dakota to the post in 1884 were the following:

> 9 July—Lieutenant Reed will arrive at Fort Sisseton 11 July;
> 1 August—Reduce number of civilians by discharging two teamsters today;
> 22 August—Send detachment to Browns Valley for three mules expected to reach there 30 August from Fort Custer;
> 6 October—Send spring wagon and escort to Browns Valley on 8 October to meet the department inspector.[5]

Another attempt was made to use telephones between the post and Webster in 1885 by stringing a second line on the poles. It did not produce the desired result and was disbanded the same year. Some of the military telegrams sent in 1888 included five to the Department of Dakota, one each to the Presidio, Chief Signal Officer in Washington, Fort Snelling, and the sheriff of Marshall County. The telegraph line continued in operation until the post closed.

Endnotes

1. Andrew Fisk Diary, January 1866. Roll 81. Minnesota Historical Society, St. Paul, Minnesota.
2. *Webster Reporter and Farmer,* 19 January 1888.
3. C. E. Bennett to Department of Dakota, 30 November 1881. Letters Sent. RG 393. V. 2. vol. 10. National Archives, Washington, D.C.
4. C. E. Bennett to Department of Dakota, 15 September 1883. Letters Sent. RG 393. 2. vol. 12:131-141. National Archives, Washington, D.C.
5. Telegrams Sent, 1884. RG 393. V. 9. National Archives, Washington, D.C.

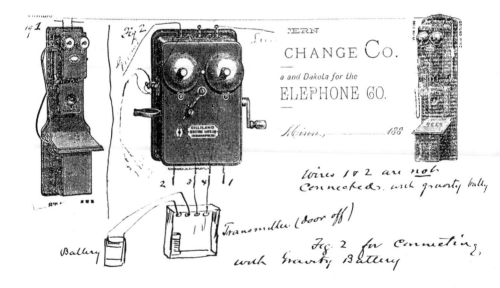

Installation notes and drawing of first telephone at Fort Sisseton, 1880.

Courtesy National Archives

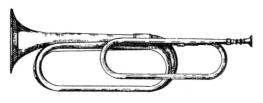

Chapter 12
Military Disbandment

Settlers Filling Area

In 1880 homesteaders began settling in northeastern South Dakota. The Federal Census that year listed ninety-seven people in Day County. At the time, Day County consisted of both Day and Marshall counties. A good part of Roberts County to the east remained closed to settlers because it consisted of the Lake Traverse Reservation. The area received a big boost in 1881 when the Chicago, Milwaukee and St. Paul Railway opened a line of track between Aberdeen and Milbank. What were stations along the route quickly became the towns of Andover, Bristol, Webster, and Waubay. A branch line was opened between Milbank and Wilmot the same year. All of this activity resulted in an influx of more homesteaders.

At the time, the Sioux were peaceful and busy on the Lake Traverse Reservation. Nevertheless, settlers felt more secure, knowing that a military post was nearby. Some settlers purchased supplies at the fort before their town was organized. In early 1882, some tension developed between the settlers and the Sisseton-Wahpeton on the Lake Traverse Reservation. That year the annuities, authorized by the 1867 Treaty, had ended. Over 200 Sioux protested by camping near Fort Sisseton. Other Sioux from the Devils Lake Reservation and Missouri River reservations began wandering into the area. Fearing trouble, Commanding General Alfred H. Terry of the Department of Dakota ordered Companies A and C, Seventh Cavalry, from Fort Meade to report to Fort Sisseton. The two cavalry companies arrived 23 May, and served as a back up to the post's two infantry companies, if needed. After this display of military force, the Sioux returned to their reservations. After peace was restored to the area, the Seventh Cavalry left the post 5 August for Fort Meade.

Settlers continued pouring into the area. In 1884 Britton was formed. Rumors circulated that Fort Sisseton would soon be closed. In fact, several area residents wrote letters of protest to United States Senator Richard Pettigrew. The senator forwarded the letters to Secretary of War Robert Todd Lincoln.

In May 1885, the people of Day County voted to split the county into Day and Marshall counties. One newspaper in late 1885 estimated the population at 2,130 in Marshall County and 5,000 in Day County. That fall the government resurveyed the nine-mile-wide by fifteen-mile-long Fort Sisseton Military Reservation, perhaps as a boundary reminder for the settlers. Post disbandment rumors continued. George Hickman in 1886 said, "The soldiers have no arduous duty to perform, and there is no apparent reason why the fort should not be abandoned and the reservation thrown open for settlement."[1]

Commanding Officer Frederick Mears advised the Department of Dakota in September 1887: "The surrounding country is about settled up to the lines of the military reservation. Time is now ripe to abandon the post."[2] An example of Webster's growth was reported by the editor of the *Webster Reporter and Farmer.* He counted 161 teams on Webster's streets one November afternoon in 1887. Prices received for farmer's products that day were as follows: wheat, $.55 a bushel; oats, $.20 a bushel; barley, $.40 a bushel; butter, $.15 a pound; eggs, $.10 a dozen; and $.25 for twenty pounds of potatoes.

Disbandment fever continued to grow in the area, especially among land seekers. Disbandment of the Fort Sisseton military reservation in Marshall County meant that 82,112 acres or 513 quarters of land would be available for homesteading. Britton's newspaper, *The Sentinel,* recognized the potential for Britton: "When the military reservation is thrown open to settlement, Marshall County will have a boom, and Britton will receive its full share of the general prosperity."[3]

Soldiers Leave Fort Sisseton

On 16 March 1889, the Secretary of War advised the Department of Dakota that Fort Sisseton would be discontinued 1 June 1889. Commanding General B. G. Ruger then issued Special Order 35, dated 8 April 1889, and sent it to the post. The order and follow-up instructions contained the following directions for discontinuing the post:

*Captain Joseph Hale, Second Lieutenant William C. Neary, and twenty-six men of Company G, Third Infantry will go by rail to Fort Snelling on 1 June;

*Serviceable property will be transferred to Fort Snelling;

*Unserviceable property, not worth the cost of transportation, including wood, coal, charcoal, grain, hay, and subsistence stores will be disposed of at the post either by sale or public auction;

*No more supplies will be shipped to the post;

*All files and records will be boxed and sent to the Department of Dakota;

*Quartermaster officer, First Lieutenant Frank B. McCoy and ten men will remain until the buildings and military reservation are transferred to an agent of the Department of Interior.[4]

Post Commander Hale then inventoried the large supplies of serviceable and non-serviceable property. Copies of the inventories were sent to the Department of Dakota for a final decision as to the status of the property. Acting on orders, Captain Hale began disposing of serviceable and non-serviceable property. After public notice, he sold 8,000 bushels of potatoes locally. He then shipped 145 wood telegraph poles and two boxes of telegraph supplies to Fort Abraham Lincoln. Also shipped were 38,000 shingles to Fort Sully, and fifty wood telegraph poles and fifty-four coils of telegraph wire to Fort Snelling.

The next task was to box all the post records for shipment. Some of the leather-bound books placed in boxes were post letters and index of letters sent, post telegrams and index of telegrams sent, post medical history, post orders, post returns, quartermaster and ordnance records, court-martial records, and post fund records. Twenty-five years of letters and telegrams received were also boxed. All records were hauled to the depot at Britton to await shipment to Fort Snelling. Eventually these records were sent to the War Department in Washington and later transferred to the National Archives. (The author reviewed all these original Fort Sisseton records in the National Archives, from which was gleaned most of the military information for this book.)

On 12 April 1889, Post Surgeon David S. Snively received medical supplies for one year, shipped before it was known that the post would be discontinued. The United States Surgeon General ordered Dr. Snively to ship the medical supplies back to the Medical Purveying Depot at St. Louis, Missouri. He was also ordered to include in the same shipment the post's medical books, instruments, and meteorological instruments. Snively also received orders to send all medicines, hospital stores, *Wood's Library of Standard Medical Authors* and *Bermingham's Medical Library* to Fort Snelling. The "Skeleton in Cabinet" was shipped to the post surgeon at Fort Maginnis, Montana Territory.[5]

On 10 May, the post received five new sets of army regulations from the War Department. The regulations were repackaged and hauled with other property to the railroad depot at Britton. A week later, Captain Hale was informed that the "railroad company platform at Britton was covered with government stores, unprotected from weather or loss by theft." Hale immediately sent a sergeant and a soldier to secure and guard the property at the station. By 22 May, all the serviceable property on the platform, including post records and medical supplies, was loaded into railroad cars and shipped to destinations.[6]

With the serviceable property shipped, Captain Hale began steps to dispose of the unserviceable property. He notified area newspapers to run advertisements listing a public auction at Fort Sisseton on 6 June 1889. Then Captain Hale, Lieutenant Neary, and twenty-six soldiers left the post 30 May for Britton. Their departure from Britton 1 June is described by the *Sentinel:* "The soldiers took the train here for Fort Snelling. It took an extra passenger coach and baggage car to accommodate them. Quite a number of our people were at the depot to see them off. These are perhaps the last United States soldiers that Britton will see for a long time, as the ten who are still at the fort will leave there via Webster."[7]

The public auction held 6 June was directed by Quartermaster Officer First Lieutenant Frank B. McCoy and assisted by ten soldiers. Surviving records, although incomplete, show some of the items that were sold at auction: 31,000 pounds coal; 4,000 feet pine boards; 1,128 feet oak lumber; 8,000 lathes; 4,500 brick made at the post; eight barrels lime; 229 pounds iron; 440 pounds plaster of Paris; thirteen gallons turpentine; six gallons harness oil; 230 gallons paint; 11,668 pounds oats; 376 pounds bran; and thirty-seven tons hay.

Obsolete medical instruments and old editions of medical books were also auctioned. A street sprinkler was purchased by the city of Webster. A table was purchased by Soren C. and Amelia Sorenson that is now in the home of their great grandson Mr. and Mrs. Russell Nickelson. One source reports that it was a large sale and that settlers from both Day and Marshall counties made purchases at "bargain-counter prices."

The Department of Interior on 10 May designated E. R. Ruggles, Webster, as their agent to receive the transfer of the Fort Sisseton military reservation. Special Order 53 of the Department of Dakota, dated 21 May 1889, outlined the transfer procedure.[8] On 9 June, after all property had been sold or shipped, First Lieutenant Frank B. McCoy obtained a receipt from E. R. Ruggles for all post buildings, as to number, character, and condition, and for the military reservation.

After an inspection of the buildings by E. R. Ruggles, the transfer of the post took place in the adjutant's office on Friday, 9 June 1889. The receipt signed by Ruggles showed that twenty-two brick, stone, frame, and log buildings were transferred to the Department of Interior. Also included were the boardwalks on four sides of the parade ground.

The receipt also listed the military reservation, which consisted of 128.3 square miles, or 513 quarters of land. The legal description, according to the 1885 resurvey, was as follows:

> Beginning at a point two miles and 2,643.4 feet north, and six miles east of the old flagstaff at Fort Sisseton, which point is on the western boundary of the Indian reservation, and marked with an iron post, and running thence south seven miles and 2,643.4 feet; thence west nine miles; thence north fifteen miles; thence east seven miles and 1,086 feet to the western boundary of the Indian reservation; thence southeast at an angle of 102 degrees 33 minutes with the north boundary line seven miles and 3,412.46 feet to the point of commencement.[9]

On Saturday morning, 10 June 1889, First Lieutenant Frank B. McCoy and ten men left for Webster. Lieutenant McCoy joined his wife, children, and one servant at a Webster hotel. The last detachment of troops departed from Webster for Fort Snelling on Monday morning, 12 June 1889. The *Webster Reporter and Farmer* described the departure: "This is the last of the troops at Fort Sisseton. For 30

HEADQUARTERS DEPARTMENT OF DAKOTA,

St. Paul, Minn., April 8, 1889.

SPECIAL ORDERS }
  No. 35.   }

   *   *   *   *   *   *   *

3. Under authority from the Secretary of War conveyed by letter of the 16th ultimo from Division Headquarters, the post of Fort Sisseton, Dakota, will be discontinued June 1st, 1889.

Company G, (*Hale's*) 3d Infantry, will on that date proceed by rail to Fort Snelling, Minnesota, and there take station.

Serviceable property, unless otherwise ordered, will be transferred to Fort Snelling.

Unserviceable property, and such as may not be worth transportation, including fuel and forage, will be disposed of in accordance with the requirements of the Regulations; the post records, securely boxed, under paragraph 714, A. R.

The post buildings will be disposed of as may hereafter be directed.

The Military Reservation will be transferred to an agent, to be designated, of the Interior Department. Until this transfer is effected, a guard of one officer and ten enlisted men will be left at the post.

The chiefs of the Staff Departments will give such detailed instructions as may be necessary to carry into effect the requirements of this order.

The quartermaster's department will furnish the requisite transportation for the movement of the troops and public property.

   *   *   *   *   *   *   *

BY COMMAND OF BRIGADIER GENERAL RUGER:

H. CLAY WOOD,

Assistant Adjutant General.

OFFICIAL:

2d Lieutenant 3d Infantry,
Acting Aide-de-Camp.

Fort Sisseton disbandment orders.

Courtesy National Archives

years [actually 25] have a detachment of army occupied the fort, and many long wearisome days have they spent there—silence reigns where once was a busy life."[10]

Endnotes

1. George Hickman. *History of Marshall County.* Britton: Dakota:1886.

2. Frederick Mears to Department of Dakota, 1 September 1887. Letters Sent. RG 393. V. 2. vol. 15. National Archives, Washington, D.C.

3. *The Sentinel*, 26 October 1888.

4. Special Orders, 8 April 1889. RG 393. V. 7. Box 4. National Archives, Washington, D.C.

5. Surgeon General to Department of Dakota, 2 May 1889. Letters Sent. RG 393. V. 7. Box 4. National Archives, Washington, D.C.

6. Joseph Hale to Department of Dakota, 21 May 1889. Letters Sent. RG 393. V. 2. vol. 16. National Archives, Washington, D.C.

7. *The Sentinel*, 6 June 1889.

8. Special Order, 21 May 1889. RG 94. Box 101. National Archives, Washington, D.C.

9. E. R. Ruggles' receipt, 9 June 1889. RG 94. Box 101. Adjutant General. National Archives, Washington, D.C.

10. *Webster Reporter and Farmer*, 13 June 1889.

Chapter 13
Fort Sisseton, After 1889

South Dakota National Guard Camp and Parade Ground

South Dakota officials, the Britton and Webster business community, and homesteaders were interested in the disposition of Fort Sisseton and its 513 quarters of land. Britton's *Dakota Daylight* proclaimed: "The military reserve will be thrown open to settlers. This means a great deal for Marshall County. It means the addition of nearly three townships to her area and wealth. Our friends in the east can make ready for an early train so as to be on hand for the best farming lands in all the Dakotas."[1]

Governor Arthur Mellette wanted the state to own the fort buildings and a section of land upon which the buildings stood. This would be used as a permanent campground for the South Dakota National Guard. Senator Richard Pettigrew in Washington introduced Senate Bill 2941 in the United States Senate to obtain the fort and one section of land for a camp and parade ground for South Dakota's National Guard. His bill passed the United States Congress and became law on 1 October 1890.

The 1 October 1890 law also provided for the disposition of the remaining 509 quarters of land in the Fort Sisseton military reservation. After the state accepted the land, some of it was reserved as endowments for state institutions. The remaining land was sold to homesteaders.

In the meantime, Edward R. Ruggles, custodian and agent for the Department of Interior, used the fort for public events. He placed this invitation in the local newspapers: "The citizens of Day and Marshall counties are invited to participate in the celebration of the

4th of July 1889 at Fort Sisseton. Everything will be done for the enjoyment of all parties attending. Ball in the evening."[2] He also authorized R. J. Glen to hold his auction sale at the fort 25 September. Ruggles had the right to use the 640 acres of land around the fort as a part of his pay.

Later, the Department of Interior deeded the buildings and Section 10, Township 125, Range 56, in Marshall County to the state of South Dakota for use by the National Guard. On 1 November 1893, Governor Charles H. Sheldon sent Adjutant General George A. Silsby to Fort Sisseton to take formal possession from E. R. Ruggles. Silsby said, "A more attractive spot, or one better adapted to a camp ground, could hardly exist."[3] Silsby signed a receipt for the section of land and twenty buildings. Custodian E.R. Ruggles had destroyed two of the old log buildings and used them for fuel.

The twenty buildings were described in the Silsby 1893 receipt:

Brick—good condition: surgeon's house, commanding officer's house, officers' quarters, hospital, library, guardhouse, powder house, oil house; fair condition: blacksmith shop;

Stone—good condition: adjutant's quarters, one barracks, sergeant's quarters; fair condition: corral or barn; bad condition: one barracks;

Frame—fair condition: sergeant's quarters, bakery, bath house, wagon shed;

Log—bad condition: teamsters' quarters, old barracks [log commissary].

General Silsby appointed Daniel Hubbard custodian for the twenty buildings and land. Interestingly, Hubbard had the right to use the facility for hotel purposes. Hubbard's receipt for the twenty buildings and custodian contract read:

I, Dan Hubbard, hereby accept the position of custodian of the property described, and agree to protect and care for the same, in a proper manner, and will always obey the instructions that may be given me by the Governor, or other proper authority, and keep the same in good condition, and properly protected from the danger of prairie or other fires. It being agreed and understood, that I shall have the right to the use of sufficient quarters, for myself and family, and be privileged to use the same for Hotel purposes, during my occupancy as above provided.[4]

Apparently, some of the farmers, settling on the quarters of land on the newly opened military reservation, used the fort as a hotel while building houses. Hubbard also had the right to use the fort land for haying.

In February 1894, Governor Sheldon approved Hubbard's request to sell some of the buildings and fixtures. The reasons for the sale are not clear; however, it appears that it was done to help control upkeep costs. The sale totaled $459.80. A list of items sold is as follows:

Storm windows—sold at an average of $1.00 each, six to Q. A. Kruger, fifteen to Frank Funtine, one to B. L. Marpe, five to T. Gunderson;

Windows—sold at $1.00 each, five to David Funston;

Lean-to [wing or extension] from various buildings—to sergeant's quarters, Andrew Larson, $5.00; to stone buildings and to commissary quarters, Q. A. Kruger, $7.00; to bakery, Ole Nelson, $5.00; to company quarters, Andrew E. Hammer, $8.00; and to lieutenant quarters, P. H. Andersen, $5.00;

Covered walk to lieutenants' quarters [four-unit officers' quarters] to Andrew Staveck, $5.00;

Storm House to Sam Walp, $5.00;

Teamster's quarters to L. Peterson, $12.00;

Wood shed and outhouse to J. H. Peterson, $13.00;

Cistern for $7.00;

Outhouses, one to J. E. Ray and one to Seth B. Richardson, $5.00 each;

Dead house to S. E. Sorenson and S. P. Christenson, $50.00;

Sergeant's house to John Waulp, $125.00;

Wagon shed to John Waulp, $75.00;

Bath house to A. E. Hammack and Anton Skadin, $100.00.[5]

During the same period, the twenty-four-foot by 145-foot old log commissary and the frame bakery were donated to Dan Hubbard as part of his pay. He sold both for scrap lumber. Adjutant General Silsby also gave authority to Hubbard to tear down four other old dilapidated log buildings. When Hubbard became custodian, he signed a receipt for twenty buildings. When he was replaced in 1896 by A. Sherin, there were fourteen buildings left.

Although the South Dakota National Guard did not train at the site because it was too far from the Webster railroad station, they believed the site had good training possibilities and did not recommend disposing of it. The buildings, however, were rapidly deteriorating. The editor of the *Marshall County Sentinel* commented about the fort's condition in February 1896: "The fort property is now sadly neglected. There is no fire break around it, the weeds and grass have been allowed to grow very rank and there is no protection whatever to the buildings from a prairie fire. The buildings that are there are not properly kept nor cared for not withstanding the extra pay the governor gives his new man, A. Sherin."[6]

Adjutant General H. A. Humphrey, South Dakota National Guard, replaced Sherin in July 1897. Humphrey in May 1900, believing the new custodian had neglected his duties, appointed another custodian. To fix more responsibility, Humphrey required a $5000 bond for the new custodian. Humphrey said, "The property belongs to the state and is not and shall not be subject material for public plunder."[7]

Leasing Fort Sisseton

Fort Sisseton Stock Company

In 1902, the South Dakota National Guard decided to accept a donation of land for a permanent summer training camp near Lake Kampeska, Watertown. Not needing Fort Sisseton, Adjutant General S. J. Conklin recommended that it be sold and the money used to equip the new camp. However, no action was taken by the South Dakota Legislature to sell the fort. Therefore, the Guard decided to lease the fort and land rather than hire a custodian to manage it.

That same year, the state leased the buildings and the 640 acres of land to the Fort Sisseton Stock Company for $275 a year.[8] The company used the buildings for housing units and various agricultural purposes. A fence was built around the fort to keep livestock off the grounds. Edith Allen Goltz visited the fort for the first time the 4th of July 1904 or 1905. Her father, Herbert Warren Allen, had been invited to visit the fort by the Sisseton Stock Company. Edith Goltz described how the Sisseton Stock Company used the buildings:

We reached the east gate of the Fort about five o'clock and found a lively barn dance in progress in one of the old barracks to the left of the gate. People from all over the area were celebrating the 4th of July and continually since. It being Sunday, they kept it up until early morning. It was amusing for me and the other children to see the dancers dancing to the tune of mouth organs and accordions.

The fort was very interesting. It was on very high ground. It was laid out in a perfect square with a gate at the east corner, one at the south corner and one at the west corner. The old army buildings, all of a cream color brick, were facing the square and a wooden sidewalk was around the four sides of the square in front of the buildings. This primitive sidewalk was deteriorating fast and was rather dangerous.

On the east side of the square were the two long barracks, behind which was the corral used by the Stock Company. One of these closest to the south gate was being used for a barn. On the south side of the square was the old guard house or prison, a small building in poor condition. Next to it were the crumbling foundations of several buildings.

On the west side were several attached two-story houses [officers' quarters] which were not usable and falling apart. Next to these was a large house, well preserved and liveable with four large rooms upstairs, four on the first floor, a nice porch in front. It was the commandant's residence. This residence had been leased by the Milwaukee Gun Club for the hunting season for a number of years and in the summers by William D. Boyce of Chicago...who brought his family there for summer vacations. My father knew Mr. Boyce and after we lived at the Fort he often visited us. It was never used by the Stock Company but boarded up until summer renters arrived so it was in excellent condition.

At the west gate a low one-story brick house [surgeon's house] had about six rooms, it was being used by the Stock Company. It was liveable but not as good as the big house. On the north side of the square...was the old hospital building, the largest of all the buildings. It had the cupola on top. It was two stories high and the rooms were very large. This was used by the Stock Company for their ranch house. Mr. and Mrs. Tom Canton

were in charge here. At the corner of the north side, at the east
gate was a small one-story building listed as the library.[9]

The Fort Sisseton Stock Company discontinued renting the fort
after 1908. The company that last year paid $305 rent to the state. It
was deposited in the Special Militia Fund, South Dakota National
Guard.[10]

Herbert Warren Allen Ranch

Herbert Warren Allen, a St. Paul attorney, was founder and president of the St. Paul and Minneapolis Gun Club. He and fellow club
members had hunted in the Fort Sisseton area since about 1900.
Allen, who was impressed with the area, began buying land around
Fort Sisseton. In 1908, he leased Fort Sisseton and the square mile
from the State of South Dakota for twenty-five years. He planned to
use the fort for a cattle operation, summer home, and fall hunting
headquarters. Allen's daughter, Edith Allen Goltz, described how her
father managed the cattle operation as well as repairing buildings at
the fort:

> [My father] then began a program of restoration of the build-
> ings. He hired a foreman and a group of cowboys. For two years
> they built new pastures, putting up new wire fences. They
> solicited herds for the summers from cattle men all over the
> states of Minnesota and South and North Dakota. The pasture
> lands were wonderful—with adequate sloughs—they soon had
> them filled with herds.
>
> For two years after leasing the Fort, my father brought in
> men to repair the buildings he needed. One of the barracks was
> repaired, roofed, so it could be used for tools and storage. Larger
> corrals were built. The old library building completely repaired
> and made liveable. The old hospital (Ranch House) was practi-
> cally rebuilt inside—replastered, new floorings, linoleum put in
> all rooms, roof repaired, screens remade and the back porch
> screened in, a new living room [old hospital ward] made on the
> east side of the house. All the rooms upstairs had new floor cov-
> erings. A new lighting system installed (before this just kerosene
> lamps were used). This was our summer home. It had four large
> bedrooms on the second floor, seven rooms on the first floor.
> Two of the bedrooms upstairs could have four beds in each one.

My father had two large cisterns built for this house, one for drinking water, one for rain water. All drinking water was hauled from a natural spring in the east pasture about four miles away. [My father]...made a game house out of the library for the hunting club he belonged to. One room was used for this purpose. The other big room with small kitchen could be used for living quarters.

New cisterns were made also for the old Milwaukee Club [commanding officer's house] which was now leased to the St. Paul and Minneapolis Gun Club, of which my father was president and founder. The small house at the west gate was replastered and put in a liveable condition. We discovered a flag pole apparatus on the center of the square so a new flag pole was installed and when we were in residence there a flag was raised each morning and lowered at sundown. The entire square was mowed every week. The ranchmen used the other buildings (all repaired) and had a permanent house keeper as some one had to be there winters. We came out the last week in May each year as soon as school was out. Our house [hospital] was boarded up when we left late in the fall and opened a week or two before we arrived.

Every time the state had land sales my father would buy sections adjoining the fort which he put into small grains. We spent our summers at the fort and my father commuted each weekend. In the hunting season he spent as much time away from his office as he could. We had a wonderful life at the fort. We had house-parties all summer, saddle horses to ride and interesting places to see.

During Wilson's presidency my father and Mr. William D. Boyce invited a group of senators from Washington to come out during the hunting season. Over forty were entertained. They came in groups, spending from two to four days. My mother was hospitalized in Webster at the time and my father and I were alone with only one housekeeper. Mr. Boyce brought out his chef and waiter to take over the house during the party. We dined each night at 9 o'clock and I was my father's hostess. A private telephone was installed to Washington so each senator was in touch daily with affairs. They left with a bag of game. Today hunters would not believe what hunting was like in these years. There was plenty of water around the fort. The mallards, canvas backs, redheads, teals and bluebills were plentiful. Before the game laws existed one could bag as many ducks as they wanted and full carryalls were not unheard of.[11]

Herbert Allen had a stroke in 1917 and died in 1921. His son Herbert Warren Allen, Jr., left Williams College and returned to Fort Sisseton to manage the ranch and hunting lodge.

William D. Boyce Hunting Lodge

William D. Boyce, a millionaire Chicago newspaper publisher, began hunting in the Fort Sisseton area about 1903. For a time he leased the commanding officer's house from the Sisseton Stock Company for a summer home. Later, he was a frequent hunting guest at the Herbert Warren Allen ranch. In 1920, Herbert Warren Allen subleased the old hospital to William D. Boyce for a hunting lodge. The rent was $600 per year. Boyce had worked on newspapers in Lisbon, North Dakota, and Britton, South Dakota, before moving to Chicago. During his successful newspaper career in Chicago, he was one of the founders of the Boy Scouts of America.[12]

Boyce remodeled the old hospital ward into an elaborate hunting lodge called "The Club Room." A large fireplace was added on the east wall. The room was furnished with a phonograph, oak card tables, book shelf, soft chairs and couches, and expensive rugs. Boyce had a special oak desk with telephone for his personal use. The walls were adorned with a bear skin and moose head. The other rooms in the hospital were used for guests' sleeping quarters. Both the bear skin and oak desk are now in the home of Herbert Warren Allen, III, who lives near the fort. Also in Allen's home is an old, large framed picture of Major Robert Rose, early commanding officer at the fort.[13]

A printed letterhead, captioned "The Fort," was used by Boyce for his correspondence. Listed on the letterhead were these communication reminders: "Railroad Station, Webster; Telephone and Telegraph, Sisseton; and Postoffice, Langford. Telegrams and mail care of W.D. Boyce."

Boyce and his guests came to Fort Sisseton each fall to hunt. Ducks and geese were in abundance in nearby lakes. Local persons were hired as guides, cooks, and helpers. Boyce died in 1929 at seventy-one years of age, ending the Boyce era. In 1933, the Allen lease

"THE FORT"

R. R. Station, Webster, S. Dak.   Post Office,
Tel. and Telephone, Sisseton, S. Dak.   Langford, S. Dak.
(Telegrams and Mail care W. D. Boyce)

Letterhead from W. D. Boyce hunting lodge.

Courtesy Herbert W. Allen, III

Artist Andrew Bowes' painting of W. D. Boyce's club room, old ward of Fort Sisseton hospital, 1927.

Courtesy Herbert W. Allen, III

1927 menu, W. D. Boyce hunting lodge.

Courtesy Herbert W. Allen, III

Artist Andre Bowes' painting of Fort Sisseton, 1927. South barracks, right side.

Courtesy Herbert W. Allen, III

of the fort expired. After the expiration, Herbert Allen, Jr., built a hunting lodge on his land just north of the northeast gate of the fort.

Restoration of Fort Sisseton

The brick and stone buildings, although in need of extensive repair, survived the agricultural and hunting lodge lease era, 1902-1933. Some buildings that were used for agricultural purposes were in worse shape than those used for living quarters. Fortunately the lessees had made some repair of the commanding officer's house, surgeon's house, library, and hospital. However, in 1928, Adjutant General W. A. Hazle, South Dakota National Guard, didn't believe that more money should be spent for the fort's preservation. He recommended to the governor that the state accumulate money to tear it down and use the rocks to build a monument on the site, when the Allen lease expired. Hazle said: "So far as the reconstruction of these buildings for any state purpose is concerned, it would be useless. They could not be made into any structure of any kind that would not cost more money than a new one. The material on the ground has absolutely no value for any other purpose than that of building a monument to mark the spot where it was."[14]

South Dakota's 1933 Legislature created a board to dispose of Fort Sisseton. The board consisted of the governor, commissioner of school and public lands, and the adjutant general. It was given authority to sell or lease the fort, provided that the fort be open to the public. After the 1933 legislative session, the American Legion Post No. 80 of Britton leased the fort and began a movement to save the old fort. They formed the Fort Sisseton Memorial Association for the purpose of raising funds to buy the grounds and maintain the property as a public park. Senator Otto L. Kaas, Harold King, and R. S. Clark drove to Pierre to "start a movement to save and restore the old fort."[15]

The Britton Legion Post and the Fort Sisseton Memorial Association persuaded the South Dakota Relief Administration to establish a transient camp at the fort for about seventy to 100 homeless men. Similar camps had been set up around the state, providing work for the unemployed. Fort Sisseton jobs included repairing and restoring the buildings. The men were paid $1.00 a day and free shelter, room, and board. The state had leased the facility to the Britton Legion, and restoration work started on the fort in the summer of

WPA Fort Sisseton restoration crew, 1934.

Courtesy South Dakota Archives

1934. Buildings were in such bad shape that the men had to live in army tents until the north barracks was repaired.

Repair work continued that summer. People in the area were excited about preserving one of its most famous landmarks. To celebrate, the Fort Sisseton Memorial Association sponsored the fort's seventieth birthday party. The Memorial Association consisted of legion posts and county commissioners from five northeastern South Dakota counties. On 23 September 1934, a crowd of about 7,000 people, in 2,300 automobiles, gathered at the fort for the celebration. Five young steers were furnished for the barbecue by the South Dakota Relief Administration. Firing squads from the American Legion posts of Milbank, Webster, Roslyn, Sisseton, and Britton participated in a flag-raising ceremony. A worn twelve-foot by fifteen-foot flag, the last one flown at the fort, was lent by E. A. Palmerlee, Havana, North Dakota. Master of Ceremonies Harold W. King of Britton introduced State Auditor George O'Neill as the speaker. The Aberdeen American Legion drum and bugle corps marched on the parade ground. A special guest speaker was George C. Allanson, Wheaton, Minnesota, a grandson of First Lieutenant John S. Allanson, stationed at the post, 1869-1870.[16]

Restoration work continued, although in one case it was lacking in historical origin. For example, a second-story hay loft with gambrel roof was added to what was originally a one-story gable-roofed horse-and-mule barn. To be sure that the remainder of the historic brick and stone buildings were restored to the original state, supervision was then turned over to the National Park Service in 1935. Money was also obtained from the Works Progress Administration (WPA). The National Park Service obtained old photos, maps, and building plans from the War Department to help with historical accuracy. Early photos taken during the lease era were also used. Hilman O. Rice, from Sisseton, was hired as the new superintendent of the restoration project on 23 November 1936. Rice continued as superintendent until 1 July 1939, when the restoration project was completed. Fourteen of the original brick and stone buildings were restored. The federal government spent $475,000 on the Fort Sisseton restoration project. Rice said, "During that time most of the buildings were rebuilt from the original plans from Washington. The work was under the supervision of the National Park Service."[17]

In February 1936, the National Park Service funded an archeological research project on the fort grounds. Over 177 artifacts were collected, boxed, and sent to the Omaha Office, National Park Service. Unfortunately, the entire shipment was misplaced. Governor Nils Boe and Robert J. Perry, Aberdeen, with the help of Senator Karl Mundt, conducted a nationwide search in the 1960s, but nothing was found.

There are many credits for the 1934-1939 restoration project. A number of organizations, different levels of government, and hundreds of people participated. However, a brass marker attached to one of the buildings simply states: "Fort Sisseton, Rebuilt by the State of South Dakota and Works Progress Administration. WPA project number 3384. 1939." The credit line on a 1936 Fort Sisseton map drawn by the National Park Service states, "Department of Interior, National Park Service and State of South Dakota, Marshall County Commissioners cooperating."

The National Guard Adjutant General, Colonel Edwin C. Coffey, in 1938 listed more credits for the restoration of the fort:

Fort Sisseton, through the cooperation of the county commissioners of that area, the American Legion posts of the district, the National Park Service, Department of School and Public Lands and the Adjutant General's Department, has been almost completely rebuilt. Just recently the Park Service has withdrawn, and a project in the amount of $48,000 for the completion of the fort has been put into effect by the Works Progress Administration, sponsored by the Department of School and Public Land. The program at Fort Sisseton is highly valuable for it retains for the area one of the oldest and most historical settings in the State of South Dakota, as well as making a fine recreational center for northeastern South Dakota.[18]

Fort Sisseton was restored, but more problems lay ahead.

United States Army Air Corps Gunnery Range

During World War II the United States Army Air Corps leased Fort Sisseton and four nearby farms for a gunnery and bombing range. The lease fee for Fort Sisseton was $1.00 a year, payable to the South Dakota National Guard. The period of the 2,700-acre lease was from 1 July 1942 to 1 July 1944. Orland Bremmon, who lived six miles north of the fort, recalled the events of that time:

Three wooden targets were erected in the shape of an airplane and placed in separate locations on the range. A P-51 Mustang would check out the targets every morning before the B-17 Bombers made their run. The gunners would start shooting their machine guns about two miles from the targets spitting clips and empty shell casings over the countryside. Every fifth round the gunners fired was a tracer that caused fires. A bulldozer was used to plow a fire break around the perimeter. The bulldozer could not get close enough to the sloughs, so the farmers had to fight prairie fires when the dry slough grass caught on fire.

The bombing was done from high altitude with small bombs leaving flour spills where they landed. Day and night practices were conducted by the Army Air Corps trainee aviators from Watertown and Bismarck. Three towers were erected at the

Courtesy Robert J. Perry

Restored Fort Sisseton, 1960 photo.

range. They were manned by a ground crew to keep a record of hits. The men stayed at Fort Sisseton and Britton.[19]

On 5 October 1944, men and army trucks returned to the area. They hauled away towers and other equipment that were abandoned when the lease expired. Some work was done at the fort, because the Army Air Corps had agreed to return it in the same condition as when the lease began.

Fort Sisseton State Park

Governmental control of Fort Sisseton was transferred from the South Dakota National Guard to the Department of Game, Fish and Parks following World War II. Adjutant General Edward A. Beckwith favored the transfer: "This fort could not be maintained by this office as funds were not available and income was not adequate. It was of little use to the National Guard."[20] The 1947 South Dakota Legislature, authorizing the transfer, stipulated that the fort be preserved as a historical feature of South Dakota and open to the public. For the first time, it became state policy to preserve Fort Sisseton for future generations.

Supporters of the fort were ecstatic at the turn of events. A public debate developed immediately as to the best way to preserve the historical fort. Funds were needed for repair work. In 1952, the state leased the fort to the National Horseman Trail Riders, who had agreed to use their fund-raising profits for repair work. The Trail Riders, led by John Olson, president, and Grace Adams, vice president, used the fort for recreational purposes. Riders were from Day, Marshall, and Roberts counties. A military ball was held in the south barracks after each riding season.

Unfortunately, the fort's buildings continued to deteriorate. Little money had been spent on them since the 1939 restoration. Some roofs were in bad shape; in fact, a part of the hospital roof had collapsed. A bill by State Representative Art Sather, to appropriate $25,000 to repair roofs at the fort, was approved by the 1953 Legislature. His bill also provided authority for the Division of Parks and Recreation to charge an admission fee for entering the fort. Hilman Rice was superintendent of the work force hired to repair the roofs.

The Department of Game, Fish and Parks did not have enough money to hire a permanent caretaker, although summer help was employed. A movement to designate Fort Sisseton as a state park was started in 1957 by members of the Britton Lions Club and its president, Robert J. Perry. Club members believed that more state funds would be available if the fort were a state park. A public meeting was held at Langford to enlist supporters for the movement. Several thousand signatures, petitioning the legislature to designate Fort Sisseton as a state park, were obtained by dedicated supporters. Robert J. Perry took the petitions to Pierre and gave them to Governor Joe Foss in January 1958.[21]

Governor Foss supported the state park concept. He turned the petitions over to the South Dakota Legislature. A legislative sub-committee held a public hearing on the matter. Legislators were told at a large hearing at Fort Sisseton on 2 June 1958 that a little money was available for maintenance, but not enough to hire a full-time caretaker. Legislators also learned that there was no central heating or running water at the fort. The sub-committee members recommended the following: that Fort Sisseton be designated as a state park (farm land excluded), that Governor Foss use emergency funds immediately to hire a caretaker, and that all revenues from the park be used for maintenance of buildings.

House Bill 677, designating Fort Sisseton a state park, was introduced in the 1959 Legislature. Robert J. Perry, Britton, new president of the South Dakota Parks Association, testified three times in support of the bill. The bill passed both houses of the Legislature. The ninety-five-year-old military fort became Fort Sisseton State Park on 2 March 1959, the day Governor Ralph Herseth signed the bill. Management of the park would continue under the Division of Parks and Recreation, Department of Game, Fish and Parks. The lease with the Trail Riders had ended in 1958.

Fort Sisseton had survived. Although its brick and cut field-stone buildings had become neglected and disarrayed, they outlasted all efforts to dismantle them. Fort Sisseton State Park was the state's eleventh park and its first historical park. A *Britton Journal* editorial stated: "Built of brick and stone, Fort Sisseton has survived both the natural and human elements which have destroyed most of the forts in the great plains region."[22]

Britton's Lion Club sponsored a dedication of Fort Sisseton State Park on 26 July 1959. The Reverend Abe Crawford, retired

Presbyterian minister, Eden, South Dakota, gave the invocation. Britton's American Legion Post presented the colors and raised the flag. Governor Ralph Herseth, after being honored with a nineteen-gun salute by the 147th Field Artillery, South Dakota Army National Guard, gave the dedicatory address.

Restoration and Preservation Continues

Restoration and preservation of fort buildings has been a continuous process. The Division of Parks and Recreation, Department of Game, Fish and Parks, spent $323,169 for maintenance and repair of various buildings between 1953 and 1990. Repair work included reshingling; replacing doors, windows, floors, and walls; and painting.

An eighteen-mile stretch of road, running along the east side of the park between Highways 10 and 23, was rebuilt and hard surfaced in 1963. The work was done in time for the fort's 100th birthday celebration 26 July 1964. The gala event was attended by 20,000 people, who watched the ceremonies begin with a jet fly-over by the South Dakota Air National Guard. After a rousing band concert by the 147th Army Band, Governor Archie Gubbrud spoke. A time capsule was buried in the center of the parade ground, not to be opened until 2064. A special centennial three-inch commemorative pin was sold at the celebration.

Former Governors Sig Anderson, Ralph Herseth, and Archie Gubbrud and Attorney General Frank Farrar were the speakers at the dedication of a new visitors' center 30 June 1968. The visitors' center, located in the north barracks, also houses a museum and interpretive panels. Improvements continued at the post, including construction of a wood blockhouse in the northwest corner of the parade ground in 1980.

In 1995, the exterior restoration of the commanding officer's house was completed. Restoration work included new doors, windows, roof, porch, and picket fence. That same year, archaeologist Todd Kapler, of the Historical Preservation Information Service, University of South Dakota, directed volunteers in the fourth archaeological survey and dig at the post.

In December 1995, Governor William Janklow approved a one-million-dollar grant for Fort Sisseton, from the Department of Transportation's ISTEA (Intermodal Surface Transportation

Trail Riders looking at collapsed hospital ward roof. Note goat on roof, 1954.
Courtesy Jack Adams

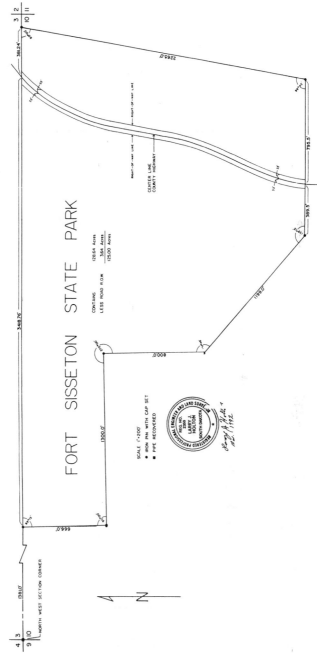

PLAT OF FORT SISSETON STATE PARK

IN THE NE 1/4 OF NW 1/4 AND IN THE NE 1/4 IN SECTION 10, T125N, R56W
OF THE 5TH P.M, MARSHALL COUNTY, SOUTH DAKOTA

FORT SISSETON STATE PARK

CONTAINS   128.64 Acres
LESS ROAD R.O.W   3.64 Acres
                  125.00 Acres

SCALE 1"=200'

● IRON PIN WITH CAP SET
■ PIPE RECOVERED

RIGHT-OF-WAY LINE

RIGHT-OF-WAY LINE

CENTER LINE
COUNTY HIGHWAY

NORTH WEST SECTION CORNER

June 7-8, 1980
PARTICIPANT PASS

S.D. Dept. of Game, Fish and Parks
Division of Parks and Recreation

Dave Daberkow, park manager, left, and Jack Adams, Sisseton, South Dakota, right, hold a plaque commemorating the donation by Jack and Marcie Adams of antique furniture for the commanding officer's quarters.

FT. SISSETON
Historical
STARR
FESTIVAL & RENDEZVOUS

25 MILES NORTH OF WEBSTER, SO. DAKOTA

SATURDAY & SUNDAY
JUNE 2-3, 1979

FOLK MUSIC · TEEPEE CAMPING · MOUNTED CAVALRY DRILL · RODEO
SQUARE DANCE JAMBOREE · NATIVE AMERICAN PROGRAM · ARTISTS
ILLUMINATION PARADE OF FORT · ALTERNATIVE ENERGY EXHIBIT · DANCE
BBQ CHICKEN DINNER · PIONEER EXHIBITS · FREE CAMPING · FOODS
CHILDREN'S ART AND ENTERTAINMENT · DRAFT HORSE PROGRAMS · TOURS

PARK STICKER REQUIRED · AVAILABLE AT GATE

Sponsored in part by: Glacial Lakes Association, Karl E. Mundt Historical and Education Foundation, Mt. Rushmore Mountain Company, National Rifle Association of America, Reptile Gardens, South Dakota Arts Council, South Dakota Department of Tourism, South Dakota Department of Wildlife, Parks and Forestry.

Produced and created by Perry Vining, Box 390, Brookings, S.D. 57006; Anne Kunze, Woonsocket, S.D. 57385, program director.

1979 Park License or Weekend Passes required, available at gate.

Interstate Publishing Co., Watertown, S.D.

Efficiency Act) program. The fund will be matched by $145,000 in state funds and $95,000 in local funds. Friends of Fort Sisseton are conducting a fund drive to raise the $95,000. The grant will be used for interior and exterior restoration of many of the buildings, as well as the installation of interpretive displays. One of the projects will be the restoration of the interior of the commanding officer's house. When completed, it will house a collection of period furniture donated by Jack and Marcie Adams of Sisseton.

Fort Sisseton Historical Festival

In 1977, the Fort Sisseton Advisory Committee of the Department of Game, Fish and Parks approved an annual Fort Sisseton celebration. No celebration had been held since 1968 when the visitors' center had been dedicated. Perry Vining of Brookings, South Dakota, was hired to plan and direct an annual celebration. Vining, who had developed Art in the Park in Brookings, advanced the historical festival idea in order to preserve and perpetuate the historical importance of Fort Sisseton.

Over 22,000 people attended the first annual Fort Sisseton Historical Festival, June 2 and 3, 1978. A mounted cavalry drill by a commemorative cavalry company from Fort Ransom, North Dakota, was one of the features. Other activities, representing the Fort Sisseton time period, included square dancing, ax throwing, draft horse pulling, and frontier cooking. A military ball was held in the hay mow of the horse barn.

Held in conjunction with the annual festival is the V. M. Starr Rendezvous, in memory of V. M. Starr, a nationally known gunsmith from Eden, South Dakota. Participants wear costumes typical of the fur-trade rendezvous era. They compete in contests such as firing black-powder muzzle-loading rifles, tossing skillets, and throwing tomahawks.

The June 1979 two-day historical festival was equally successful when 29,000 people attended. Featured that year was a parade, rodeo, Fort Ransom cavalry drill, fiddler's contest, and a black-powder muzzle-loader shootout.

The festival has continued to grow in popularity. Each year between 1978 and 1990 an average of 32,398 people, including 1,286 campers, attended the Fort Sisseton Historical Festival. During those years, performers reenacted fort life as well as other aspects pertinent to the time period. A melodrama by the Britton Community Theater was one of the programs. Some of the events consisted of folk arts, craft making, flag raising ceremony, fiddlers' jamboree, barbershop chorus, and post cutting. Concession stands sold period food and clothing items. Contests typical of the period continued to be highlighted: tomahawk throwing, black-powder muzzle-loading rifle shooting, and horse pulling, to name a few.

In June 1992, 40,000 people attended the festival. There were many white tents housing concession stands located on the west side of the buildings and south of the horse barn. A number of the concession stands were billed as trading posts. Some of the period items sold were buffalo skulls, beads, fry bread, traps, camp cooking equipment, black-powder supplies, leather-craft items, Indian dolls, knives, wood carvings, Indian jewelry, western art, and moccasins. One frontier-kitchen food stand was selling fry bread, Indian tacos, and egg rolls. During the two-day event, swarms of people enjoyed sightseeing, in addition to watching contests or dramatic plays, eating period food, buying pioneer items, and visiting with friends. All of the restored Fort Sisseton brick and cut-field-stone buildings and wood blockhouse were open to visitors.

The festival continues to reveal the historical significance of the fort. Between 1991 and 1995, an average of 43,000 people each year have attended the annual festival, held the first weekend in June. In 1995, for example, 44,750 people, including 1,843 campers, attended the historical festival. Campsites for campers and recreational vehicles are provided west of the fort near the cemetery. In addition to the annual festival, the fort is open during the summer for visitors. The Division of Parks and Recreation, of the Department of Game, Fish and Parks in Pierre, is in charge of all state parks. The management of Fort Sisseton State Park is under the direction of the park manager, Roy Lake State Park, Lake City, South Dakota.

Epilogue

Fort Sisseton was a United States Army post in northeastern South Dakota between 1864 and 1889. Following military disbandment, it was transferred to the State of South Dakota. During years of neglect, the post buildings slowly decayed.

A state official in 1928 recommended that the brick and stone ruins be leveled and used to build a commemorative monument in the center of the parade ground. Historically minded area people, however, were successful in saving the old fort from demolition. They led a movement resulting in restoration of the fort by the National Park Service in the mid 1930s. Marshalling their forces again, area people convinced the 1959 South Dakota Legislature to designate the fort as a state historical park.

Under the able direction of the Division of Parks and Recreation of the Department of Game, Fish and Parks, Fort Sisseton State Park has become a landmark of frontier military history. The fort's stately brick and stone buildings stand as an important link to a past era. Fort Sisseton has become a classroom of frontier military history for thousands of visitors each year. The old post will continue as a showplace of frontier army life for generations.

Standing on Fort Sisseton's parade ground, one can visualize a bustling scene, as soldiers pursued their daily tasks. A guard in full-dress uniform stands at his post near the stable on a cold winter night. The cry of "present" moves down the line as morning roll call is answered. "To the rear march" echoes across the grounds as a sergeant drills a formation of marching men. The command "attention" rings out as rows of troops prepare for inspection. At sunset the bugler sounds "retreat" while the national flag is lowered, followed by the booming of the cannon. At day's end the bugler's "tattoo" drifts across the scene.

Fort Sisseton stands as a tribute to thousands of frontier soldiers and civilians who helped shape the history of South Dakota and the nation. Future generations will be able to appreciate their work, thanks to the efforts of the men and women who worked to restore and preserve this historic fort.

Endnotes

1.*Dakota Daylight*, 2 May 1889.

2. *Webster Reporter and Farmer*, 20 June 1889.

3. South Dakota Adjutant General's Report, 1893:5.

4. National Guard Files, H74.28. South Dakota Archives, Pierre, South Dakota.

5. Fort Sisseton sales list, H74.28. South Dakota Archives, Pierre, South Dakota.

6. *Marshall County Sentinel*, 20 February 1896.

7. South Dakota Adjutant General's Report, 1900:6.

8. Special Militia Fund. State Treasurer's Report, 1902. State Archives, Pierre, South Dakota.

9. "As I Remember Fort Sisseton," Edith Allen Goltz. *Marshall County*. Marshall County Historical Society. Dallas, Texas: Taylor Publishing Company, 1979:12. (Hereafter cited as *Marshall County*.)

10. Special Militia Fund. State Treasurer's Report, 1910. State Archives, Pierre, South Dakota.

11. *Marshall County:*12.

12. *World Book Encyclopedia*, p. 444.

13. Herbert Warren Allen III, Interview with author, 14 September 1992.

14. South Dakota Adjutant General's Report, 1928:15.

15. *Marshall County Journal*, 30 March 1933.

16. *Fort Sisseton*. Fort Sisseton Memorial Association, Britton, South Dakota:1935.

17. Hilman O. Rice to Robert J. Perry, 8 July 1967. Robert J. Perry Papers, Aberdeen, South Dakota.

18. South Dakota Adjutant General's Report, 1936:8.

19. Orland Bremmon interview with author, 14 September 1992.

20. South Dakota Adjutant General's Report, 1944-1946.

21. Robert J. Perry interview with author, 5 June 1992.

22. *Britton Journal*, 2 July 1959.

Appendix A

Commands and Commanders, Fort Sisseton Era, 1864-1889

General in Chief of the Army—Headquarters, Washington, DC.
 1863-1869, Ulysses S. Grant
 1869-1883, William T. Sherman
 1883-1888, Philip H. Sheridan
 1888-1894, John M. Schofield

Military Division of Missouri—Headquarters, St. Louis until 1868, after that Chicago
 1865-1866, Maj. Gen. John Pope
 1866-1868, Lt. Gen. William T. Sherman
 1868-1883, Lt. Gen. Philip H. Sheridan
 1883-1886, Maj. Gen. John M. Schofield
 1886-1888, Maj. Gen. Alfred H. Terry
 1888-1890, Maj. Gen. George Crook
 1890-1894, Maj. Gen. Nelson A. Miles

Department of Northwest—Headquarters, St. Paul in 1862, after that Milwaukee
 1862-1865, Maj. Gen. John Pope
 1865-Maj. Gen. Samuel R. Curtis

 District of Minnesota
  1862-1865, Brig. Gen. Henry H. Sibley
 District of Wisconsin
  1862-1864, Brig. Gen. T. C. H. Smith
  1864-1865, Brig. Gen. Bell
 District of Iowa
  1863-1865, Brig. Gen. Alfred Sully

(Department of Northwest absorbed by Department of Dakota in 1866)

Department of Dakota—Headquarters, Fort Snelling
   1866-1869, Brig. Gen. Alfred H. Terry
   1869-1872, Maj. Gen. Winfield S. Hancock
   1872-1878, Brig. Gen. Alfred H. Terry
   1878-Bvt. Maj. Gen. John Gibbon
   1879-1886, Brig. Gen. Alfred H. Terry
   1886-1891, Brig. Gen. Thomas H. Ruger

Appendix B

Post Commanders, Fort Sisseton, 1864-1889
Year or Part of Year Served, Name, Rank, Unit

1864	Clowney, John, Maj., 30th Wisc. Inf.
1864-66	Rose, Robert H., Maj., 2nd Minn. Cav.
1865	Everest, Aaron S., Capt., 2nd Minn. Cav.
1866	Davy, Peter B., Capt., 2nd Minn. Cav.
1866-67	Hayman, S.B., Maj., 10th Inf.
1867-69	Hampson, Jesse A. P., Capt., 10th Inf.
1868	Stanley, William, Capt., 10th Inf.
1869-72	Bates, J. C., Capt., 20th Inf.
1871-72	McNaught, John S., Capt., 20th Inf.
1871	Hawley, William, 1st Lt., 20th Inf.
1872-73	Yard, J. E., Maj., 20th Inf.
1872-73	Stanley, William, Capt., 20th Inf.
1873-74-76-77	Crofton, Robert E. A., Maj., 17th Inf.
1874	McArthur, Malcolm, Capt., 17th Inf.
1874-76	Pearson, Edward P., Capt., 17th Inf.
1875	Carlin, William P., Lt. Col., 17th Inf.
1876	O'Brien, Lyster M., 1st Lt., 17th Inf.
1877	Patterson, John H., Capt., 20th Inf.
1877-79	Van Horne, William W., Capt., 17th Inf.
1878-79	Burns, J. M., 1st Lt., 17th Inf.
1878-84	Bennett, Clarence E., Capt., 17th Inf.
1880	Roberts, Cyrus S., Capt., 17th Inf.
1880-83	Roach, George H., 1st Lt., 17th Inf.
1884	Chynowith, Edward, 2nd Lt., 17th Inf.
1884-88	Schooley, David, Capt., 25th Inf.
1885-87	Mears, Frederick, Maj., 25th Inf.
1888	Sanborn, Washington I., 2nd Lt., 25th Inf.
1888-1889	Hale, Joseph, Capt., 3rd Inf.

Officers temporarily in command during the absence of the commanding officers are not included in this list.

Appendix C

Officers Serving at Fort Sisseton, 1864-1889
(Unit, Name, Rank, Year, or Part of Year Served)

Thirtieth Wisconsin Infantry
Baker, Edwin O., 1st Lt., 1864
Burton, Lewis S., Capt., 1864
Cassimen, Samuel, 2nd Lt., 1864
Clowney, John, Maj., 1864
Devlin, Edward, Capt., 1864
Gill, William H., 1st Lt., 1864
Hubbard, Myron F., 1st Lt., 1864
Jones, John T., 2nd Lt., 1864
Klatt, John, Capt., 1864
Overton, George A.J., Capt., 1864
Priestly, Thomas, 2nd Lt., 1864
Smith, Samuel W., 1st Lt., 1864

Second Minnesota Cavalry
Andrews, George, 1st Lt., 1864
Bonham, Isaac, Capt., 1865
Briley, William L., Capt. 1865-66
Cutler, Frederick L., 2nd Lt., 1864-65
Davy, Peter B., Capt., 1864-65-66
Darrow, Jonathan., 1st Lt., 1865-66
Everest, Aaron S., Capt., 1864-65
Field, Albert R., Capt., 1865-66
Gardner, Patrick E., 1st Lt., 1864-65
Griswold, Frank C., 2nd Lt., 1864-65
Hanley, John C., Capt., 1864-65
Jones, B. F., Capt., 1864
Howe, Henry S., Capt., 1865-66
Hunt, Richard O., 1st Lt., 1864-65
Larke, Thomas, 2nd Lt., 1865-66
Lidden, John, 2nd Lt., 1864
McGibe, A., 1st Lt. 1865
McGill, Archibald, 1st Lt., 1865-66

McKusick, Jonathan, E., Capt., 1864-65
McKusick, William F., 1st Lt., 1864
Mills, Arthur H., Capt., 1865-66
Paine, James M., Capt., 1864-65
Patch, Louis, J., Capt., 1864-65
Phillips, Henry F., 2nd Lt., 1865
Plowman, Henry, 2nd Lt., 1864-65
Rose, Robert H., Maj., 1864-65-66
Sanborn, Robert W., 2nd Lt. 1865
Sherman, Wm. L., 1st Lt., 1865
Smith, Lyman B., 1st Lt., 1864-65
Stevens, Wm. F., 2nd Lt., 1865-66
Strong, William F., 2nd Lt., 1865
Tilton, John, 1st Lt., 1864
Thompson, Joseph S., 2nd Lt., 1864-65-66
Thompson, Thomas, 1st Lt., 1864-65
Wood, Robert, 2nd Lt., 1864

Third Minnesota Battery
Daniels, Don A., 2nd Lt., 1865
Dwelle, Tad M., 2nd Lt., 1865-66
Jones, John, Capt., 1865-66
Western, Horace H., 1st Lt., 1864-66
Whipple, John C., 1st Lt., 1865-66

First Regiment United States Volunteers Infantry
Evans, A. C., 1st Lt., 1864-65
Handy, George E., 2nd Lt., 1864-65
Weitzel, Lewis, Capt., 1865

Tenth United States Infantry
Bottsford, Charles E., 2nd Lt., 1867-68
Broatch, Wm., 1st Lt., 1866-67
Carroll, S.S., Capt., 1866-67
Crosman, George H., Capt., 1866-67
Davis, Chas L., 1st Lt., 1866-67-68
Dumme, Wm. McKee, 1st Lt., 1866-67
Edwards, Charles M. 2nd Lt., 1866-67
French, Thomas H., 1st Lt., 1868
Geoghegan, John D., 1st Lt., 1866-67-68
Hampson, Jesse A.P., Capt., 1866-67-68

Hayman, S. B., Maj., 1866-67
Hines, John W., 2nd Lt., 1867-68
Hopwood, J. H., 2nd Lt., 1866-67
Hunter, John, 1st Lt., 1866-67
Jewett, Charles E., 2nd Lt., 1866-67-68
Kelton, Dwight H., 2nd Lt., 1866-67-68
Macy, John P., Capt., 1866-67-68
Stanley, William, Capt., 1867-68
Taylor, Lewis, Lt. Col., 1867-68
Tracy, John P., Capt., 1868

Twentieth United States Infantry
Allanson, John S., 1st Lt., 1869-70
Bates, J. C., Capt., 1869-70-71-72
Coe, J. N., Capt., 1869-70
Cushman, Herbert, 1st Lt., 1877-78
Fletcher, William, Capt., 1877-78
Hawley, William, 1st Lt., 1870-71-72-73
Howgate, Wm. H., 2nd Lt., 1869
Howgate, H. W., 1st Lt., 1877
Maize, William R., 1st Lt., 1872-73
McCaskey, W. S., 1st Lt., 1869-70
McNaught, John S., Capt., 1870-71-72-73
Patterson, John H., Capt., 1877
Potter, John H., Capt., 1878
Rodman, John B., 2nd Lt., 1870-71-72-73
Schreiner, Herman, 1st Lt., 1869
Sharps, G. Dent, 2nd Lt., 1877-78
Stanley, William, Capt., 1872-73
Tilton, Palmer, 2nd Lt., 1877-78
Turnock, Edwin, 2nd Lt., 1869-70-71-72
Wishart, Alexander, 1st Lt., 1871-72
Wood, Walworth N., 2nd Lt., 1870
Yard, J. E., Maj., 1872-73
Yeckley, Jonathan A., 2nd Lt., 1872-73

Seventeenth United States Infantry
Bennett, Clarence E., Capt., 1878-79-80-81-82-83-84
Burns, James M., 1st Lt., 1878-79
Brush, Daniel, 1st Lt., 1878-79
Carlin, William P., Lt. Col., 1875-76

Chynowith, Edward, 2nd Lt., 1880-81-82-83
Cook, William I., 2nd Lt., 1877-78
Crofton, Robert E.A., Maj., 1873-74-76-77
Dowdy, Robert W., 2nd Lt., 1879-80
Garritty, Frank D. 1st Lt., 1873-74-75
Garretly, Edwin F., 1st Lt., 1877
Grumley, Edward I., 2nd Lt., 1880-81-82-83-84
Howe, Edgar, 2nd Lt., 1878-79
Howell, D. L., 2nd Lt., 1881
Kilpatrick, Andrew E., 2nd Lt., 1878-79
Lyons, Robert T., 2nd Lt., 1873-74-75
Mann, William A., 2nd Lt., 1875-76-77
McArthur, Malcolm, Capt., 1873-74-75-76-77
Metcalf, Charles, 2nd Lt., 1873-1874
Nickerson, James, D., 2nd Lt., 1877-78
O'Brien, Lyster M., 1st Lt., 1873-74-75-76-77
Pearson, Edward P., Capt., 1873-74-75-76-77
Roach, George H., 1st Lt., 1880-81-82-83-84
Roberts, Cyrus, S., Capt., 1880-81-82-83-84
Ruhlen, George, 1st Lt., 1879-80-81-82-83-84
Van Horn, William W., Capt., 1877-78-79

Twenty-fifth United States Infantry
Edwards, Eaton A., 1st Lt., 1887-88
Farnsworth, Charles, 2nd Lt., 1887-88
Glenn, E.F., 2nd Lt., 1885
Green, James O., 2nd Lt., 1884-85-86-87-88
Kendall, Frederick A., Capt., 1884
McMartin, John, 1st Lt., 1884-85-86-87-88
Mears, Frederick, Maj., 1884-85-86-87
Reade, Harry, Capt., 1888
Reed, H. D., 2nd Lt., 1884-85
Ritzius, Henry P., 1st Lt., 1884-85-86
Sanborn, Washington I., 2nd Lt., 1884-85-86-87-88
Schooley, David, Capt., 1884-85-86-87-88

Third United States Infantry
Hale, Joseph, Capt., 1888-89
McCoy, Frank B., 1st Lt., 1888-89
Neary, William C., 2nd Lt., 1888-89

Appendix D

Army and Citizen Surgeons Serving at
Fort Sisseton, 1864-1889

June 1864-September 1864	Dr.Lamberton
July 1864-September 1864	Edwin O. Baker
October 1864-May 1866	1st. Lt. Charles J. Farley
June 1866-July 1866	E. E. Braun
July 1866-October 1866	F. C. O. Roehrig
November 1866-March 1867	Major H. R. Silliman
April 1867-June 1867	James M. McMaster
July 1867-August 1867	William P. Lambert
September 1867	Major B. Knickerbocker
October 1867-January 1868	Lt. Col. Lewis Taylor
February 1868-April 1868	James M. McMaster
May 1868-March 1869	A. I. Comfort
April 1869-November 1870	Major B. Knickerbocker
December 1870-September 1872	Capt. C. E. Munn
October 1872-March 1873	J. N. Coonan
April 1873-October 1873	W. E. Turner
November 1873-June 1878	Charles E. McChesny
July 1878	C. C. Miller
August 1878	E. W. Dubose
September 1878	C. C. Miller
October 1878-August 1879	Charles E. McChesny
September 1879-June 1883	James B. Ferguson
July 1883-February 1884	Victor Biart
March 1884-June 1884	1st. Lt. Robert B. Benham
July 1884-October 1884	O. M. Archibald
November 1884-April 1885	1st. Lt. C. Macauley
May 1885-May 1886	Capt. W. T. Spencer
June 1886-October 1886	1st. Lt. John L. Philips
November 1886-September 1888	David S. Snively
October 1888-February 1889	Capt. Benjamin Munday
March 1889-June 1889	David S. Snively

Appendix E

Hospital Stewards Serving at Fort Sisseton, 1864-1889

June 1864-September 1865	A. H. Marston
October 1865-February 1866	Charles H. Lewis
March 1866-October 1868	D. A. Craven
November 1868-April 1872	Cassius B. Cullen
May 1872-October 1876	Charles Kennan
November 1876-February 1883	Augustus Gecks
March 1883-December 1885	Herman Wilkendorf
January 1886-July 1886	Frederick H. Russell
August 1886-September 1887	George D. Belk
October 1887-June 1889	John H. Sanborn

Appendix F

Chronology

1851

* Treaty of Traverse des Sioux signed by officials of the Minnesota Sioux and United States government. A reservation was created along the Minnesota River between Lake Traverse and New Ulm, Minnesota.

1862

* Minnesota Sioux War.

* Military Department of Northwest created in Saint Paul, with Major General John Pope commanding.

* Colonel Henry H. Sibley's force subdued Chief Little Crow's force at Wood Lake, Minnesota. Many Sioux fled into Dakota Territory.

1863

* General Pope moved Department of Northwest headquarters to Milwaukee and created three military districts: Wisconsin, Minnesota, and Iowa.

* Brigadier General Alfred Sully, Commanding Officer of Iowa District, led expedition against the Sioux in Dakota Territory.

1864

* In May the new military post was named Fort Wadsworth, in honor of General James W. Wadsworth, who died in the Civil War. The post's primary mission was to keep the Sioux from returning to Minnesota.

* Major John Clowney and four companies of the Thirtieth Wisconsin Infantry located Fort Wadsworth 1 August 1864 and began construction.

* Brigadier General Alfred Sully led second expedition into Dakota Territory. Included in the expedition was Colonel Minor T. Thomas and the Minnesota Brigade.

* Colonel Thomas and Minnesota Brigade, returning to Minnesota in late September, left Major Robert H. Rose and four companies of the Second Minnesota Cavalry to replace Major Clowney and

Clowney and men of the Thirtieth Wisconsin Infantry. Major Rose and men continued construction of Fort Wadsworth.

* Three officers and eighty-two enlisted men, First Regiment United States Volunteers Infantry (former Confederate deserters and prisoners), stationed at the post between November 1864 and September 1865, helped Major Rose with post construction.

* Major Rose established Frontier Indian Scout Force and set up camps in Fort Wadsworth area. At its peak, between 1864-1867, the Frontier Indian Scout Force consisted of 200 scouts, stationed in sixteen area scout camps.

1865

* A fifty-stall cut-field-stone stable was completed.

* A brick guardhouse and prison were built.

* Enlisted men moved into two cut field-stone barracks on 9 December.

1866

* General William Tecumseh Sherman, Commanding Officer of the Military Division of Missouri, ordered that Fort Wadsworth be continued as a permanent military post.

* Captain Albert R. Field and forty men of Company A, Second Minnesota Cavalry, were caught in a February blizzard at the foot of Coteau, north of post. Captain Field and three men perished in the storm.

* Major S. B. Hayman and four companies of the Tenth United States Infantry replaced Major Rose and his men 7 June 1866. Major Hayman and men continued post construction.

1867

* War Department General Order No. 41 provided authority for a 86,400-acre Fort Wadsworth military reservation. Later, a sliver of land along the northeast side was transferred to Lake Traverse Reservation, leaving an 82,112-acre military reservation.

* A two-and-a-half-story brick commanding officers' house was built.

* A four-unit, story-and-a-half brick officers' quarters was completed.

* A field-stone and brick magazine were built.

* Cut field-stone adjutant's office finished.

* Sisseton Wahpeton Treaty was signed. Lake Traverse Reservation of 918,780 acres was created.

* Fort Wadsworth was changed from a four-company infantry post (about 200 men) to a three-company infantry post in 1867 and to a two-company infantry post (about 106 men) in 1869.

1868

* School for children and enlisted men opened.

* A new one-and-a-half-story brick hospital was opened. It was remodeled in 1886.

* Fort Laramie Treaty was signed. Signors agreed to the creation of the Great Sioux Reservation, consisting of all land west of the Missouri River in present-day South Dakota.

1874

* A band of Hunkpapas from the Grand River country raided Fort Wadsworth and stole some horses.

1875

* Fortification embankment and ditch around the post were leveled.

1876

* Fort Wadsworth, to avoid confusion with Fort Wadsworth on Staten Island, NY, was renamed Fort Sisseton in honor of the nearby Sisseton tribe, according to General Order 94.

1878

* Northwest blockhouse was dismantled. The wood was used for fence posts behind the officers' quarters.

1880

* New brick building housing a school, library, and court-martial room was completed.

* A brick blacksmith shop and a carpenter shop, with a covered space between, were constructed.

1881

* Chicago, Milwaukee and Saint Paul Railway began serving Webster, D.T., twenty-two miles south of the post.

* Town of Webster was established.
* A new one-story brick surgeon's house was completed.
* Soldiers built the post's first telegraph and telephone line to Webster.

1882

* One new three-inch rifled cannon and carriage was received. The four worn-out twelve-pound mountain howitzers and prairie carriages were returned to the Rock Island Arsenal.
* Cut field-stone commissary sergeant's quarters was constructed.
* Troops A and C, Seventh Cavalry from Fort Meade, were sent to Fort Sisseton to assist the post's two infantry companies in maintaining order in the area.

1884

* Town of Britton was established.

1885

* The people of Day County voted to split the county into Day and Marshall counties.

1886

* Chicago, Milwaukee and Saint Paul Railway began serving Britton.

1888

*A cut field-stone oil house was the last building erected at the post.

1889

* War Department officials announced that Fort Sisseton would be discontinued on 1 June 1889.
* Twenty-two brick, stone, frame, and log buildings and the 82,112-acre military reservation were turned over to the Department of Interior, 9 June.
* Last detachment of Fort Sisseton soldiers left Webster for Fort Snelling 12 June 1889.
* South Dakota became a state.

1890

* President Benjamin Harrison on 1 October signed the bill sponsored by United States Senator Richard Pettigrew transferring Fort Sisseton and one section of land to South Dakota for use as a permanent campground for the South Dakota National Guard.

1892

* Officials of the United States government opened for settlement 668,000 acres of land previously purchased from the Sisseton and Wahpeton tribes, leaving 250,780 acres for the reservation.
* Town of Sisseton was formed.

1893

* On 1 November, Fort Sisseton, including its twenty remaining buildings and one section of land, were transferred from the Department of Interior to the State of South Dakota.

1902

* South Dakota National Guard officials, after managing the fort since 1893, leased its remaining fourteen buildings and one section of land to the Fort Sisseton Stock Company.

1908

* Fort Sisseton and its one section of land were leased to Herbert Warren Allen for twenty-five years, for agricultural and hunting purposes.

1920

* Herbert Warren Allen subleased the hospital to William D. Boyce for use as a hunting lodge. Boyce died in 1929 and his lease expired.

1923

* The South Dakota Senate passed Senator Otto L. Kaas's Senate Bill No. 183, providing a $75,000 appropriation to convert Fort Sisseton into a penal institution. The post would be intermediate to the penitentiary in Sioux Falls and the reformatory in Plankinton. First offenders between the ages of sixteen and thirty would be sent there for training and farm work to reclaim them for society. The bill failed to pass the Legislature.

1933

  * The South Dakota Legislature created a board for the purpose of disposing of Fort Sisseton.

  * American Legion Post No. 80 of Britton leased the fort and began a movement to save the decaying buildings.

1934

  * Officials of the Britton Legion Post No. 80 and the Fort Sisseton Memorial Association arranged to have the South Dakota Relief Administration establish a transient camp at the fort for about eighty to 100 homeless men. The repair of the buildings was started.

  * About 7,000 people gathered at the fort and celebrated its seventieth birthday.

1935

  * Management of the project for restoration of Fort Sisseton buildings was turned over to the National Park Service. The restoration project was completed in 1939.

1942

  * Fort Sisseton land and buildings were leased to the United States Army Air Corps for use as a gunnery range, 1 July 1942 to 1 July 1944.

1947

  * The South Dakota Legislature transferred the management of Fort Sisseton from the South Dakota National Guard to the Department of Game, Fish and Parks. The Legislature also stipulated that the fort be preserved as a historical feature of South Dakota.

1952

  * Fort Sisseton was leased to the National Horseman Trail Riders.

1954

  * Representatives of nine northeast towns met at Roslyn to promote Fort Sisseton as a site for the United States Air Force Academy, and elected Albert R. Johnson as president of the group.

The fort was among the top finalists for consideration by the national selection committee.

1959

* South Dakota Legislature designated Fort Sisseton as a state park. Dedication ceremonies were held at the fort on 26 July. The lease with the Trail Riders ended.

1964

* Fort Sisseton's 100th birthday celebration was attended by 20,000 people.

1968

* A new visitors' center was dedicated by former Governors Sig Anderson, Ralph Herseth, and Archie Gubbrud, and Attorney General Frank Farrar.

1973

* Fort Sisseton was placed on the National Register of Historic Places.

1978

* First annual Fort Sisseton Historical Festival held on the grounds attracted 22,000 people. The crowd numbers soared to 40,000 in 1992.

1995

* A record-breaking crowd of 44,750 people attended the Fort Sisseton Historical Festival held the first weekend in June.

1996

* Governor William Janklow approved a one-million-dollar ISTEA (Intermodal Surface Transportation Efficiency Act) grant for further restoration of Fort Sisseton.

Bibliography

Adams, Jack. Interview, 14 September 1992. Publisher of *Sisseton-Courier*. Sisseton, SD.

"Administration of Public Domain." *South Dakota Historical Collections* 20:240.

Allen, Herbert W. III. Interview, 14 September 1992. Britton, SD.

American Military History, 1607-1958. Department of the Army, July 1959.

"Archeological Report of Fort Sisseton." National Park Service, 1936. South Dakota Archives, Pierre, SD.

Billings, John D. *Hardtack and Coffee*. Boston: George M. Smith and Co., 1887.

Billings, John S. "Report on the Hygiene of the United States Army." Circular No. 8. Surgeon General's Office, Washington: GPO, April 25, 1875.

Billings, John S. "Report on Barracks and Hospitals." Circular No. 4. Surgeon General's Office, Washington: GPO, December 5, 1870.

Bremmon, Orland. Interview, 14 September 1992, Britton, SD.

Brown, Joseph R., Museum. Browns Valley, MN.

Brown, Samuel J. Manuscript. Doane Robinson Papers. Folder 44. South Dakota Archives, Pierre, SD.

Camp Release Monument. Montevideo, MN.

Carley, Kenneth. *The Sioux Uprising of 1862*. St. Paul: Minnesota Historical Society, 1976.

Cartographic Division, National Archives. Alexandria, VA.

Census, Federal, 1870 and 1880.

Comfort, A.I., MD. "Old Potteries at Kettle Lakes." *Monthly South Dakotan*. Vol. 5. No. 12. April, 1903.

Coggins, Jack. *Arms and Equipment of the Civil War*. Garden City, NY: Doubleday and Company, 1962.

Cullum, Major General George W. *Biographical Register of Graduates of the United States Military Academy*. 2 vols. New York: Van Nostrand, 1868.

Daberkow, Dave, Phone Interview, 8 January 1996. Manager Roy Lake State Park, Lake City, SD.

Dakota Daylight. All issues through 1889.

"Dakota Lakes Region." Directors of the National Horseman Trail Riders, 1954.

Day County Museum. County Courthouse. Webster, SD.

DeWitt, Marty. Fort Sisseton Materials. Division of Parks and Recreation, Department of Game, Fish and Parks. Pierre, SD.

DeTrobriand, Philippe. *Army Life in Dakota*. ed. Milo Milton Quaife. Chicago: The Lakeside Press, 1941.

Doud, George W. Diary. South Dakota Archives, Pierre, SD.

Edward, Paul M. "Fort Wadsworth and the Friendly Santee Sioux. 1864-1892." University of South Dakota Master's Thesis. *South Dakota Historical Collections* 31:74-156.

Fisk, Andrew, Pocket Diary. Minnesota Historical Society, St. Paul, MN. Roll 81.

"Fisk Expedition of 1864." North Dakota Historical Society 2, 1908.

Folsom, S.P. and H. Von Minden Fort Sisseton Map, 1866. File 2229A, South Dakota Archives, Pierre, SD.

Fort Lowell Museum, Tucson, AZ.

"Fort Ridgely." Nondated. Minnesota Historical Society, St. Paul, MN.

"Fort Sisseton." Britton, SD: Fort Sisseton Memorial Association, 1935.

Fort Sisseton Original Records in Record Group 92, 94, and 393, National Archives, Washington, DC.

Fort Sisseton. Schumucker, Paul, Nohr & Associates, Consulting Engineers. 1974. Unpublished. South Dakota Archives, Pierre, SD.

Fort Sisseton. Graham, Ruth. National Park Service. 1935. Unpublished. South Dakota Archives, Pierre, SD.

Fort Sisseton Selected Materials. Minnesota Historical Society, St. Paul, MN.

Fort Sisseton Museum. Visitors' Center, Fort Sisseton, SD.

Fort Sisseton, Vertical Files. South Dakota State Historical Society, Pierre, SD.

Heitman, Francis B. *Historical Register and Dictionary of the United States Army.* 2 vols. Washington: GPO, 1903.

Hershler, N. *The Soldier's Handbook.* Washington: GPO, 1884.

Hickman, George. *History of Marshall County.* Britton, Dakota: 1886.

Hicks, Major James E. *United States Military Firearms.* La Canada, CA: James E. Hicks and Son, 1962.

Historical Festival, Fort Sisseton, 1992.

History and Biography of Central and Northern Minnesota. Chicago: Ogle and Co., 1904.

Holabird, Lieutenant Colonel Samuel B. "Reconnaissance in the Department of Dakota." 15 October, 1869. Ex. Doc. 8, 41st Cong. 34th Sess. Washington: GPO.

Hubbard, Lucius F. and Return I. Holcombe. *Minnesota in Three Centuries.* 3 vols. Mankato: Publishing Society of Minnesota, 1908.

Indian Scout Enlistments. Register of Enlisted Men in the U.S. Army, 1789-1914. RG 94. Microcopy 233, Roll 70 and 71. National Archives, Washington, DC.

Johnson, Norma. *Wagon Wheels.* Vol. 1, 1981; Vol. 2, 1982; Vol. 3, 1983; Vol. 4, 1985; Vol. 5, 1986; Vol. 6, 1989. Courier Publishing Company, Sisseton, SD.

Johnson, Norma and Oliver Swenumson. "Across the Years." *History of Sisseton, South Dakota.* Watertown, SD: Interstate Publishing Co., 1992.

Johnson, Norma. "The Colonel and the Fort." Dakota History Conference. Madison, SD: Karl E. Mundt Foundation, 1982.

Kapler, Todd. "The Past and Present: A Summary of Archaeological Excavations at Fort Sisseton, 1992-1994." June 2, 1995, Dakota History Conference, Center for Western Studies, Sioux Falls, SD.

Karie, Karen. *Fort Sisseton Our Living Heritage.* Sisseton, SD: Courier Printing, 1979.

Kingsbury, George W. *History of Dakota Territory.* 5 vols. Chicago: S. J. Clarke Publishing Co., 1915.

Lee, Robert. *Fort Meade and the Black Hills.* Lincoln: University of Nebraska Press, 1991.

Lewis, Wendy, Interview, 5 June 1992. Naturalist, Division of Parks and Recreation, Department of Fish, Game and Parks. Fort Sisseton, SD.

Lounsbery, Clement A. *Early History of North Dakota.* "The Buffalo Republic." Washington: Liberty Press, 1919.

Maps and Drawings used for Restoration of Fort Sisseton. National Park Service. File 2229A. South Dakota Archives, Pierre, SD.

Marcy, General R.B. "Outline Description of the Posts and Stations of Troops in the Geographical Divisions and Departments of the United States." Washington: GPO, 1872.

Marshall County. Marshall County Historical Society. Dallas, TX: Taylor Publishing Co., 1979.

Medical History of Fort Sisseton. Record group 94. National Archives, Washington, DC.

Meyer, Roy W. *History of the Santee Sioux.* Lincoln: University of Nebraska Press, 1967.

Minnesota in Civil War and Indian War, vol. 1. 1861-1865. St. Paul: Pioneer Press, 1890.

Military Library. South Dakota National Guard Museum, Pierre, SD.

Military Reference Branch. National Archives, Washington, DC.

Morris, H. S. "Historical Stories Legends and Traditions." Sisseton, SD: *Sisseton Courier,* 1939.

Nankivell, John H. *25th Infantry.* Reprint. Fort Collins, CO: The Old Army Press, 1972.

Northwestern Bell Newsletter, "How Robert J. Perry Saved the Fort." April 1959.

"Official Correspondence Pertaining to the War of the Outbreak, 1862-1865." *South Dakota Historical Collections* 8:100-596.

Ochsenreiter, L. G. *History of Day County* 1873-1926. Mitchell, SD: Educator Supply Company, 1926.

Ordnance, Fort Sisseton. Room 400. M1281, Stack 32, Shelf 4, Roll 8, National Archives, Washington, DC.

Paxon, Lewis C. Diary. North Dakota Historical Society. 1908:146.

Perry, Robert J. Personal Papers on Fort Sisseton, Aberdeen, SD.

Perry, Robert J. Interview, 5 June 1992. Aberdeen, SD.

Peterson, Harold L. *Round Shot and Rammers.* Harrisbug, PA: Stackpole Books, 1969.

"Plan on Visiting the Colorful Dakota Lake Region." Sisseton South Dakota Chamber of Commerce, 1953.

Post Returns of Fort Sisseton, 1864-1889. National Archives. Microfilm Role 1179, South Dakota Archives, Pierre, SD.

Reese, N. L. South Dakota WPA Writer's Group. Daytona Beach, FL.

Register of Deeds Office. Marshall County, Britton, SD.

Renville, James. "Recalls Early Day Happenings at old Fort Sisseton." *Sisseton Courier,* September 17, 1953.

Renville, Victor. "A Sketch of the Minnesota Massacre." *North Dakota Historical Collections* 5:271.

Regulations of the United States Army, 1863, 1881, 1889.

Reports of the Commissioner of Indian Affairs, 1862-1892.

Reports of the Secretary of War. Volume 1, 1862-1890.

Rickey, Don Jr. *40 Miles a Day on Beans and Hay.* Norman: University of Oklahoma Press, 1963.

Roberts County History. Roberts County Centennial Committee. Sisseton, SD: *Sisseton Courier*, 1961.

Robinson, Doane. *Encyclopedia of South Dakota.* Pierre, SD: by author, 1925.

Robinson, Doane. Personal Files. Folder 44. South Dakota Archives, Pierre, SD.

Robinson, Doane. *A History of the Dakota or Sioux Indians.* 1904. Reprint. Minneapolis: Ross & Haines Inc., 1967.

Robinson, Doane. *History of South Dakota.* 2 vols. Aberdeen, SD: B. F. Bowen and Co., 1904.

"Rose, Major Robert H." *St. Paul Daily Press*, April 10, 1866.

Rothamer, Siegmund. Diary 1863. South Dakota Archives, Pierre, SD.

Sather, State Representative Art. Phone Interview, 26 April 1994. Sisseton, SD.

Schuler, Harold H. *The South Dakota Capitol in Pierre.* Pierre, SD: by author, 1985.

Schuler, Harold H. *A Bridge Apart, History of Early Pierre and Fort Pierre.* Pierre, SD: by author, 1987.

Schuler, Harold H. *Fort Pierre Chouteau.* Vermillion, SD: University of South Dakota Press, 1990.

Schuler, Harold H. *Fort Sully: Guns at Sunset.* Vermillion, SD: University of South Dakota Press, 1992.

Schuler, Harold H. *Camp Rapid.* Camp Rapid, SD: South Dakota National Guard, 1995.

Scott, Marvin. "History of Fort Sisseton." Omaha, NE: National Park Service, Region II. Not published.

Schell, Herbert S. *History of South Dakota.* Lincoln, NE: University of Nebraska Press, 1975.

Sheridan, P. H. *Army Posts in the Military Division of Missouri.* Chicago: Military Division of Missouri, 1876.

Sheridan, P. H. *Record of Engagements with Hostile Indians.* Division of Missouri, 1868-1882. Washington, DC: GPO, 1882.

Sisseton & Wahpeton Bands versus the United States. Washington, DC: Court of Claims.

Sisseton Land Claims. Senate Document 23. 56th Congress, Second Session. December 5, 1900.

Sentinel, Britton,SD. All issues through 1889.

South Dakota Archives, Pierre, SD.

South Dakota State Historical Society, Pierre, SD.

South Dakota State Engineer's Reports, 1947-1960. State Archives, Pierre, SD.

South Dakota State Treasurer's Reports, 1902-1959. State Archives, Pierre, SD.

South Dakota Adjutant General's Reports, 1887-1947, State Archives, Pierre, SD.

Sterling, Dr. Everett, Personal Papers. Box 1, Folder 13, South Dakota Archives, Pierre, SD.

Stevenson, C. Stanley. "Buffalo East of the Missouri in SD." *South Dakota Historical Collections* 9:389.

Sturnegk, F. Map of Fort Sisseton, 1871. File 2229A. South Dakota Archives, Pierre, SD.

Tarbell, Wright. "Early History of Codington County." *South Dakota Historical Collections* 24.

"The Scout Camps." *Sisseton Courier,* June 8, 1967.

Trende, Fred. "Fort Sisseton, South Dakota Reburials at Custer Battlefield National Cemetery." Report on File in South Dakota Archives and Fort Sisseton.

Vandenberg Jr., General Hoyt Sanford. 1993 Letter. USAF, Retired, Tucson, AZ.

Webster Reporter and Farmer. All issues through 1889.

Woolworth, Alan R. Fort Sisseton Selected References, Minnesota Historical Society, St. Paul, MN.

Yard, Major J. E. "Annual Report of Fort Wadsworth, 1873." National Archives, Washington, DC.

Index